A Dictionary of Concepts on American Politics

Preface

No topic of political science is more adequately covered than American government. Most textbooks are quite good and, as subsequent editions appear, become even better if only because of the stiff competition they encounter. A valuable insight or new approach is seldom ignored and significant new literature on any institution of national government is almost immediately incorporated. Aids to learning such as narratives, case studies, contemporary methodologies, cartoons, and road maps, enhance the presentation of material.

However, there is an urgent need for a concentrated primer on the main ideas, events, concepts, and institutions of American government. This need is all the more acute when texts offer points of view and narratives to the near exclusion of a basic discussion of government. My purpose in this dictionary is to provide the student with a readable and useful source book that, in as little space as possible, tells what an idea, concept, event, or institution is and why it is important.

All of us who teach American national government can and do offer overviews and perspectives on the concerns that shape the American political tradition. This is essentially the "profess" part of being a professor. I believe that we have an obligation to place our own viewpoints before students in the free marketplace of ideas. Certainly, most of our textbooks offer such perspectives.

Still, many of us have the definite feeling that the basics are often neglected. We know and understand American national government so well that, at times, we pass over a fundamental idea that is and remains unclear in the minds of our students. This book is aimed at that audience. If students need to know precisely what an idea is or what an institution does, they may look it up here.

There are several techniques for organizing a dictionary of this kind. One can organize it thematically as I have chosen to do, or one may simply list the terms alphabetically, as some other dictionaries have done. In choosing the general topic headings I have risked creating an organizational framework that might not correspond to the instructor's or to that of the text being used. But certain general themes, such as the presidency, Congress, and the courts, are almost universally accepted.

The instructor who assigns this dictionary as "required" or as "recommended" will likely suggest how its chapters correspond to the class needs in the syllabus. Additionally, an index is provided. It is not unusual for a teacher to recall or to anticipate a term from another section out of normal sequence. The student who wishes more information or a refresher may look for the term in the general index.

It is possible to teach a course in American government from a dictionary alone. In that instance, the instructor may choose to offer his or her own narrative and perspective, grounding the student in the basics from the dictionary.

Not all of the entries in this volume may be considered vital or important. No attempt has been made to rank them according to importance. Because of the wide diversity of books and teaching methods, I have tried to be inclusive rather than exclusive. I welcome suggestions from students and professors alike on additions to the book.

Often agencies have multiple purposes and acts, and treaties and resolutions have many clauses. I have only identified the most important portions of the concepts concerning them. One might discuss the Budget and Impoundment Control Act in several places and with different emphases. In discussing the Congress, the emphasis might be placed on the creation of the powerful Congressional Budget Office, whereas in teaching the presidency one might point out the attempts to control the impoundment of monies. I have reduced the duplication of entries and have provided cross-references throughout the book. The actual choice of placement of entries is, for the most part, arbitrary.

In teaching our courses, both primary and advanced, most of us encourage discussion within our classes. The best type of discussion is one that is based on fundamental knowledge of the ideas and concepts of American government and on an understanding of its functions and institutions. The aim of this dictionary is to provide such knowledge and understanding.

I was guided in my work by the authors of prior dictionaries and by the authors of the many American government textbooks available. I based my choices of terms on those previously published materials, noting especially those concepts that recur in all or nearly all of the standard ones. However, no list of terms is final or complete. I thank those who read my typescript and provided suggestions for improving it, especially those who suggested the addition of terms I had initially overlooked. In this vein, my special appreciation goes to my editor, Wayne Anderson of Wiley and his reviewers, George A. Schutte of San Diego City College and Richard H. Foster of Idaho State University. Of course, I alone accept full and complete responsibility for errors.

James B. Whisker

Contents

1

Political Ideas

Absolutism: Absolutist governments exist where democracies have either not been developed or where they have failed. Such governments have almost totally unrestrained political powers given to single individuals, such as dictators or kings, or to single political parties that are rigidly controlled by elitist groups. There are few, if any, rights guaranteed to citizens over and against government.

Accountability: In modern, democratic states we believe that leaders are responsible and accountable to the people. The people as the electorate have placed leaders in office and they have a right to know how these leaders have fulfilled their positions of public trust. Closely tied to accountability is the concept of placing all men, leaders included, under the control of the law. When the Nixon administration fell, it was because it had failed to be limited by the law and be accountable to those who had placed it in power.

Alienation: First used by Proudhon and Marx, the term refers to the estrangement of persons from their political and social environment. When individuals are alienated they no longer function as responsible citizens. Political sociologists since Marx have used this term to describe the natural by-product of political corruption and the disillusionment of individuals with corrupted or impotent political systems. When societies find their government is unable or unwilling to deal with crises, members of society may become alienated from the state mechanism.

Anarchism: Governments are thought to be necessary and desirable in every mode of political thought except anarchism. It is the negation of government. Society would exist in a much happier way if it were not restrained by government. The founder of modern anarchism, Pierre Joseph Proudhon, taught that government granted monopoly powers to some at the expense of all others. Thus, he advocated the partial, but not total, abolition of government. The most eloquent spokesperson of *peaceful anarchism* was Peter Kropotkin, who taught that a society of mutual cooperation was possible without government. Some advocated violent revolution, beginning with acts of individual violence directed against the general population, as a way to achieve *terroristic anarchism.* Either way, the general program of anarchism is the abolition of the state mechanism.

Aristocracy: In medieval societies, and in those still accepting such medieval ideas, there is supposedly a "superior" class of persons chosen by God to govern. Such persons are *aristocrats by birth.* Jefferson, John Adams, and others in colonial America spoke of a *natural aristocracy* who were naturally more talented than other men, and who should govern. Some, like Adams, wanted to build devices into the Constitution to guarantee government by aristocracy, while others, like Jefferson, merely hoped that men would naturally tend to select such men for office. There are some men whose natural talents allow them to accumulate more wealth than other men. These *economic aristocrats* (or "aristocracy of wealth") were held by some to have a natural right to govern, or at least to have the right to a greater say in governance by, for instance, having more votes or votes in accordance with their property value or the taxes they paid.

Authority: This is the legal power given to a public agency or body that enables it to perform the functions assigned to it. In a democratic state, authority is given to the government and its many departments and divisions by the people. Authority may be defined by the Constitution and bylaws made according to that basic document.

Autocracy: This is a governmental system in which political power is found in the hands of one individual, or, occasionally, a small group of persons. Unlike kingships, autocracies are often accompanied by mass indoctrination, political propaganda, mass support trumped up by the leaders, and political ideology. Kings generally have some legitimate claim to their thrones, as in the case of a son of a king who follows his father to power. Autocrats seize power and hence are not necessarily "legitimate" rulers. This often accounts for the mass rallies autocrats hold, as these rallies serve to ensure popular support of the autocratic regime.

Bill of Rights: Several nations have basic and fundamental written documents that guarantee basic civil liberties and rights to their citizens over and against government. The first modern document of this type was the English Magna Carta (Great Charter), signed in 1215. In republican governments these documents are of fundamental importance, for they limit government and remove from it certain preogatives. These documents protect the minority from the tyranny of the majority.

Bourbon Democrat: This term usually refers to conservative Democrats, especially in the South or in the Border States. The term is archaic. Presently, one identifies such conservatives as conservatives.

Bourgeoisie: This is a largely archaic term for the business class in western societies. Its use is rather restricted today to communist rhetoric. Communists describe the capitalistic systems as "bourgeois capitalist" meaning that the pseudo-democracies of the West are actually run by and for the profit of the capitalist class. It is opposed by the workers who are called "proletariat."

Capitalism: This is the modern economic system generally found in the Western or free world. Private property exists as do property rights for the owners. Individual enterprises are owned by private investors who seek to compete with similar enterprises owned by other private parties for the sale and distribution of goods and services. In a modern state, the state itself produces nothing, for this is the job of private enterprise, not the government. Extensive government intervention in the free enterprise system through regulatory commissions and boards has changed capitalism significantly from its earlier forms.

Central Economic Planning: In his book, *Road to Serfdom*, Friedrich Hayek has suggested that the road to totalitarianism is prepared by beginning centralized economic planning not only for the governmental functions but for those things that have traditionally been done by private enterprise. Under centralized planning the goals of society are set by the state, which then develops plans to achieve these goals. Precious resources are allocated to industries and projects according to the value of the project within the government's total plan. In its final form centralized planning, with direct allocations of investment, industrial consumption, and production becomes antithetical to capitalism.

Centrism: This term is much more at home in European (especially continental Europe) politics than in America. While our political tradition leads us toward political center, thus avoiding extremes, we seldom use the term centrism to describe this tendency. In Europe, centrism means political movements that tend to gather in the middle of the political spectrum, avoiding such extremes as facism, communism, monarchism, or socialism.

Charisma: This term has been borrowed from the field of religion. There it is applied to the reception accorded some especially outstanding individual by his followers over whom he exercises no particular power save that of his ideas and personality. It is a rare attribute of a great leader. All of the founders of the great religions are said to have been charismatic figures whose ideas and leadership shaped and formed the world (or a significant portion thereof). Today the term is applied to almost any political leader of public opinion who maintains a substantial following. Since the advent of radio and television, image makers have been able to manufacture "charisma" in near wholesale quantities. The term thus has lost most of its true meaning.

Class: In aristocratic societies of Europe class distinctions were drawn according to birth (nobility) and position (title). The more democratic a society the less class is emphasized, so that modern democratic states are moving toward classlessness. Most societies show significant disparities in wealth and some find that this can be a base for class distinctions. In America we often speak of "upper class," "middle class," and "poor class." Political sociologists are more likely to use the term "socioeconomic status (SES)" than "class."

Collectivism: In modern, alienated society some individuals seek protection and escape from individualistic isolation through collective movements. Those political ideologies that offer mass escape from the rigors of individualism are termed collectivism. Quite often, collectivists preach some form of socialist ownership and operation of the factors of production and of the land. Mass values are chosen over individual conscience, and mass liberties are preferred to individual rights.

Communism: In its pure form, communism means that all things are held in common, with the individual possessing at best a residual right to use what he or she needs. Such pure communism may occasionally be found in strict religious organizations. The term is more commonly used to describe the "scientific" socialism of Karl Marx and his followers. Marx taught that history is divided into epochs and that dialectical laws propel history necessarily toward the last epoch of mankind, communism. Before communism can triumph there will be a series of frightful collisions between the workers and their capitalist "masters." The Communists will necessarily triumph in the end. After a series of preludes, the final stage of communism will be developed wherein each will receive what he or she needs while contributing what he or she can to the whole.

Concurrent Majority: This theory was developed by John C. Calhoun during his search for a means of protecting the slave states from the growing antislavery sentiments in the North. Each society has two major climates of opinion. In his time one of these developed in the North and the other in the South. Each should be protected from the possible tyranny of the other. To do this each group should be given a kind of veto power over the other in matters that touch their respective special concerns. Thus, major decisions could be reached only with the approval of each group.

Consensus: Amerindians developed a method of reaching a conclusion without the formality of voting. Each individual or at least each leader of the group talked in favor of his or her view. As the issues were discussed each individual looked for common areas of agreement and eventually a consensus was reached which all could support. In any society a consensus is an ideal that the society should strive for. It is the ideal replacement for majority rule, an idea that threatens the minority with the tyranny of the majority. To the degree societies can reach consensus on issues, their policies will be strengthened. It is an ultimate form of regime support.

Conservatism: In European traditions, conservatism supported the idea of natural or traditional aristocracies. This form of *aristocratic conservatism* was defeated by integral or French liberalism, but it never made much impact in America. Europeans developed a *traditional conservatism*, which was popularized in the writing of Edmund Burke, especially in his condemnation of the French revolution. Many of his ideas were popularized in America by Alexander Hamilton and John Adams. *Modern conservatism* emphasizes limited government, republican ideals, constitutional government, judicial restraint, and stability through maintenance of present conditions. Many contemporary conservatives are really remnants of 19th-century or laissez-faire liberalism. One major tenet of Burke's conservatism accepted by modern conservatives is the notion that society is a continuum, a partnership, involving the living, the dead, and those yet to be born. Society breaks this chain if it practices total revolution, and this is the ultimate sin, for it dispossesses the future generations from their natural heritage.

Constitution: In any state a constitution is the fundamental statement of principles under which government operates and by whose authority laws are made. Constitutions determine the type of state to be formed, as unitary or federal. They specify the offices to be created and the method to be used in filling those offices. They explain the basic rationale of government. Some constitutions are strictly applied by some authority such as the courts; in other states constitutions are only a general guide to action and may be violated at will by the government. Most constitutions are written, but some are "traditional." In ancient Greece a constitution was merely a history of the politics of the nation.

Constitutionalism: In a limited state a constitution is a basic statement of the powers of government and the rights of citizens. It is central to republican thought, for it provides a bulwark against constant change emanating from a series of temporary majorities. It is the protector of minority rights, for it ideally contains the basic principles of a free nation that are not subject to change by 50 percent of the population.

Consumerism: The self-appointed leader of American consumer interests, Ralph Nader, has sought to obtain laws from Congress and rulings from bureaucratic and regulatory agencies which might protect individuals and small businesses from the larger, more powerful corporations. Areas where Nader and his Raiders have sought action include: truth in lending and full disclosure of finance terms; limitations on food additives and protection from allegedly dangerous chemicals; controls over auto engine emissions and safety devices in autos; regulation of certain areas of medicine and law; truth in labeling, packaging, and selling of merchandise; and installation of air bags in autos. Nader's efforts have popularized consumerism to some degree and of course, Nader has inspired imitators.

Democracy: This Greek idea is formed by the combination of two works "demos" meaning "people" and "kraots" meaning "authority." In *pure democracy* the people rule directly, deciding issues among themselves. In *representative democracy* the people select others to represent them.

Democratic Socialism: In this system of government the state takes over the factors of production, owning them in the name of the people. The extent of governmental ownership is determined by the people using democratic means. Actually, the democracy of such systems is more like a republic than a democracy, for most such systems have bills of rights and other constitutional safeguards associated with republics. Several European nations have democratic socialist systems, including England and Sweden. The most important feature of democratic socialist systems is the absence of authoritarian government. In this it differs from Marxist or scientific socialist systems.

Demagogue: In our descriptions of leaders of totalitarian states, a demagogue is a leader who has come to power by trickery, revolution, or intimidation and who has no legitimate claim to power. Hitler might be considered the archetype of a demagogue. The term may also be applied to a ruthless politician who has been elected to office, but whose rule seems to be authoritarian and intimidating. Huey Long of Louisiana was called a demagogue at times during his tenure in office in the 1930s.

Direct Democracy: Most democratic systems depend on representatives chosen from among and by the people at large. On some occasions the entire population may become involved in the law-making process. Devices for popular democratic participation in government include initiative, recall, referendum, and plebiscite. In a very small area direct democracy may occur regularly, as in New England town meetings.

Divine Right of Kings: James I of England wrote the best known defense of the divine right of kings, the *Trew Law of Free Monarchies.* All rights in the state belong to, and may occasionally be dispensed by, the king. No one but the king has any kind of right by nature's law. God ordained that kings should rule and any attempt to alter that situation would be sin. Kings are God's messengers to men for their good.

Economic Determinism: Although principally associated with the ideology espoused by Karl Marx (dialectical and historical materialism of communism), there have been many political philosophers who believed that the economic system of the times determined the way political systems would be set up. Among the modern non-Marxist thinkers who taught economic determinism were James Harrington and Charles A. Beard. Harrington taught that the way property is distributed among the classes determins the political forms people adopt in government. Beard taught that the Founding Fathers were economically determined, as members of the economic aristocracy, to frame a constitution that was conservative and protective of property rights.

Fascism: This political ideology was originated by Benito Mussolini in reaction to socialism and French liberalism. It was supernationalistic and militaristic. It taught the unity of theory and action, but failed to develop a viable theory during its existence (1933–1943). It shared a strong commitment to state control of major enterprises and central economic planning with socialism. However, most property remained in private hands. Its party adherents gloried in paramilitary training and uniforms ("Black Shirts"). There are several varieties of fascism. The German form, nazism, was racially based. Pseudofascist governments were created in Spain under Franco, Portugal under Salazar, and Argentina under Peron. Fascism is a postdemocratic, postindustrial, highly nationalistic ideology.

Government: The political and administrative authority of a state is called a government. These organizations exercise full political authority in executive, judicial, and legislative matters. Government may be democratic, authoritarian, or totalitarian.

Ideology: This unique development of the 20th century teaches a kind of "secular religion." It offers a closed system of thought about man, society, and the state. It is based on one or more fundamental books, such as Marx's *Capital* or *Communist Manifesto* or Hitler's *Mein Kampf*. In its rightist versions (fascism, nazism) it teaches supernationalism while its leftist version (communism) teaches internationalism and the brotherhood of the working class. True ideology denies the possibility of further development of knowledge beyond applying the principles of the philosophical system to new situations or sciences. Even science may be subject to ideological constraints.

Integral Liberalism: Popularized by Jefferson and his followers in this nation, this 19th-century form of liberalism triumphed over old, aristocratic conservatism by preaching a philosophy of freedom of conscience and natural rights of man. Much of American liberalism of the 19th century came from the writings of English philosopher, John Locke. Man, Locke taught, is endowed with certain inalienable rights. Among these are life, liberty, and property. Jefferson used this idea in the Declaration of Independence, a fundamental work of American liberalism of the 19th century.

Jefferson and his followers believed in very limited government that would do very little except act as policeman and protector from foreign invasions. Government should not interfere with the lives of private individuals any more than was absolutely necessary.

Jacksonian Democracy: The term is associated with the expressions of political power by frontiersmen, newly liberated from disenfranchisement by property qualification to vote. Jacksonian democracy taught equality of men and rejected the Jeffersonian notion of a natural aristocracy. The frontier spirit and experience were fundamental to the development of the individual. Alexis de Tocqueville, visiting America during this time, noted the individualism of the people of the frontier. Jackson ran the nation by "gut feelings" rather than political philosophy. He despised strong government and complex institutions that he did not understand. He felt that the president was the coequal of the Supreme Court in determining the constitutionality of laws and that the president was morally obligated to invalidate laws that were incorrectly framed or that violated the public trust.

Jeffersonian Democracy: Those who followed the ideas of Thomas Jefferson were said to be Jeffersonian Democrats. These ideas included: natural aristocracy among men; fundamental and basic civil liberties and the rights for all men; very limited government; dependence on local self-government; minimum controls by government over individuals; subordination of military to civil authority; fear and distrust of standing armies; preference for an agrarian, not an industrial society; and a belief in natural rights placed in nature by God. This is sometimes called Jeffersonian liberalism.

Laissez-faire Capitalism: Laissez-faire is a French expression meaning "to leave something alone." In this, the earliest form of capitalism, the state was to allow capitalism to develop on its own without state interference. It was advocated by Adam Smith in his *Wealth of Nations* (1776). He saw a society filled with small producers and small shopkeepers and merchandisers, and filled with individual laborers. Each sold his or her own labor to these small businesspersons, and purchased locally produced goods and services. Smith's ideas clearly influenced the development of American capitalism.

Left: The political spectrum is often divided into right, center, and left. Those of the political left include liberals, socialists, communists, and radicals. Those of the political left subscribe, in varying degrees, to ideas of change and alteration in the political system. They generally favor, or pretend to favor, mass democracy and popular sovereignty. In Europe, the distinction is seen more clearly than in America. One might not speak of a "liberal" as a "leftist" here so frequently as one might in Europe. Continental European parties tend more toward political extremes whereas American parties tend toward the political center.

Legitimacy: Governments and rulers prefer to exercise power that is recognized by the people and by foreign powers. A government has achieved legitimacy when it is accepted as a legal and full representative of the people by other major powers, by international organizations and, most of all, by the vast majority of its citizens. Governments believed to be illegitimate often find that diplomatic recognition is not afforded them by civilized nations, by the international community, and by world organizations.

Liberal: Liberals are those who seek to change the status quo. *Nineteenth century liberalism* as it was known in the United States opposed government intervention in the lives of men and in governing more than was minimally necessary to preserve public order. The principal exponents of this form of liberalism were the Antifederalists and the Jeffersonians. *Modern (interventionist) liberalism* seeks constantly more governmental controls over areas that were heretofore considered the private concern of free enterprise or of individuals. Liberals generally have great faith in the intellectual abilities of men. Evils of society exist only as privations of goods that ought to be present. Hence, poverty can be eliminated by applying governmental powers and moneys to the problems of society. They place much emphasis on civil liberties and civil rights and seek governmental intervention to ensure such rights. Human rights are preferred to property rights.

Majority Rule: This is closely associated with theories of democracy. If the people are truly sovereign then the majority of them ought to be able to decide policy. In legislature and in most other places where ballots are taken 50 percent + 1 are said to constitute a majority. In many votes not nearly all eligible to cast votes choose to do so. Thus, the result of a ballot may not equal a majority that is committed to a policy. In representative democratic systems the legislature may not truly represent the population. Some groups, such as religious or racial minorities, may be under-represented (or over-represented). Majority rule is frequently mitigated by the republican device of protecting minority rights by building into fundamental laws and constitutions a requirement that a simple majority cannot be used to tamper with certain rights and freedoms. Levies affecting property frequently must be approved at the local level by a vote substantially larger than a simple majority.

Melting Pot: The United States has been the land of immigrants with the exception of the Amerindians. All nationalities and races of the world have entered this nation and been assimilated into the population. Israel Zangwill wrote a popular play that used this term to describe the process of assimilation of various national and racial groups.

Mercantilism: In the 16th and 17th centuries the monarchs of Europe assumed that the wealth of their nations was best expressed in terms of gold, silver, and jewels held in state treasuries. Hence, they set out to acquire colonies and with them the wealth that could be brought to their courts from around the world.

Monarchy: The rule by one individual who has legitimately come to power and is known as king, sovereign, or monarch is commonly called monarchy. *Hereditary monarchy* allows son to follow father on the throne. *Elected monarchy* permits a group of special electors to choose the best of their peers to serve as king or emperor. *Constitutional monarchy* mitigates one-person rule by setting constitutional guidelines and by creating other political institutions such as parliaments to share in governing. Present-day monarchies are generally constitutional governments wherein the kings perform few if any functions beyond those required traditionally as parts of ceremonies.

Nation: Traditionally, a nation is a group of people possessing one or more of the following characteristics: common mores, folkways, customs, and traditions; common ethnic origin or race; common language or languages spoken by all or most of the inhabitants; defined geographic area that the people view as their own; common religion or social philosophy; and common views of the public good. The state is the political expression of the nation. If the state properly contains a single nation it may be called a nation-state. The factors listed above, which are shared by the inhabitants, are sometimes called centripetal forces, that is, factors that pull the state together and give it unity. Those factors that tend to pull the state apart, frequently the opposites of the desired values listed above, are called centrifugal forces.

Nationalism: One of the most powerful forces known to people, nationalism is the combination of sentiments and irrational feelings people possess about their state. One might speak of his or her state as "the fatherland" (or "motherland"). He or she treasures the symbols, such as the flag or those animals or birds that stand for the nation. Nationalism may be healthy, but it may also cause wars and other harmful acts. Some have viewed nationalism as an ideology, although more frequently in the 20th century it is a component of ideology.

National Socialism: Commonly called "nazism" this form of fascism added a strong racial bias to the usual attributes of fascism. It was bound up with German mythology as popularized in the operas of Richard Wagner and the frustrated nationalism of 19th-century Germany. It taught the racial supremacy of the "Aryan" peoples and the racial inferiority of nonwhites, especially Jews. (Germany maintained Jews were not caucasian). It participated in the elimination of racially "undesirable" peoples of Europe, including Jews and Gypsies.

Natural Law: This is the philosophical view that holds that there is a law (or a set of laws) to be found in nature which ought to underlie the laws of a state. Those laws may simply be a part of the natural setting, such as the law of gravity is for physical scientists, or it may be thought of as the handwork of God revealed to men. Some have claimed it to be simply one form of divine or eternal law, the law that coexists with the diety. Others find it to be immutable only because Nature itself is permanent. It is often thought to be identical to such revealed laws as the Ten Commandments. Many believe that any state law that is in conflict with natural law is null and void. This idea of a "higher law" was most important in the philosophical views of nearly all the Founding Fathers.

New Left: In the late 1950s and early 1960s a "free speech" movement began at the University of California—Berkeley and its ideas and often violent tactics spread to other college campuses. It was politically quite left of center, but its ideology rejected (traditional) Marxism and socialism. It found ideological support in the writings of such leftist professors as Herbert Marcuse. During the middle to late 1960s it was a powerful force, especially on college campuses. While it seldom attracted even 10 percent of the student body it was able to close colleges at times and, of course, attract considerable multimedia coverage. Its protests against the war in Vietnam hastened American withdrawl from southeast Asia. Many of its demonstrations were really "media events" rather than actual major demonstrations. Its most vocal supporters frequently supported civil rights and minority rights causes at times.

Nihilism: After the revolution, what will society be like? There are many schools of thought which could be incorporated under the title of nihilism in that they advocate the abolition of the state by force, but have no idea whatsoever of what the future will bring. It is the nihilist who preaches a philosophy devoid of values save for the destruction, by any and all means, of what presently exists. Nihilists have been used by Communists, Nazis, and Fascists as a tool for the destruction of the state. After the revolution the Nihilist is frequently destroyed.

Oligarchy: The corrupted rule of the few was classified by Aristotle as oligarchy. Today we might associate it with the misrule of a self-appointed elite, rather than with a corrupted aristocracy. Roberto Michels, in his "iron law oligarchy," taught that all governments are controlled by the few. Even in democracies we have, at best, competing political parties that are controlled by oligarchies. In common usage, any political elite may be called an oligarchy.

Oligopoly: Monopoly exists when markets are controlled by only one producer. Oligopoly exists when markets are controlled by only a few corporations. The few oligopolistic producers are in collusion with one another to fix prices at a certain level, which assures each of the noncompeting corporations high profits. Consumerists have objected that many areas of economic life are today controlled by oligopolies, notably energy areas.

Participatory Democracy: This is an offshoot of the older idea of direct democracy. It has become associated with the New Left, but many individuals and groups had recommended direct participation in the decision-making process long before the 1960s. The object of direct and/or participatory democracy is direct control of social, political, economic, and cultural life by the masses of the citizenry. This was, effectively, one of the aims of the populist and progressive movements in the nation from the 1880s through the 1930s. It is precisely what one finds in venerable American institutions such as the New England town meetings.

Paternalism: In some philosophies of government the individual is believed to be incompetent to govern him or herself and thus must be directed by the governmental structure. The state must then act for the people in nearly every way. It is the function of the government to constantly be developing new policies to protect us from ourselves and to guarantee us the good life. Mild paternalism is found even in the most democratic state, such as in this country in the Social Security program. In modern states, paternalism has been furthered by liberal programs. In authoritarian states "cradle to the grave" welfare systems provide for the citizens in every possible way, but at considerable cost in terms of loss of control over one's destiny.

Pluralist Democracy: This term is used by political scientists to acknowledge the existence of many competing groups in society, all of which are looking for some favors from the political system. If one is less optimistic about democracy, one could express the same idea by speaking of competing political, social, and economic elites. One assumes that in a basic political environment such as ours there are nearly infinite numbers of competing ideas and ideologies and values. All recognize that power is needed to secure their goals and only the political system offers such power to be used to authoritatively allocate their values. Our heterogeneous society is the source of competing elites and it will always be thus. Any conception of the state must necessarily allow for such competition as will exist among groups. Major interest and pressure elites and groups arise and they tend to balance one another. All of this activity is part of pluralism. We consider a democratic structure the best to cope with our pluralistic interests.

Popular Sovereignty: This doctrine assumes complete, supreme, final, and unlimited power on behalf of the people. Under this doctrine the people are empowered to create and to alter the basic institutions of government. Ideas of popular sovereignty were advanced by natural rights thinkers to counter claims to kingly prerogatives and unlimited powers.

Populism: In the late 1870s a movement grew primarily out of the Midwest and spread through farming areas, which had strong popular democratic and socialistic overtones. It advocated government operation of many utilities and the railroads. It was based somewhat in the "free silver" movement, which advocated unlimited purchases and coinage of silver. It captured the Democratic Party by the election of 1896 when its principal spokesman William Jennings Bryan emerged as the party's presidential candidate. It failed in most of its more radical demands. It was revived in the 1920s in the reformist campaigns of such statesmen as Robert LaFollette. Many hold that the promise of populism was fulfilled, at least in part, in the New Deal. The campaigns of George Wallace in 1968 and George McGovern in 1972 had overtones of populism. Generally, populism has been favored by small farmers and the poor who want more democratic government and nonorthodox liberal governmental programming.

Proletariat: The workers of the world are called the proletariat in communist ideology. Supposedly, the workers have triumphed in a great victory in the Soviet Union and its East European satellites over the capitalist or "bourgeois" forces. The revolution, which Communists believe will come inevitably, will pit the workers (proletariat) against the capitalist (bourgeoisie).

Protestant Ethic: Calvinism, as it was taught in America, instructed that a few men were to be saved for reasons known only to God, and for reasons beyond their power to alter, whereas others would fall into hell for their sins. God's chosen people would be rewarded in this life as well as in the next. The rewards of this life would be material in nature. The God-fearing man or woman who worked hard, saved his or her money and invested it carefully might be one of the elect. To show that one was a member of the elect, and thus deserving of membership in the visible church (and thus allowed to participate in politics), one might attempt to succeed in the material sense. The Protestant ethic was held by sociologist Max Weber to be the basis of capitalism and the principal reason for its success in America.

Radical: On the normal political spectrum the radical is to the left of the most liberal ideology. He or she seeks change, frequently favoring revolution as the principal instrument of change, and frequently chooses to use other extra legal means of accomplishing goals. Few political parties of a radical nature exist in the United States, but the ones that do exist frequently receive much media attention. Examples of radical movements would include: Yippies, Students for a Democratic Society (SDS), and the various Marxist and Communist parties.

Republic: While we may use "democracy" and "republic" interchangeably in the United States, a republic differs, if only slightly, from even representative democracy. Republics qualify the democratic processes by removing certain things from changes that can be wrought by simple majorities. Our republican constitution protects, especially in its Bill of Rights, certain freedoms. These rights can be altered or abridged but not by simple majority vote. Republican governments are associated with written constitutions and the rule of laws, not of whims of men. They have the conservative feature of providing guidance for future actions by preserving past records (for example, the courts are bound by *stare decisis*).

Right: Those who tend toward conservatism or other protectionist or reactionary political ideas are said to be on the right of the political spectrum. Generally, rightists tend, in varying degrees, to accept ideas of nationalism and traditionalism. The past is a general guide to present and future action and change is generally destructive of the political system in rightist views. On the far end of the rightist side of the political spectrum are fascism and nazism. In Europe rightists may support the restoration of traditional monarchies.

Rugged Individualism: This concept is traced to the presidency of Theodore Roosevelt. "Teddy" was a weaking as a child who struggled to develop himself mentally and physically without help from or the support of welfare or governmental programs. Alexis de Tocqueville who visited America during the presidency of Andrew Jackson noted the self-sufficiency of the backwoodspeople of the frontier and coined the term "individualism" to describe their robust attitude in the daily struggles with nature. Roosevelt believed that it was such individualism that made America great and he championed it publicly.

Rule of Law: Despite former President Nixon's claim that the president is above the law, the American Constitution makes all of us, president or poor person, equally subject to the law. We adopted this philosophy to avoid the excesses of kingly government wherein the king could decide on a mere whim what the law might be. Laws are to be an expression of the community, made in an orderly fashion, and promulgated broadly among the people. Laws are to be applied justly and equally to all people by courts sitting in fixed places and staffed by competent judges.

Social Contract: In modern political thought social contract theory is associated with three writers: Thomas Hobbes, John Locke, and Jean-Jacques Rousseau. They taught that the state was founded as a result of willful political acts of those who consciously chose to leave the stateless "state of nature" where people existed with obligations, rights, and morality. There was a compelling reason for establishing the state, be it protection, property rights, or education and culture. Americans were steeped in Locke's contractual theory, founding their early political communities (especially in New England) by mutual covenant. One early contract was the Mayflower Compact.

Socialism: This system of thought holds that the major (or perhaps even the minor as well) factors of production are to be held in common. The state, as trustee for the general public, controls all factors of production. Generally the state holds title to all property, and it alone can allocate the use of land through a centralized plan. The state takes on a paternalism that provides a wide range of social services to the individual.

Sovereignty: The term popularized by Jean Bodin in 1576 is defined as the supreme power over citizens and subjects. Bodin had spoken of two qualities of sovereignty: inalienability and indivisibility. There is no idea of morality necessarily connected to sovereignty. In American federalism we speak of "divided sovereignty" shared by the federal and the state governments. There is also the concept of popular sovereignty, where citizens are, in the final analysis, sovereign.

Theocracy: As suggested in the Old Testament, God rules over men in a theocracy. God may directly select one (or a group) to rule in his stead, or his will may be made known indirectly through a group of priests or others specially selected. God is the final sovereign and the people may attempt to enter some sort of contract with him. The Puritan experiment in New England was based largely on the concepts of theocracy and covenant with the deity.

Totalitarianism: This is the latest form of tyranny over the minds of the people. It is generally developed in postindustrial and postdemocratic societies. The industrial base is used to exploit class conflicts between workers and owners by mass media such as radio and television. The nation probably had a brief flirtation with democracy, which was proven to be ineffective and impotent in dealing with crises. A significant portion of the population has become alienated from its government and seeks salvation outside the normal political parties and processes. Totalitarianism is based on an exclusive political party which is the custodian of a book of knowledge that alleges that the party has the cure-all for all political problems. An oligarchy comes to power, probably by illegitimate means, and seeks a monopoly of power and prerogative. Communism, fascism, and nazism are recent examples of modern totalitarian systems.

Traditional Authoritarianism: Human history has seen more authoritarian regimes than democratic ones. Kingships are the principal example of traditional authoritarian government. Oligarchy, the corrupted rule of the few, is a second traditional form of authoritarianism. Absolute power is held by one person or a few individuals to the exclusion of the remainder. Such regimes are supported by professional armies that swear personal loyalty to the ruler(s). The masses not only may not participate in government, but they are generally denied even the most basic rights.

Unitary State: In this centralized governmental system, local or regional governments exercise only such powers as are granted to them by the central government. This kind of state provides unified and consistent administration. It does not permit local or regional governments to operate as "laboratories" wherein experiments with different types of government or governmental institutions can be tried out. Law and legal interpretations are uniform throughout the system.

Uprooted and Disinherited: In any society there are those who have been unable to establish permanent relationships with faith or ideology and who have come to regard the existing state as evil. These persons have no future in the state and thus they are willing tools in its destruction. Some are able to establish meaningful relations with the state after a time, such as when economic conditions allow their employment, thus giving them ties with the economic and political system. Others remain permanently alienated from both the state and society. Some come to accept dissident ideologies, such as communism or fascism. Others accept nothing and become nihilists. The S.A. in Nazi Germany was drawn from this group.

Utopia: The term was first used in Thomas More's novel of the same title (1516) and it has been used ever since to describe an imaginary society. Utopias are used frequently as vehicles to express the novel social, economic, and political ideas of various writers. Most frequently, a traveler has visited the utopian state and returned to describe the institution to the reader. Occasionally, our society is described to the inhabitants of the utopia. A utopia is a model that allows contrasts to be made between conflicting types of state mechanisms. This also allows disguised criticism of present societies. The other society is generally held to be superior to that of the writer's era, but on occasion the future society is described as a place of horror. In antiutopias such as George Orwell's *1984* or Aldous Huxley's *Brave New World* technology has been misused to destroy the individual.

Welfare State: In its final and complete form, the welfare state is the ultimate form of the paternalistic attitude that has produced complete cradle-to-grave care of the individual. The government over-rides property rights in order to provide for human needs and wants. It is the product of years of liberal-protectionist programs. It is often identified with the liberal, democratic socialist state, but it need not take precisely that form. States that have created social programs such as welfare systems, aid to the elderly and the handicapped, social security, and the like, have begun to move toward the welfare state. No state is precisely equal to any other state in degree of welfare planning and operations.

2

The Founding of the Republic

Albany Plan: This plan to unify the colonies primarily for military purposes was proposed by Benjamin Franklin in 1754. It provided for a governor-general as executive and an elected assembly from the 13 colonies. As proposed it had proportional representation with 48 seats, and it was to have real legislative powers.

Annapolis Convention: This convention was called by the Congress to amend the Articles of Confederation to allow for some measure of control from the central government over interstate commerce. It met in Annapolis, Maryland, in 1786, and its recommendations culminated in the Constitutional Convention in Philadelphia in 1787. Only five states sent delegates.

Antifederalists: Originally this term included those who opposed ratification of the new federal Constitution circa 1787. The members of this group opposed any centralization of powers away from the states and/or local communities toward the federal government. After the adoption of the Constitution they supported the Jeffersonian opposition to Alexander Hamilton's centralization of powers in the Washington administration. They opposed judicial review of legislation by the Supreme Court.

Articles of Confederation: This basic document of American government was drafted by the Continental Congress on June 11, 1776, and approved on November 15, 1777. It was ratified by all the states March

1, 1781. The Congress created by the Articles ceased to function March 2, 1789 when the new Constitution was declared to be ratified. It was a weak confederate government which gave executive and legislative authority to the Congress, but it had no power to tax and no means with which to compel the states to contribute those amounts of money apportioned to them. It could not control interstate commerce. Efforts to amend the document failed because amendments required the approval of all 13 states.

Aristocracy: The Constitution expressly forbids the granting of aristocratic titles. Because of the way this nation was founded few English or other European aristocrats had direct relations with the colonies. There were those who wished to have an aristocratic government in America. The demand was for an aristocracy of merit, not of title. John Adams, Thomas Jefferson, and Alexander Hamilton all discussed government by the most able and many devices such as indirect election of senators and the selection of the president by the electoral college were attempts at ensuring government by aristocracy of merit.

Assumption of State Debts: This was a cornerstone of the fiscal policies of Alexander Hamilton, who, in 1789, as secretary of the treasury, proposed that the federal government assume all state debts still outstanding and related to the War of Revolution. This plan was approved by the Congress but not without bitter opposition from states such as Virginia, which had already retired their debts.

Boston Tea Party: On December 16, 1773, a group of colonists, disguised as Amerindians, dumped 342 chests of tea in Boston Harbor as a protest against British taxation. This is the most famous act of civil disobedience in American history.

Charter Colony: The English king granted certain charters to groups that established colonies in the New World. These charters usually exempted the colony from all but incidental control by the king's ministers. Such charters were guarded by the colonists. Rhode Island and Connecticut were charter colonies. The charters were nominally agreed upon by both the colonists and the crown. Legislatures in charter colonies were elected by the colonists, and the governors were chosen by the legislatures, nominally with the consent of the king. So successful were these governments that their constitutions survived until well after independence.

Checks and Balances: In *Federalist 51* the author described this as a system "so contriving the interior structure of the government as that its several constituent parts may, by their mutual relations, be the means of keeping each other in their proper places." This describes the relations between the executive, legislative, and judicial offices of government, with each checking on the other, thus preventing corruption in the whole government.

Commerce-Slave Trade Compromise: In the Constitutional convention of 1787 there were a number of compromises reached by the delegates that allowed the new charter to be drawn up. None was more important at the time than this one which, on the one hand, gave the new, proposed central government control over interstate commerce and, on the other hand, prohibited the federal government from interfering with the slave trade until after 1808. Further, the Senate was given the power to reject treaties, by requiring that it approve all treaties by at least two-thirds vote.

Concurrent Power: This is a power to act in the public interest held jointly by the federal and state governments. The power to tax is concurrent power.

Connecticut Compromise: Two major plans for representation in the legislature under the new constitution were proposed in the constitutional convention of 1787. One would base representation on population and the other would give states equal voice in the legislature irrespective of population size. The Connecticut Compromise allowed for the creation of two houses, with representation in the one based on population (House of Representatives) and the other with equal representation for each state (the Senate). This is the basic formula on which our present system of federalism and representation is based.

Confederation: Twice in American history we have known confederate governments: under the Articles of Confederation and during the Civil War in the Southern states. A confederate government has component members, as does a federal state. In a federal state the central or national government is superior in power and sovereignty to the components whereas in a confederacy the components individually are, in the final analysis, sovereign and superior in power to any central or national government. In a confederacy the central government has very few, specified powers.

Constitutional Amendment: This refers to changes in the basic and fundamental document under which the United States is governed or under which a state is governed. Sometimes the Constitution is amended to correct a deficiency. More often it is amended to create a new power heretofore prohibited to government. It may be amended to delete a function of government, or guarantee fundamental rights to citizens. The Bill of Rights is really a set of ten amendments to the federal Constitution.

Amendments may be either proposed by the Congress (two-thirds vote of each house) or by special conventions called by application of two-thirds of states. Amendments may be ratified either by 34 state legislatures or by three-quarters of the states in special conventions.

Constitutional Convention: This is a meeting held to propose amendments to the U.S. Constitution or, perhaps, even to propose a new federal constitution. While the Constitution allows for the calling of a convention to draft changes in it, this device has never been used.

Constitutional Convention of 1787:   After discussing the possibility of changes to the Articles of Confederation at the Alexandria and Annapolis meetings, delegates from most of the 13 original states met in Philadelphia, originally to propose the needed amendments. Very quickly the delegates decided to propose a new constitution rather than amend the old one. The delegates met from May 25 until September 18, 1787. By the end of the convention, all states but Rhode Island sent delegates. The president of the convention was George Washington and its secretary was James Madison. Fifty-five men of the 74 elected served at the convention. Where the Articles of Confederation had required all states to consent to changes, the new Constitution extralegally allowed the document to become operational after only nine states approved.

Continental Congress: The First Continental Congress met with representatives of the 13 colonies in Philadelphia in 1774 for the purpose of petitioning the British government for redress of grievances. The Second Continental Congress again met in the same city to plan resistance to the British government. The Continental Congresses met periodically until 1781 and were the principal political and governmental power directing American efforts to establish independence and orderly government.

Declaration of Independence: This document was drafted largely by Thomas Jefferson in response to a resolution given by the Second Continental Congress, June 7, 1776. The draft was accepted on July 4,

1776. It argued that the king of England and his officers had committed many offenses against the American colonists and that the colonists ought to be free and independent of British rule. Most importantly, it argued in most eloquent fashion that the colonies were sufficiently prepared and politically sophisticated enough to become an independent power. The Declaration has no legal standing today but is highly valued as a statement on liberty and equality.

Delegated Powers: When the federal Constitution was drafted in 1787 it was assumed that all powers were originally invested in the states. The states chose to grant some of those powers to the new federal government, delegating them to the central regime. Other powers were shared by both levels of government, called concurrent power; still others were retained by the states called reserved powers. Finally some powers were prohibited altogether to government, these being reserved as rights of the people.

District of Columbia: Territory was given to the federal government by Maryland and Virginia (land given by Virginia was later returned) to become the seat of the new central government. The district is not given representation in Congress although an amendment allowing for congressional representation has been submitted to the states. The district has three electoral votes in the electoral college.

Division of Powers: In American government there are two divisions of powers: (1) between the states and the federal government; (2) between the legislative, judicial, and executive branches of the government. It is the second to which we most frequently refer. Powers are also divided by selecting the personnel to serve in the three branches of the new government by different methods. All powers are also limited by various checks and balances and by generally prohibiting certain powers to government.

Economic Interpretation of the Constitution: In 1913 Charles A. Beard proposed a thesis that the Constitution was framed by men who were economically motivated by virtue of their membership in the economic aristocracy to create a conservative document that would protect their property rights over and against the poorer classes. Much of Beard's *Economic Interpretation of the Constitution of the United States* has been discredited by Forrest MacDonald and others, although many still accept

Beard's thesis as one of the several major modes of explaining the formation of the federal union as we know it today.

Enumerated Powers: Those powers granted to the Congress in Article I of the Constitution are enumerated powers. Enmerated powers may also be those powers specifically granted to the federal government, or to some branch of it.

Faction: As commonly used today a faction is a branch or a wing or a portion of an existing political party which has broken or partially broken from the main body. Hence, in 1948 the southerners who deserted President Truman to support J. Strom Thurmond for president were a faction. The term has also been used by Madison in the *Federalist Papers* to describe what today would be called interest or pressure groups.

Federalist Papers: Eighty-five essays were written in defense of the newly proposed Constitution by "Publius." The real authors were soon discovered to be John Jay, Alexander Hamilton, and James Madison. The articles appeared in New York newspapers in the fall and winter of 1787–1788 and were widely reprinted. Most scholars agree that these essays represent the finest political theory every produced in this nation. They espouse the cause of the new Constitution and explain its meaning and application.

Hartford Convention: From December 15, 1814 until January 5, 1815, delegates from the New England states met at Hartford, Connecticut, in secret session. They proposed seven amendments to the Constitution and suggested that the states consider using the doctrine of interposition. This doctrine was alleged to permit the states to interpose themselves between federal law and its operation on the citizens of a state. This doctrine is no longer considered to be viable. The convention really accomplished nothing concrete.

Implied Powers: There are powers not expressly granted by the Constitution, which are nonetheless real. Such federal powers were first noted by Chief Justice John Marshall in the case of *McCulloch v. Maryland* (1819) where he wrote, "Let the end be legitimate, let it be within the scope of the Constitution, and all means which are appropriate, which are plainly adapted to that end, which are not prohibited, but consist with the letter and spirit of the Constitution are Constitutional." These powers then are not to be found explicitly in the Constitution, but they are necessary in order to carry into effect some expressly granted power.

Import Duty (Imposts): This is a tax levied on goods entering this nation and manufactured or assembled in another nation. For many years this tariff, theoretically designed to protect our beginning industries, was the mainstay of the federal income. Such duties are primarily used to make imported goods cost as much as or more than domestically produced items. There are many factors affecting the rate of tax to be placed on such imports. The Constitution requires that import duties (imposts) be uniform among the states.

Letter and Marque and Reprisal: This is an archaic term still contained in the Constitution. The practice was abandoned in 1856 by all nations as a result of a Declaration of Paris. These letters had granted the right to engage enemy vessels and capture commercial cargoes on the high seas to private vessels.

Loyalist: In the American Revolution many colonials, especially the wealthy, the aristocratic, and the educated, favored continuance of British rule. They remained loyal to the crown. After much bitter fighting with the colonials who favored independence, many loyalists fled America. Some went to Canada and others returned to England or went to other British colonies. The Jay Treaty supposedly halted the confiscation of their property and ended their mistreatment. Historian Samuel Eliot Morison has estimated that approximately 10 percent of the colonials were loyalists.

Madison's Journal: James Madison was the secretary of the Constitutional Convention of 1787. He kept two sets of notes. The formal notes contained only the formal motions made and the votes taken on these motions. Forty years after he died his diary was published and it has become an invaluable record of the debates and discussions of the convention. It has been augmented by a few other diaries and notes taken from the personal papers of other delegates. Still, the journal provides by far the clearest insight into the secret sessions of the convention.

Mayflower Compact: On November 21, 1620, the colonists who intended to found the Plymouth colony created a compact among themselves and with God for the governance of the future community. This served as the basis for the Puritan colony until 1691. It is one of the very first natural rights-based compacts in the world.

Paterson Plan: This is often called the "Small State Plan" or the "New Jersey Plan." It was one of the proposals for the new constitution proposed in the Convention of 1787. It would have strengthened the power of the states in the legislature by having equal representation from all states rather than by having representation according to population. The plan contained a supremacy clause making federal laws superior to those of the states.

Preamble to the Constitution: These famous words, "We the people..." preface the federal Constitution. They give a concise statement of the principles of American democracy and state the reasons for creating the federal union as we know it today. The U.S. Supreme Court has failed to find legal meaning in the preamble, but the general public sees the words as the basis of our republican system. Much has been made of the fact that the preamble speaks of a covenant among the people rather than of an agreement among the states to form the federal government. It is one of the principal arguments used to dismiss "states' rights" arguments of state sovereignty.

Prohibited Powers: Article I, section 9 of the Constitution prohibits certain powers to Congress. It may not suspend the writ of *Habeas Corpus* unless the nation is invaded or in a state of civil war, or unless public safety requires it. It may not impose ex post facto laws or pass bills of attainder. It may not give ports of one state preference over ports of another state. Congress may permit moneys to be drawn from the treasury only on direct appropriation.

Proprietary Colony: The English king granted charters to companies or individual proprietors to found and administer colonies in the New World. These proprietors held grants of land in the New World from the crown. Pennsylvania, Delaware, and Maryland were proprietary colonies. Lower houses of the legislatures were chosen popularly, but the membership of the upper house and the colonial governor were chosen by the proprietor with the consent of the king. William Penn's "frame of government" for Pennsylvania was quite democratic, but, generally, these colonies were run by the proprietors in the mother country.

Public Domain: These are lands over which the government exercises control and/or holds title. It includes national parks and forests, grazing areas, American Indian reservations, and the like. The sale of public lands helped to finance many land grant universities over the past 125 years. The homestead sales in the 19th century depleted the vast land reserves.

Quartering Act: The British Parliament required the housing of British troops in the homes of American colonials. It was one of the most hated pieces of legislation passed by the Parliament and its passage helped to prepare the colonials for separation from the mother country. The Third Amendment to the Constitution forbids the quartering of troops in private homes in peacetime except with the permission of home owners.

Royal Colony: Some British colonies were administered by the crown. A royal governor would be appointed by the king. As a result of years of benign neglect royal colonies in America achieved some considerable degree of self-government and resented later attempts to bring back the more direct governance of the crown. The legislatures had lower houses that were popularly elected and upper houses appointed by the king. Eight of the original colonies were royal colonies.

Separation of Powers Doctrine: American government is characterized by the doctrine of the separation of powers. Each governmental division has its own method of selection, each has its own powers, each has its own checks on the other two, and each has its own functions to perform. The system allows the executive to propose legislation, the legislature to amend and/or pass or disapprove the legislation, and the courts to interpret and apply the legislation. The executive oversees the operations of government while the courts interpret and restrict such actions and the legislature controls the budget and grants powers through law.

Shays' Rebellion: After the Revolutionary War Daniel Shays led a rebellion of debtors in the western part of Massachusetts. In the fall and winter of 1787–1788, Shays' followers resisted the collection of debts and the foreclosure of mortgages against former soldiers of the war. The militia was called out and the former army captain and his followers were arrested. The message of the revolt was clear: the federal government had to be strengthened, so that public order could be maintained. This was one event that precipitated the Constitutional Convention.

Sons of Liberty: There were several groups of American colonists who opposed a number of acts of the English Parliament, most especially its taxing of the colonists in the Stamp Act. This group, which existed from 1765–1766, was collectively called the Sons of Liberty.

Stamp Act Congress: In 1765 the English Parliament imposed a tax on the colonies, requiring the affixing of stamps on all legal and commercial documents, newspapers, and other written materials. Delegates from nine colonies met in New York on October 7, 1765, and rejected the alleged power of the Parliament to tax the colonies.

Three-fifths Compromise: This is a wholly archaic portion of the Constitution, but it is significant in seeing how the Constitution was put together as a "bundle of compromises." Black slaves were to be counted as three-fifths of a freeman for purposes of apportioning the House of Representatives and for levying direct taxes according to state populations. The Thirteenth Amendment destroyed the slave system, rendering this obsolete.

Tory: See *Loyalists*, Chapter 2, p. 26.

Town Meeting: In early New England principal decisions were made in a purely democratic setting wherein the townspeople voted directly on measures before them. It remains in effect in some sections of the nation, but its opinions today are more likely to be advisory than binding.

Townshend Acts: Charles Townshend was chancellor of the exchequor in the British cabinet in 1767 when a series of duties were imposed on glass, paper, tea, and paint. These acts also suspended the New York legislature. They were the cause of much friction between the colonies and England.

Virginia and Kentucky Resolutions: A series of 10 resolutions drafted by Thomas Jefferson in 1797 and 1799, passed by the Kentucky legislature, and sent to other states for approval, the resolutions held that states may render acts of the federal government to be null and void within the boundaries of the dissenting states. The delegated powers granted by the sovereign states to the central government were clear and precise. No undelegated powers existed. If the federal government tried to implement other powers the states could render such acts passed under implied powers null and void.

Virginia Plan: This is also called the Large State Plan and is sometimes known by the name of its sponsor, Edmund Randolph. This plan for a new constitution, presented in Philadelphia at the constitutional convention, gave extensive powers to the larger states by apportioning the lower house of Congress according to population. In the plan, as drafted primarily by James Madison, the lower house would choose the Senate.

Whiskey Rebellion of 1797: In 1791 Secretary of the Treasury Hamilton obtained legislation from Congress to tax the production of whiskey. The farmers and backwoodspeople opposed this tax. As a test of strength for the new Constitution Washington's suppression of the Whiskey Rebellion proved conclusive. The federal government had the power to enforce the laws it made. Hamilton had bought the loyalty of the rich by selling federal bonds to them at favorable interests rates. He forced the poorer classes to obey the Constitution and its new government by taxing them and then suppressing their revolt. This test was designed to show that a revolt such as Shays' Rebellion would not be repeated under the new government.

Writ of Assistance: The English, in order to stop the smuggling of goods, allowed general search warrants to be issued. These warrants neither specified the goods to be sought out nor the premises to be searched. They were widely discussed and certainly fueled the flames of revolution. These writs undoubtedly provided some rationale for the Fourth Amendment protections against unreasonable searches and seizures.

CASE

Coleman v. Miller (307 US 433, 1939): All amendments but one (the Twenty-first) have been approved by state legislatures. The Supreme Court in this case was asked whether a state legislature might, after having previously rejected an amendment to the Constitution, be able to reverse itself and approve the proposed amendment. The court answered in the affirmative. It also held that Congress alone can determine how long the states might have to approve a proposed amendment. Congress may set a time limit on the amending process within which an amendment would have to be ratified or it would otherwise die from lack of approval.

3
Federalism

Admission of New States: Article IV, section 3, of the Constitution allows new states to be admitted to the union on equal footing with all other states. A territorial assembly must petition the Congress for admission and the Congress then passes an enabling act to be signed by the president. The territory then forms a constitution and presents this to the Congress which then presents the president with a bill to admit the new state, which the president signs. The Congress may create conditions for admission, but after a state is admitted it is free to repudiate the provisions in its constitution required by Congress. No state may be formed out of other, existing states without the permission of the states involved and of the Congress. States may not withdraw from the union once admitted.

Amendment: No matter how perfect one may consider a basic document like the Constitution to be there will always be need for some changes. At other times changes may be made for reasons that may seem to be less than perfect. An amendment to the federal constitution may be offered by the Congress by a resolution passing two-thirds of both houses or offered by a special convention convened by two-thirds of the states. The latter method of proposal has never been used. Amendments must be approved either by three-quarters of the states or in special conventions. The latter method has been used but once, in the case of the Twenty-first Amendment. Congress has begun to stipulate periods of time within which amendments must be ratified. The deadline for ratification of the

Equal Rights Amendment was extended by Congress, the first time an extension was granted.

Centralization: The greatest danger to federalism is the tendency of the central government to set up programs for the social, economic, and political welfare of its citizens which have tended to decrease the importance of the states. Federal court rulings have limited state prerogatives in court proceedings and in civil rights areas. Expansion of federal powers through the increased use and broadened interpretation of the commerce clause has also weakened state powers.

Comity (states): This refers to the Constitutional provision that "the citizens of each state shall be entitled to all privileges and immunities of citizens in the several states." This allows the full recognition of judicial, executive, and legislative acts of one jurisdiction by another.

Cooperative Federalism: This is a product of modern rhetoric which holds that the states and the federal government are cooperating partners in a common quest for the good life for the citizens of the United States. It is thus a means of defending the grants-in-aid programs carried on by the federal government, defending these programs as vital and sustaining ways to ensure the survival of the states. An example of cooperative federalism in action is the interstate highway program.

Creative Federalism: This term is associated with the administration of President Lyndon Johnson. It emphasized mutual decision making and joint planning in intergovernmental affairs. It is a form of cooperative federalism, but its creators insisted that it was one step beyond cooperative federalism because it required federal officials not only to help states fund programs but to join with the states in planning and implementing these programs. It also spoke of revenue sharing and of other ways to provide states with moneys with few if any standards or requirements attached. It also emphasized regional planning as in the Appalachian area, thus allowing one agency to serve only a specified group of states. Opponents argued that most of the cooperative federal programs failed to live up to the promised cooperation while the regional organs served to weaken, rather than strengthen, states.

Exclusive Power: Certain powers are expressly reserved to the states for their control and other powers are granted to the federal government to the exclusion of the states. Those powers given over to one or the other level of government in the federal system are called exclusive powers. The opposites are those prohibited to either level of government and those shared by both levels of government. States have exclusive control over local and (if applicable) county and township governments. The federal government controls foreign affairs to the exclusion of the states.

Federalism: This is a system of dual or divided sovereignty in which both the states and the central government participate in the process of governing Americans. It is a unique scheme which allowed for an orderly transfer of major powers to a centralized government while allowing the states to retain their identities and some of their former powers.

Full Faith and Credit: Article IV, section 1 of the Constitution requires that "full faith and credit shall be given in each state to the public acts, records, and judicial proceedings of every other state." This applies only to civil proceedings and not to criminal ones. One major area falling under this clause relates to divorces granted by some states. This clause was designed to protect personal and property rights of individuals.

Grant-in-aid Programs: To encourage states to undertake projects the federal government believes will prove to be beneficial to its citizens, the federal government provides moneys to the states. These moneys frequently carry with them certain basic and fundamental requirements of performance that must be maintained in order for the state to continue to receive these grants. Programming undertaken with these grants include the construction of highways, welfare systems, airport construction, agricultural experimentation, and the like. This involves the federal government in heretofore reserved functions of the states while enabling the states to take on programs they otherwise could not afford. How these grants are to be handled is one of the major problems in determining the nature of federalism in the future.

Horizontal Federalism: States undertake to establish relationships with one another. Some of these relations are prescribed under the Constitution, such as granting full faith and credit to the acts performed by one another. Other relations are undertaken voluntarily as in interstate compacts.

Implied Powers: The powers of the federal government have grown in relation to state powers. A part of this expansion has taken place because of the use of implied powers. The Supreme Court discovered the existence of such powers in *McCulloch v. Maryland* (4 Wheaton 316, 1819). The court ruled that implied powers were to be sustained so that they might be used to implement direct grants of power made by the states to the central government. Implied powers are suggested in the Constitution, Article I, section 8, the "necessary and proper" clause. Had the courts not discovered implied powers it appears most unlikely that the powers of the central government could have grown to the proportions found today.

Inherent Powers: Most powers enjoyed by the federal government come about as a result of direct grants of powers from the states in the Constitution or from those powers implied under the "necessary and proper" clause as needed to implement the specific constitutional powers. The United States is a sovereign nation. That fact alone provides for certain powers, for there are powers that accrue to the sovereign power of any independent state. When the states surrendered their sovereignty in creating the federal union these inherent powers naturally accrued to the new central government even without direct constitutional action.

Intergovernmental Tax Immunity: See Chapter 10, p. 203.

Interposition: This statement of states rights and state sovereignty held that the states may "interpose" themselves between a federal law and its intended operation on the citizens of a state. In essence, the doctrine of interposition is merely a device that was to be used to try to overturn final national sovereignty. It was propounded by James Madison and Thomas Jefferson as a means of opposing the Alien and Sedition Laws in what became known as the Virginia and Kentucky Resolutions. It was used again by the South prior to the Civil War, and was discussed again after the *Brown* case as a means of preventing desegregation. It is essentially the same as nullification in intent and presumed application.

Interstate Commerce: Congress was given power to legislate the regulation interstate commerce. The lack of such authority had been a serious defect in the Articles of Confederation. Interstate commerce is defined as commercial transactions that cross over state lines, thus involving two or more states.

Interstate Commerce Powers: The principal way the federal government has moved into control over areas heretofore reserved to the states has been in and through its power to control interstate commerce. Under the guise of regulating the flow of interstate commerce the central government has been able to desegregate public facilities and set basic standards for minimum wages and working hours and working conditions. The expansion of such power began under John Marshall during his long term as chief justice of the Supreme Court and continued through Justice Taney up to the contemporary Warren Court.

Interstate Compact: Article I, section 10 of the Constitution permits states to make agreements among themselves, although the Congress must approve these arrangements. In *Virginia v. Tennessee* (148 US 503, 1893) the Supreme Court held that any compact that tends to increase the powers of states relative to other states of the federal government must be approved expressly by the Congress. Others may be approved indirectly or by implication. Congress has, at times, given blanket approval to whole areas of interstate compact action, such as in civilian defense arrangements.

Intrastate Commerce: Generally, this is commerce that takes place wholly within the boundaries of one state. Federal regulation of interstate commerce may extend to transactions that have taken place wholly within one state if these are a part of a chain that carries them across state boundaries. States ordinarily may regulate the commercial transactions that take place intrastate.

Kingpin Clause: See *National Supremacy*, Chapter 3, p. 35.

Matching Funds: See Chapter 10, p. 203.

National Supremacy: This "kingpin clause" of Article IV of the Constitution makes federal laws, treaties, and the Constitution superior to state laws and constitutions. In *McCulloch v. Maryland* (4 Wheaton 316, 1819) the Supreme Court also defended "implied" as well are constitutionally mandated powers as superior to state powers. In *Cohens v. Virginia:* (6 Wheaton 264, 1821) the Supreme Court allowed the federal courts to review decisions of state courts and to overturn these. The Fourteenth Amendment was interpreted by the Court in *Gitlow v. New York* (268 UES 652, 1925) as giving the federal courts supremacy over state courts, laws, and constitutions in fundamental guarantees of civil liberties and civil rights.

Necessary and Proper Clause: Article I, section 8 of the Constitution gives to the Congress the power to make all laws that are "necessary and proper" to carry out the specific grants of power found in the Constitution. The powers discovered here were accepted by the federal courts beginning with the **McCulloch v. Maryland** precedent (4 Wheaton 316, 1819). These powers add to the position of federal supremacy over the states.

Nullification: This is the archaic allegation of power as espoused by the writings of John Calhoun which stated that the states could declare acts of the Congress null and void within their respective boundaries if the state legislatures chose to do so. South Carolina attempted to nullify tariffs in 1828 and 1832. Operationally, there is little difference between interposition and nullification. Both are archaic states rights positions and are without legitimate constitutional base.

Police Power: Although many foreign nations operate national police forces, Americans have come to regard police power as a prerogative of state and local governments. The Founding Fathers wished to keep police power near to the people and avoid possible authoritarian uses of such police by the central government. Since Watergate-related revelations about misuse of federal police powers domestically as in the case of the CIA, we have strengthened our dedication to the maintenance of state and local control over domestic police forces. Under police powers states may control public health, safety, and morality, and provide for the welfare of the general population. The federal government has entered the field of police power, by providing for individual and collective well-being under the guise of controls over interstate commerce.

Privileges and Immunities: In Article IV, section 2 and in the Fourteeneth Amendment the Constitution speaks of\various "privileges and immunities" enjoyed by citizens of the United States and of the states. The text of the Constitution is speaking of obligations states have to treat citizens of other states with courtesy equal to that accorded their own citizens. The Fourteenth Amendment was designed to guarantee certain rights to citizens of the nation against state encroachment. The full meaning of both of these states of "priviliges and immunities" has yet to be exploited by the courts.

Referendum: This is one of the popular democratic devices which allows the average citizen to participate directly in the legislative process. Where it is permitted in the states a petition must be signed by a fixed number of voters, usually a certain percentage of eligible voters. The issue is then presented to the voters on a ballot on a regular election. Voters may accept or reject the proposition. The famous tax limitation amendment in California, Proposition 13, was approved by referendum. Referenda may be proposed to the voters. This is the common way states amend their constitutions. New state constitutions may be offered to voters in a referendum. There is nothing comparable to a referendum on the national level. Some state referenda may be advisory only, expressing the sentiment of the public on an issue. Such a referendum was held in 1976 in Massachusetts on handgun control.

Regionalism: With founding of programs such as the Tennessee Valley Authority and the Appalachian Regional Commission the federal government has begun to look at groups of states and their collective problems rather than at the individual states and their individual problems. Some have come to view these regional arrangements as decentralization of the federal authority whereas others see these institutions as a threat to the existences of the individual states. The growth of regionalism has provided us with a graphic lesson in federalism for it rests on the assumption that the real points of differentiation among the components of the federal union are regionally, not state, based.

Rendition: This is the proper term for the rendering up of a fugitive from justice by one state to another where the alleged crime took place. It is the federal equivalent of extradition which, properly, is the rendering up of prisoners by one sovereign state to another sovereign state. The obligation of state governors to render up prisoners to another jurisdiction has been held by the courts to be a moral or political, but not a ministerial, obligation. Prisoners may request a formal extradition hearing before being rendered up.

Republican Form of Government: Article IV, section 4, of the Constitution provides that the federal government shall guarantee a republican form of government to each of the states. The Supreme Court (*Luther v. Borden*, 7 Howard 1, 1848) has found this guarantee to be a political, not a judicial, matter, and has thus placed the matter in the hands of the president and the Congress. Reconstruction of the South after the Civil War was justified, in part, by invoking this provision of the Constitution. Its precise meaning is not clear and it is doubtful that the federal government will ever define it more clearly.

Resulting Powers: There are powers granted directly to the Congress in the first article of the Constitution and there are powers that are implied directly from the enumerated powers, as the Supreme Court discovered in *McCulloch v. Maryland* (4 Wheaton 316, 1819). The Congress also has powers which are neither directly granted nor directly implied, but which result from a combination of these two types of powers. These powers that are discovered as a result of a combination of other powers are called resulting powers.

States' Rights: Technically, all states have rights that result from the reservation of certain powers by the states at the time of the framing of the federal Constitution. The term has come to imply a form of resistance to federal encroachment to areas that rightfully belong to the states. Many states' rights advocates maintain that the states are sovereign and that they may void, by nullification or interposition, acts of the federal government. This position is without constitutional justification. Others argue that the central government should be curtailed in some of its actions by constitutional amendment. Their arguments will become meaningful if their amendments should ever be proposed by the Congress and presented to the states. Many states' rights advocates object to federal involvement in civil and voting rights activities within the states.

Tenth Amendment: The Tenth Amendment reads, "The powers not delegated to the United States by the Constitution, nor prohibited by it to the states, are reserved to the states respectively or to the people." The precise meaning of the amendment is unclear and the Supreme Court has thus refused to interpret or apply it. Presumably, it was meant to limit state governments, and to restrict the use of what we call implied or resulting powers. If this is the case then it has failed in its mission. The phrase "or to the people" makes the amendment quite unclear.

Twenty-first Amendment: While repealing national prohibition by rescinding the Eighteenth Amendment, the Twenty-first Amendment gave powers to the states to restrict the sale and distribution of beer and liquor. Much time and attention has been given in several states to the way in which they will control such sales. While the states have the power under the Twenty-first Amendment to wholly prohibit such sales or to sell such products themselves, the federal government has maintained that public sales of such products are at best quasigovernmental functions. Hence, liquor sold in state stores may still be taxed by the federal government.

Vertical Federalism: States have relationships with the central government. Some of these are prescribed in the Constitution, such as the federal guarantee of a republican government in each of the states. Others are established voluntarily as in the grants-in-aid programs.

CASES

Ableman v. Booth (21 Howard 506, 1859): See Chapter 8, p. 154.

Ashwander v. Tennessee Valley Authority (297 US 288, 19-36): See Chapter 8, p. 154.

Bailey v. Drexel (259 US 20, 1922): See Chapter 10, p. 210.

Baker v. Carr (369 US 186, 1962): See Chapter 3, p. 71.

California v. LaRue (409 US 109, 1972): In this curious decision, the Supreme Court gave the states the power to regulate lewd or obscene public performances in establishments serving liquor or beer under the Twenty-first Amendment, which gave the states the power to regulate the importation and sale of liquor. The regulation of such performances is generally and otherwise not possible. Thus, the Twenty-first Amendment expanded state powers, albeit to a very small degree.

Champion v. Ames (188 US 321, 1903): The Supreme Court used the interstate commerce clause to broaden federal police powers, thus giving the federal government the power to regulate certain activities under the interstate commerce clause. This case involved interstate sales of lottery tickets, but as a precedent it has allowed the federal authorities to move into many other areas with police power, especially against organized crime.

Charles River Bridge v. Warren Bridge (11 Peters 420, 1837): This was a broadening of the interstate commerce power allowing the federal government to regulate under that clause of the Constitution, individual entities that existed only in interstate commerce, provided that they formed a part of a chain vital to the movement of interstate commerce. Thus, a public authority was permitted to build a free, public bridge despite the fact that a privately owned bridge with an apparent exclusive franchise would be injured by the opening of the free one.

Coyle v. Smith (221 US 599, 1911): All states are equal in every respect to all other states. Even those admitted to the federal union after the creation of the Republic are equal to the original 13. The Supreme Court found them to be "horizonally equal." In the enabling legislation permitting a territory to apply for statehood the Congress may set any condition it chooses for admission. But once a state is admitted it may ignore any condition set by Congress unless it is a restriction that applies constitution- ally to all states. Thus, new states have the same reserved powers as those retained by the original 13 states, even though the states had never been sovereign entities as had the original states.

Doran v. Salem Inn (422 US 922, 1975):   The Supreme Court held that federal courts may issue preliminary injunctions against the enforcement of local laws if the plaintiff can show compelling need for such interim relief.

Edwards v. California (314 US 160, 1941):   California had passed legislation restricting immigration to that state of poor persons from other states. Commonly known as the "Okie" law, the intent was to restrict the migration of the economically disadvantaged who might become the un- employed poor living on welfare subsidies. The Supreme Court struck down this law, holding that a state might restrict the movements of per- sons only if it were to be done rationally, as in the case of criminals or carriers of disease. The migration of humans is not "commerce" which the state may control. One state was not to be permitted to isolate itself from the difficulties common to all by restraining the transportation of persons and property across its borders.

Ferguson v. Skrupa (372 US 726, 1965):   In sustaining a Kansas law prohibiting individuals from entering the debt consolidation business, the Supreme Court held that the rationale of the state legislature in adopt- ing public police was the exclusive concern of the public bodies of that state and not of the federal courts. It is wholly immaterial that the business was useful, not inherently immoral, or not contrary to the public welfare. The economic theories of state legislature is of no interest or consequence to the federal courts. If the people of a state wish to do something they may do so without federal interference unless that activity is expressly forbidden by the federal Constitution. Kansas could, if it chose, absolutely prohibit the plaintiff's business.

Gibbons v. Odgen (9 Wheat 1, 1824):   This is a fundamental case in the regulation of interstate commerce. The Supreme Court, headed by John Marshall, defined interstate commerce powers in such a way as to permit federal regulation of entities that existed wholly in one state if they formed a vital link in the free transportation of goods in interstate com- merce. The power to regulate interstate commerce thus did not stop at the boundary of a state, but was applicable within a state's territory. The term commerce was defined so as to include navigation.

Goldberg v. Kelly (397 US 254, 1970): In this case the Supreme Court placed welfare benefits under "due process" protections. Welfare benefits may not be terminated without first having a "pretermination hearing." Such a hearing would have some of the characteristics of a trial in that the recipient would have the right to an attorney, be confronted with witnesses against him, be allowed to cross-examine witnesses, and have the standard protection of rules of evidence as used in the courts. The case recognizes that social and economic benefits of the welfare system have some characteristics of a right rather than being simply public doles of the nature of privilege.

Graves v. New York ex rel. O'Keefe (306 US 466, 1939): In this case, reversing previous precedents, the Supreme Court held that states may tax the wages of federal employees. Prior decisions, following basic reasoning of *McCulloch v. Maryland,* had held that the states may not tax federal employees; and that the federal government may not tax state employees.

Hawke v. Smith (253 US 221, 1920): When an amendment to the Constitution is proposed and sent to the state legislature for action, the Supreme Court ruled in this case, the states cannot substitute the results of a referendum for action of the legislature.

Helvering v. Gerhardt: Reversing previous decisions rendered following *McCulloch v. Maryland,* the Supreme Court found that the federal government had the power to tax state employees' wages.

Johnson v. Maryland (254 US 51, 1920): Maryland law required all drivers to have a valid operator's license. A U.S. Post Office employee was arrested because he did not have a license. The federal courts ruled that the federal government was wholly competent to judge the qualifications of its employees to perform their assigned duties and thus overturned the conviction of the driver. The federal employee was free from state control and the state could not examine him on its own accord. A federal employee would be required to obey state laws when these laws did not interfere, or interfered only incidentally, with his or her job, as in obeying state traffic laws.

Kahn v. Shevin (416 US 351, 1971):   State law had permitted certain property tax exemptions for unremarried widows, but not for widowers. The Supreme Court sustained this preferential treatment of widows finding this benign classification to be fair. A widow, the court reasoned, is faced with greater difficulties in a male dominated culture than is a widower. State tax law was reasonably designed to ease the burden of the loss of a husband and wage-earner. Justice Brennan noted that more rational discrimination might have been made on the basis of income and financial position than on sex.

Kansas v. Colorado (206 US 46, 1907):   The United States Supreme Court held that, in the absence of any specific limitations, the federal courts are vested with all the judicial power that the nation is capable of exerting. The case itself dealt with the settlement of a dispute over water rights between two states.

Kentucky v. Dennison (24 Howard 66, 1861):   The Supreme Court found that the obligation of a governor to render up prisoners or fugitives from justice to the police of another state was merely a moral, but not a legal, obligation. The Court was unable to decide on how it would force a governor of a state to comply with the Constitution. Thus it found this duty to be political or moral, but not ministerial, requiring compliance.

Leisy v. Hardin (135 US 100, 1890):   Under the rule established in this case, states may regulate interstate commerce as the Congress permits. The Congress may validate state laws restricting commerce of a national character provided the federal law is silent on the area to be regulated. Absence of such congressional authorization would invalidate these laws in the courts. Congress may thus permit state police laws to operate even when they are in violation of interstate commerce. Where the Congress is silent the state may not operate.

Luther v. Borden (7 Howard 1, 1948):   One constitutional obligation of the central government to the states is a guarantee of a republican form of government. In this case, the Supreme Court held this to be a political matter, not a judicial one. Hence, the president and the Congress must decide whether a republican form of government exists within a state.

Martin v. Hunter's Lesee (1 Wheat 304, 1816):   The Supreme Court extended its appellate jurisdiction over state courts when cases came within the scope of the judicial powers of the federal government.

Massachusetts v. Mellon (262US 447, 1923): The Court found that (1) a state cannot protect its citizens who are simultaneously citizens of the United States from the enforcement of federal laws; (2) acceptance of federal grants-in-aid monies by states is a political not judicial act; (3) taxpayers' suits, attempting to establish injury due to taxation for a federal purpose, will not be entertained in federal courts; (4) only if an individual can show that Congress exceeded its authority in constitutional powers or violated the separation of church and state may he or she sue to stop federal programs, thus intruding into areas reserved to the states, was held to be invalid.

McCulloch v. Maryland (4 What 316, 1819): The operations of the Bank of the United States were subjected to a Maryland tax. The Supreme Court held that states may not tax such federal institutions. Further, the court sustained the creation of the bank in its famous defense of implied powers. The bank was not specifically authorized in the Constitution, but its existence was allowed under implied powers that are necessary and proper to stabilize fiscal operations that were authorized in the Constitution.

Missouri v. Holland (252 US 416, 1920): Congress passed an act regulating the hunting of migratory birds. The Supreme Court struck down the law, saying that the states alone had the right to regulate the taking of wild game. The United States then entered into a treaty with Great Britain in which it agreed to regulate the same hunting. This time the Supreme Court allowed the accretation of power to the Congress as a result of its attempting to carry out the treaty provisions. What had been a reserved power before the treaty became a proper area of federal operation after this latest expression of the will of the American people, the treaty with Britain.

New State Ice Co. v. Liebmann (285 US 262, 1932): This case is notable for Justice Brandeis' promotion of the principles of federalism. He wrote, "It is one of the happy incidents of the federal system that a single courageous state may, if its citizens choose, serve as a laboratory; and try noble economic experiments without risk to the rest of the country." Brandeis was underwriting one of the most famous and often repeated arguments for federalism: that it allows, even encourages, diversity of practice. Thus states may choose a number of experimental democratic devices such as referendum, initiative, and recall.

A decade before Justice Holmes had suggested the same thing in *Truax v. Corrigan* (257 US 312, 1921). The Fourteenth Amendment may not be used "to prevent the making of social experiments that an important part of the community desires, in the isolated chambers afforded by the several states, even though the experiments may seem futile or even noxious to me and to those whose judgment I most respect."

San Antonio School District v. Rodriguez (411 US 1, 19-73): There is no constitutionally guaranteed right to a public school education. The federal courts may not subject the state or local school budgets to judicial scrutiny. The Supreme Court thus upheld the public school finance system used in Texas based on property taxes. It recognized that school districts that have higher property valuations may raise and thus expend more money than can poorer areas with lower property values. These powers to sustain schools are localized, based in reserved powers.

Schechter Poultry Co. v. U.S. (295 US 495, 1935): In invalidating a portion of the New Deal economic recovery program in this case, the Supreme Court found that portions of the trade the legislation sought to control were not interstate, but intrastate, hence the proper area only for state remedy. This case is commonly called the "Sick Chicken" case for it dealt with the shipment of allegedly diseased or sick poultry within intrastate commerce. This is one of the most restrictive of the more modern cases dealing with the "interstate commerce" clause of the Constitution.

South Carolina Highway Dept. v. Barnwell Brothers (303 US 177, 1938): The state of South Carolina had laws limiting vehicle size and weight that were more restrictive than federal or other state standards. The Supreme Court upheld the state laws as legitimate safety restrictions even though they impeded the free flow of goods in interstate commerce. This was mitigated somewhat in *Southern Pacific Railroad v. Arizona* (325 US 761) where the court weighed the total effect of weight limit laws on interstate commerce; here it invalidated the Arizona law because it was too restrictive of the free flow of goods in interstate commerce.

South Carolina v. United States (199 US 437, 1905): The state of South Carolina owned and operated liquor dispensaries. These were taxed under a federal excise tax. South Carolina objected since the federal government was not permitted to tax the states, except as provided in the Constitution, that is, equally. The Supreme Court held that the liquor business was extraneous to the operation of state government, and that the business enterprise was not an instrument of government. Thus, the federal government is presumed under this precedent to be able to tax state owned or operated businesses.

Steffel v. Thompson (416 US 452, 1974): The plaintiff had been ordered to stop distributing antiwar handbills by local police despite the fact that his right to do so was recognized constitutionally. He was not arrested, but only threatened with arrest. The federal government afforded him protection in the federal courts. The Supreme Court argued that the principle of comity was violated, albeit only slightly, by offering him protection. Comity policy is not as seriously undermined by federal relief when no state action is pending as when relief is offered after state action has begun. The reception of the case by the federal courts does not imply that state courts might not apply the proper law to the case; nor is the federal action designed to destroy federalism.

Steward Machine Co. v. Davis (301 US 548, 1937): The Supreme Court held that there is no invasion of the powers reserved to the states by systems of taxing and spending under which the states are induced to cooperate with federal policies in relieving social needs that are national in scope. By placing pressures on the states to adopt various programs, such as through tax and credit benefits, the Congress cannot be said to have intruded on areas alien to its purposes or to have destroyed the principles of federalism.

Texas v. White (7 Wall 700, 1869): After the Civil War had already proved the point with bloodshed, the Supreme Court held that the states could not leave the union. Once a state always a state. The court called the American system "an indestructible union composed of indestructible states."

United States v. Butler (297 US 1, 1937): In another case in which the Supreme Court invalidated New Deal economic recovery legislation, the Court found that the Agricultural Adjustment Act had appropriated monies illegally and in advance for an unlawful purpose. The real motivation, the Court found, for the AAA was to purchase the acceptance of federal programs in areas reserved to the states, and prohibited to the central government, for legislative remedies. The court found that the "general welfare" clause of the Constitution was a call to spend monies for public use to better the general welfare, but within prescribed guidelines. It was not an independent source of power that might invalidate state powers that they had reserved to themselves.

United States v. California (297 US 175, 1936): The federal government may regulate state activities if these activities are not normally a part of the exercise of the state's sovereignty. In this case, the Supreme

Court upheld the safety inspection and regulation of a railroad operated and owned by the state of California. The danger to be apprehended under the law is as great if the railroad is state owned as if it is privately owned and the federal may then control the state government.

Welton v. Missouri (91 US 275, 1876):   The state of Missouri had attempted to tax dealers of goods produced out of state, and it had not required the tax from dealers of goods produced intrastate. The Supreme Court found this to be a burden on the free flow of interstate commerce that was not constitutionally permitted. States may not discriminate in tax policy between goods produced in state and out of state.

West Virginia v. Sims (341 US 22, 1951):   States may make interstate compacts with other states, but state courts then may not themselves be the ultimate judges in cases of controversy with sister states in terpreting the meaning of such compacts. Upon entering into such a compact to which the consent of Congress is required, a state accepts legal obligations that can only be solved by the Congress or the federal courts.

Wisconsin v. Constantineau (400 US 433):   The Supreme Court held that where a state law has violated both state and federal laws or constitutions the federal courts need not wait until after state courts had ruled on the issues to begin proceedings. Where the state law is ambiguous the federal courts (following *Railroad Commission v. Pullman,* 312 US 496, 1941) should await the decision of state courts and not interfere in the hope that state courts would act on the statute. Only after state courts have rendered a decision sustaining the law which allegedly violated federal law or the Constitution should the federal courts act. In the *Wisconsin* case the law was held to be unambiguous and thus the federal courts could act without waiting.

Younger v. Harris (401 US 36, 1971):   In this case the Supreme Court found that there is a reasonable presumption to be made that state courts will protect and defend the constitutional rights and liberties of its citizens on a basis equal to the federal courts. The court chose to defend the federalist principle and the integrity of state legislative, judicial, and executive offices. To over-ride this presumption the plaintiff must be prepared to show that he or she would be unduly jeopardized without hasty federal intervention. Under the federalist principles, U.S. courts should not interfere with state processes. Only after state court remedies are exhausted should federal relief be sought.

4

Politics and Political Parties

Absentee Ballot: When an individual cannot go personally to a voting place to cast his or her ballot because of illness or necessary absence, he or she may be permitted to vote by mail in a special absentee ballot. The exact conditions of such ballots are determined by the laws of the state in which the individual is registered to vote.

Ancillary Activities of Political Parties: Although political parties are formed to win elections, nominate candidates, and mobilize public opinion, they often perform other functions. These ancillary functions include holding picnics and banquets, listening to speakers, developing youth movements, promoting social activities, and practicing charity. Frequently, political parties will have adjunct groups involving youth, women, or senior citizen groups. They may publish journals, magazines, and newspapers. They may sponsor voter registration drives or support community activities such as visits by bloodmobiles. Some may host special events. On occasion they may help with extraordinary expenses, such as funerals of long-time members.

Apolitical Persons: Some individuals have no interest in politics whatsoever. They are unlike nonvoters who choose to remain away from the polls, but whose interest in politics is genuine if limited. Those having no discernible interest in the political processes may constitute 1 or 2 percent of the adult population of the nation.

Apportionment: In the context of federal government, apportionment refers to the method the states use to create districts from which members of the House of Representatives are elected. Every 10 years a census is held to determine the number of seats each state may have in the House. The state legislatures, or in certain cases, the courts, create congressional districts within the states as units in which elections may take place. Some states may have only one representative in the House; then, of course, apportionment is not required. Each state is guaranteed at least one representative by the Constitution. The state may also apportion itself within the state for purposes of creating districts from which state legislative representatives and senators are elected. The Supreme Court has required that all districts be equal in population to all other districts created within a state for purposes of electing classes of officials.

Australian Ballot: This is a secret ballot containing the names of all persons legally running for office within a given area. Ordinarily it contains space to write in names that do not appear on the printed sheet. Some states prohibit write-ins on primary election ballots. Originally, as used in Australia, party identifications were not given. As used in the United States, candidates are identified by party affiliation. An Australian ballot may also contain propositions to be voted on in referendum.

Available Person: Individuals who wish to hold political office play many games during the selection process. One game is played where prospective candidates make it known that while they are theoretically not seeking office they might be available for a "draft" by their party. Those who sit back and wait to see what develops while not publicly campaigning for office are called available persons. The first available man was commonly assumed to be Warren G. Harding, perhaps our worst president ever. When the Republican Convention of 1920 deadlocked over two worthy candidates, Harding's manager made it known that Harding was the available man and he was nominated.

Balancing a Ticket: Traditionally, vice-presidential nominees have not been chosen for their presumed ability to serve as president if needed. Rather they have been chosen to "balance" the ticket. This means that the candidate is selected to represent a different area of the nation, to offer political balance in ideological views, or to offer support in a crucial area (geographic or ideological). Thus some very strange tickets have been offered, as in 1952 when the Democrats nominated liberal Adlai Stevenson as the presidential standard-bearer and conservative John Sparkman as the vice-presidential nominee.

Bandwagon: This is a psychological device that is often encountered in politics. A candidate's managers and adviser try to create a winning atmosphere which convinces uncommitted delegates or politicians that their candidate is about to win and that they ought to "climb on his bandwagon" now. Presumably everyone likes to support the winner and the right presentation of the candidate as the sure winner can aid in a number of things, including raising money and gathering support from all quarters. If a candidate is certain to lose it becomes very difficult, if not impossible, to obtain overt support or campaign donations.

Campaign: In the process of electing candidates to office, Americans have required those hopefuls to appear before the voters in a wide variety of roles. They may be received as honored guests in a city or as adversaries in a debate or as featured speakers at some political event. They may meet with special groups such as the workers in a factory or senior citizens to discuss pertinent problems. They distribute bumper stickers, pins, brochures, posters, position papers, and other materials. All this is directed by a professional manager, financed by contributions (or the candidate's own money), and orchestrated by professional staffs. This, in its totality, is what we call a political campaign Campaigns occur anytime there is opposition, whether in a primary election or in a general election.

Campaign Fund: This is money available to a candidate or a political party to use in the attempt to influence voters in a primary or a general election. Such funds are normally used by parties or candidates to pay the costs of office space, television and radio spots, newspaper ads, campaign literature, buttons, and bumper stickers.

Candidate Orientation: Voters often express an interest in a particular candidate irrespective of other factors, such as his or her political party identification. This interest may take the form of a simple matter of liking the candidate's good looks or youth and vigor or it may be expressed in terms of a trust which the voters place in the individual. Most recent studies have shown that the image projected by a candidate is seldom the primary, and almost never the single, motivating factor in voting for that person.

Census: The Constitution requires an enumeration of the population for purposes of apportioning the House of Representatives every 10 years. The census has been used to reapportion state legislatures since *Baker v. Carr* involved the federal courts in "one man, one vote" apportionment of those bodies. In recent years the census has also provided the federal government with a mass of other information on the living style of its citizens through complex questionnaires given out with the census.

Certificate of Election: This is an official document given by the appropriate public official certifying the election of candidates to the various public offices voted on by the public in a general, special, or primary election.

Chain Ballot: This is a method of invalidating the electoral process when it uses the Australian ballot. The first person in the chain illegally obtains a ballot. It is then marked by the election manipulator. Each subsequent participant hands in the marked ballot and returns his or her own blank ballot to the manipulator, thus continuing the chain. The reward is often money, whiskey, or some commodity. Realistically, for a chain ballot to work, the election officials must be involved in the illegal operation.

Challenge: This is an allegation made by someone at the election site that a prospective voter is ineligible to vote in that election. In many jurisdictions the challenged voter may cast a ballot, but that ballot is segregated from all others until the challenge is satisfied. When a challenge is issued one must be reasonably certain that the voter is ineligible because the law ordinarily prohibits capricious challenges.

Closed Primary: Scholars disagree about the role of the rank and file in the selection of party candidates. Often, the masses are closed off from the selection process. This is not done in this nation by law. It is often accomplished in fact by powerful party operatives, such as the late mayor of Chicago, Richard J. Daley. Some political manipulators draw up slates of candidates. If they can control the vote especially by illegal or immoral means, they may be able to practice closure, cutting off the majority of party members from active participation in the selection of candidates.

Coalition: In continental Europe where there are many parties in most of the countries, seldom does any one party hold a majority of seats in the nations' parliaments. Several parties may then join in a coalition to create a parliamentary majority. In our system we have always had a majority from one or another major political party in our state and federal legislatures, so coalition often takes on a different meaning. One might speak of "conservative (or liberal) coalition" made up of members of both parties, speaking in ideological instead of party terms or one might find a sectional coalition made up of members of both parties from the same geographical area. One might also find, at times, rural coalitions in opposition to urban coalitions, again cutting across party lines. Most of these coalitions exist only temporarily, in opposition to specific legislation or in support of particular programs.

Conflict of Interest: Persons elected to public office generally have private interests in professions or industries or businesses. If they are forced to act in the public interest in areas where they also have private interests there is a possibility of the two interests conflicting. A lawyer may have a coal company or miners' union as a client. A bill may be presented to a legislature wherein he or she is a member, which seeks to regulate some aspect of mining. The client may directly or indirectly ask the lawyer-legislator to serve the client's interest when voting on the proposed legislation; or the law-legislator may feel self-compelled to try to represent his or her client rather than the general public. What is far less obvious is whether the conscientious lawyer-legislator is consciously or subconsciously following self economic interests by voting the way the client desires; or if he or she is consciously or unconsciously compensating for this possible conflict of interest by voting in the opposite way.

Compromise: The essence of politics is compromise. One must be willing to settle often for but a portion of what he or she wants so that his or her fellows may be satisfied also. One adjusts positions to allow for adjustments in the positions of others and out of this comes law. Our federal Constitution is often called, and with some large measure of justice, a "bundle of compromises."

Consistent Pressures: Individuals are often motivated to vote by a number of organizations and institutions to which they belong or on which they depend. When these pressures motivate one to vote in only one way, that is, when these pressures to vote are consistent in one direction, the individual has little difficulty in voting. Problems in determining how to vote are caused when these pressures work in opposing directions.

Contested Elections: Two (or more) individuals may claim to have been elected to a given office. The results reported in an election may be contested by one (or more) of the participants in an election. In either case they may contest the election. Legislative bodies may often determine the winners of contested legislative elections. Some disputes are carried into the courts for final settlement.

Contesting Elections: The heart and soul of the democratic processes, as we know them in this nation, are found in candidates competing for the support of voters in contesting elections. When a candidate is unopposed, his or her selection is virtually guaranteed. Only rarely can a write-in candidate win a major election. Our democratic government is based on the assumption that two (or more) political parties will present qualified candidates to the voters for their selection. Winning contested elections is the purpose of a political party. The opposite of this is an uncontested election.

Corrupt Practices Acts: All states and the federal government have sought to create legislation designed to prevent the fixing of elections by using illegal or immoral means. Since 1925 the federal government has passed significant legislation to stop corrupt electoral practices. Many of these bills aim at the wrong problems or at minor infractions while allowing major corruptive practices to continue. The main objection to most corrupt practices laws is that they are unenforceable, are easily circumvented, or that they set standards so unrealistically high that no attempt is made to enforce them. The laws will not be effective until the general public is willing to cooperate with the law enforcement officials to stay the use of illegal devices. One must also remember that bosses and manipulators could not buy votes if there were not individuals willing to sell their votes.

Countervailing Pressures: There is a general assumption made about pressures that are exercised on the legislators, presidents, and other public officials which holds that for each force that seeks to move sentiment in one direction there will also be a force that seeks to move opinion in another direction. If management pushes a view, labor might propagandize the opposite view. Industries tend to work at cross purposes. Farmers and industrialists may work against one another. Consumer groups and industries may clash on issues. Only in a very few areas, such as veterans' affairs, do we not find strong contervailing powers.

Credentials Committee: At times states may send two or more delegations to the national conventions of the major political parties. It is the function of the credentials committee to decide what delegation to seat, although these decisions are subject to the approval of the convention as the highest authority in a political party. The courts have generally held that conventions, through their credentials committees, are the final judges of the credentials of delegates. Generally, the work of these committees are routine. At some conventions the established delegations of the bosses, manipulators, and entrenched political establishment are challenged by counter-delegations representating racial, sexual, or other minorities. Occasionally, the convention will over-rule the credential committees.

Cross Pressures: An individual may be buffeted about by a number of conflicting pressures which seemingly require him or her to vote in different ways. A Catholic Republican in 1960 was cross-pressured to vote for Kennedy as a Catholic and for Nixon as a Republican. Most voters are motivated to vote by a number of contradictory demands which stem from any number of sources.

Dark Horse: Occasionally a political party will choose an unknown or little known candidate to head its ticket. That person is commonly called a dark horse. Most frequently, the term is applied to a presidential nominee, but there is no reason why it cannot be applied to a gubernatorial or senatorial candidate. A convention becomes deadlocked between two (or more) major figures. A lesser known figure may then be suggested as a compromise figure. James Knox Polk is frequently called the first dark horse although it seems unfair since he had defeated Henry Clay previously for the speakership of the House of Representatives. Clearly, Warren G. Harding was a dark horse compromise candidate when the Republican Convention of 1920 deadlocked.

Direct Primary: Most states allow the voters to choose the nominees of the major political parties by direct voter choice. Most require only a plurality, not a majority, of voters to approve a nominee. This device gives the rank and file party members greater voice in party affairs and it tends to diminish the powers of statewide party bosses. Direct primaries may be used whether a state has a closed or an open primary.

Electoral College: Electors are chosen for the purpose of selecting the president and vice-president of the United States. In theory they are free to vote for those individuals who in their opinion will best serve in the two offices. In practice they are chosen to cast their ballots for the winners of the preferential presidential elections held in their states. In essence, the individual voters do not elect these officers; the electors of the electoral college do. These electors are generally not popularly chosen by the voters and are pledged to vote for the winners of the presidential election in their state. Each state has the number of electors equal to its congressional delegation. The District of Columbia has three votes as well. An absolute majority is required in the electoral college for it to elect the president and vice-president.

Electoral Count Act of 1887: In the election of 1876 Samuel J. Tilden defeated Rutherford B. Hayes in the popular vote, but in a blatant partisan move the special election committee appointed by Congress ruled that certain challenged electoral votes were all to be given to Hayes, allowing Hayes to win in the electoral college 185 to 184. To avoid such a mess in the future the Congress passed this law, allowing the Congress in its separate houses to consider challenged ballots. If the findings of the two houses differ the delegation certified by the state's governor will be accredited.

Favorite Son: An individual supported by his own delegation for the presidential nomination of one of the two major political parties is called a favorite son. It is unlikely that he will have support outside his own state's delegation. It is a way of conferring honor on the individual and he is realistically not a candidate for the office. Such an arrangement does allow the individual to control his delegation's vote, giving him considerable bargaining power with the more serious candidates.

Federal Election Campaign Act of 1972: This ill-fated piece of legislation was designed to prevent individuals from "buying" political office. It set a maximum of $0.10 per eligible voter for expenditures in federal elections and set limits on the amount an individual and his or her immediate family could spend of their own money on the election. It required disclosure of contributions over $10 and of expenditures over $100. It did not and could not prevent the circumvention of the law by very wealthy candidates. Other committees could be created, such as "Democrats for X" or "Professors for X," and so on.

Federal Elections Campaign Act of 1974: For a long time there had been discussion of governmental funding for elections and this law fulfilled some of those recommendations. Taxpayers may elect to give $1 of their tax money to a special fund. To receive money a candidate must raise at least $5000 in contributions of $250 or less in each of 20 states. Individuals were limited to $1000 to any one candidate in a general or primary election and to $25,000 maximum in political contributions in any one year. Interest groups were limited to a $5000 contribution to any one candidate in a general or primary elections. New limits were set on expenses in federal elections. State and local employees paid by federal money were exempted from the nonparticipation clause of the Hatch Act of 1940 (although they may still be regulated by state laws).

Filing: In order to seek the nomination of his or her party, a candidate is required in most states to declare officially that he or she is seeking office. The act of filing is the formal declaration. State law may require a petition to be attached to the filing statement showing a specified number of voters who wish to see the candidate run for the office. In some states candidates must file with a cash deposit that may be refunded if the candidate receives a certain number of votes. The process was designed to make certain that only serious candidates seek their party's nomination for office. In some states a candidate may be nominated by write-in and this circumvents the filing statement.

Fluctuations: In many nations, unlike our own, parties themselves are constantly realigning their views and changing their ideologies and commitments. Occasionally, an American political party may take on a new cause, as the Democrats did in assuming the populist cause in the last decade of the 19th century. Individuals may change party associations as a result of fluctuations in their own lives. A Democrat may assume that he or she ought to be a Republican if he or she is successful in life. Disillusionment over something associated with one party, such as the Watergate Scandal, may convince individuals to change parties. Parties seek stability normally and they seldom change their appeals to account for fluctuations in voter status.

General Election: After parties have nominated their candidates, frequently by use of the primary election, a final election involving the candidates of the principal political parties must be held. Traditionally held on the first Tuesday after the first Monday in November, this general election selects those to serve in government. In some cases involving the selection of local officials, especially in local nonpartisan elections, the general (usually only) election may be held on a different date, although this is generally not the case.

Gerrymandering: See Chapter 7, p. 120.

Hyphenated Parties: In choosing to join one of the principal political parties, some Americans feel they must qualify that membership in some way. An individual might choose to call him or herself a "moderate

Republican" or "liberal-Democrate." He or she may choose to self-identify with a particular leader, such as "Regan-Republican" or "Wallace-Democrat." On occasion a party may split at least partially and temporarily. Thus, one might call him or herself "states rights-Democrat." This method of qualifying one's party association suggests that the individual might not support a candidate of his or her party if that candidate does not accept the qualification the member has added.

Ideological Parties: Although common in Europe, these parties are unpopular in America. There are "third parties" in this nation which accept some political ideology as a closed system of thought, such as the Communists and the Nazis. They are really disinterested in participating in elections and when they do run candidates they fare poorly. They seek primarily to propagandize their ideology and to indoctrinate the few who might join in the ideological beliefs.

Image: See Chapter 5, p. 82.

Incumbent: The office holder who seeks reelection is called an incumbent. Political scientists attach great significance to the incumbency, especially when election time rolls around. Campaign managers attach great importance to the incumbency, expoiting it in campaign mottos such as "re-elect Congressperson X" or "Keep Senator Z on the job." Occasionally, an office is filled by appointment, following the death or resignation of the elected office-holder. There is no general agreement on whether a nonelected office holder is truly an incumbent. Nonetheless, the fact that the candidate holds the office can be practically exploited so that is purely an academic question.

Independent: When registering to vote, individuals may list a political party identification or they may choose to register independent of any political party. Except in those states that have open primaries, this means that the voter can vote only in the general election. He or she has no choice in the selection of the party nominees and thus must choose between the candidates chosen by others.

Indicator Precincts: When one watches the television commentators predicting the results of an election when only a few percent of the votes have been counted one often wonders how this can be accurate. In order to make such a projection the statisticians rely on the vote from a few key precincts. These indicator precincts are also used by political scientists to study voting behavior. Careful analysis of past voting trends leads the experts to choose these precincts over all others for their purposes.

Interest Group: This is a group of persons, who may or may not be organized, who share common interests. As concerns the legislative or political processes, interest groups may have reason to be concerned with the passage/defeat of a piece of legislation or with the victory/defeat of a political candidate.

Issue Orientation: Ideally, candidates should be chosen by a responsible electorate which is interested in how the candidates stand on the issues that are important to the office they seek. Voters must learn to recognize issues and to discern how the candidates differ on these issues. They must learn to weigh an issue to see its relative importance in their lives as opposed to other issues discussed in a campaign. Elections are only rarely decided on the basis of how candidates stand on issues. Voters are more conscious of their party identifications and candidate appeal than of issues. Candidates occasionally develop issue-oriented campaigns with elaborate position papers and the like. It is a difficult task to convince voters that a candidate should be elected on the basis of the candidate's stand on the various issues.

Literacy Tests: It is reasonable to assume that voters are able to read and write as a precondition to voting. Literacy tests were often unequally applied to disenfranchise blacks or other minorities or nations.

Lobbyist: Various groups seek to influence policy at both the state and federal levels of government. They frequently find that their causes are best stated by professionals who specialize in influencing legislators and executives. These professionals are called lobbyists. Frequently, lobbyists were legislators themselves or were professional staff members of legislative or executive offices before beginning careers as influence brokers.

Long Ballot: One of the more frequently debated questions in politics is how to determine how many public officials should be elected to office. Many voters favor electing virtually all local, state, and national officers while others feel that only legislators and the executives should be elected. An election involving many officials necessitates the use of the long ballot while the election of fewer officers allows the use of a short ballot. In Europe one finds a longer ballot because of the existence of many political parties, all of which are attempting to elect public officers. Many political scientists favor the rational and reasonable selection of fewer officers by ballot because voters tend to know less about the candidates for lesser offices, such as state auditor or state attorney general.

Lunatic Fringe: A term coined by President Theodore Roosevelt to describe the adherents to unusual causes, the term has had wide acceptance as a label for anyone holding unorthodox political views. Over the years it has been used to describe Anarchists, Syndicalists, Nazis, Fascists, Communists, and Socialists.

Machine Politics: Machines are generally the creation of political bosses. No boss can long control large numbers of voters or large geographical areas without an assortment of helpers. These include: (1) *bag persons* who carry the moneys, most of it illegally obtained by graft, kickbacks, and extortion, to be used to manipulate elections; (2)*record keepers* who keep track of monies and materials that can be used to force others to follow the boss; (3) *ward heelers* and precinct workers who help line up the votes in the various districts the machine controls; (4) *drivers* whose job it is to bring voters to the polls; (5) *enforcers* who use terror and the threat of terror to keep voters in line; (6) minor *political officials* who support the boss in every way. Machines control patronage and help secure those who follow in their jobs and in other ways. They may even practice charity toward less fortunate members of their constituency.

Mandate: When a campaign has been issue-oriented the victor will often claim that his or her election shows that the will of the electorate has been shown and that it supports his or her stand on the issues. The victor thus claims a voter mandate to fulfill campaign pledges. This supposed mandate may be quite general or it may be reasonably specific.

Massachusetts Ballot: This is a form of the Australian ballot. Offices are listed with the candidates being placed in each office block in alphabetical order.

Mending Fences: In political jargon this means that a politician is trying to patch up feelings back home, presumably because he or she needs the support of those who have felt themselves injured for the next election.

Muckraking: Theodore Roosevelt coined this term, applying it to the actions of journalists who were exposing misbehavior in the corporations of the day. It comes from John Milton who spoke of raking up muck.

It is now applied to any journalistic inquiry in which wrong-doing is uncovered.

Multimedia: Sometimes called "mass media" the term applies to all the various spoken and written forms of making an idea known to the public. By reporting or not reporting news events, the radio and television stations, newspapers and magazines, and the like focus attention (or deny attention) on an event. When candidates or interest groups wish to bring their messages to the public they do so by advertising in the written and spoken media. Even motion pictures or television or radio programs may focus attention on a story or idea and provide an editorial statement on it by presenting the idea or story in a certain way. There have been many challenges to the way news events are presented on television and on radio. Generally, these media outlets are bound by the "fairness doctrine" which requires them to give equal time to the other viewpoint. Such fairness is not required of newspapers or magazines.

National Chairperson: Each of the major political parties has a chairperson who is a kind of permanent staff member, selected by the political party's national convention or executive committee, usually on the advice of the presidential nominee. This person coordinates the party's campaigns, raises money, directs party activities, and plans party strategy. This chairperson really cannot do much in the state party organizations, save what he or she can accomplish by personal mission.

National Committee: This is the highest permanent organ of a national political party. It coordinates the activities of the party in the time between the conventions. The Democrats have one man and one woman from each state, the District of Columbia, and certain territories. The Republicans also have one man and one woman from each state, but they add state chairpersons from states in which the party has had success (as in carrying the state for the presidential nominee, in having a majority of the congressional delegates from the Republican party, or in winning the most recent gubernatorial election). The delegates are chosen by the state parties or delegations to conventions or by popular election by the party. In some states the leading member of the party may choose to stand for committee selection. From 1968 to 1976 Governor Arch Moore of West Virginia was also Republican Committeeman.

National Convention: This is the highest authority of each major national political party. Traditionally the conventions are held every four years to nominate the presidential and vice-presidential candidates, but there is no reason why conventions cannot be held more frequently. The convention also adopts its party platform. Both major parties admit delegates to their conventions from territories even though these areas have no vote in the presidential elections. This input is the one chance territories have to make inputs into the selection of presidents.

Nomination: Before a person can hold office he or she must normally be nominated. Candidates for elective office may be named by their parties in convention, as is the case with presidential candidates. They may be nominated by the voters in the party primaries as is generally the case with senatorial or House of Representatives candidates. Individuals who are nominated for nonelective office are generally recommended by the executive branch and confirmed by the Senate. In the rare case of a write-in candidate the process of nomination may be bypassed.

Nonpartisan Election: While all elections for federal offices are partisan, there are elections at the local level wherein candidates run for office without being identified by party affiliation. Nonpartisan elections are frequently used to select judges for state courts and for memberships of school boards.

Nonvoters: These are the people who seldom or never vote in elections. They may choose to protest the choice of candidates or to object to the existing political parties because they are not representative of their views. They may simply have no interest in politics and they may distrust the entire political system. Habitual nonvoters make up about a quarter of the adult population of this nation.

Office-block Ballot: This is a form of ballot in which the names of candidates are grouped by office for which they are contending. The candidates may or may not be identified by party affiliation.

Oligarchy: Robert Michels, a Swiss political sociologist, in his *Political Parties* (1915) argues that groups of militants direct political parties. They are not effectively isolated or checked by the rank and file of the party. These members of the oligarchy advance their own selfish interests at the expense of the rest of the party. How well this "iron law of oligarchy" fits American political parties is the subject of much debate among scholars. If one accepts Michels' thesis then one must conclude that power is always held by the few, never the many, and that parties are merely tools in the hands of such competing oligarchical groups.

One Party Democracy: The idea was first presented by Vladimir Orlando Key, Jr. in his study of Southern politics. Key suggested that in certain areas of the United States, especially in the Southern states, only one party really has any chance of winning an election. Indeed, frequently there is no opposition party, or, if one does exist, it fails to nominate candidates for any or most offices. Still, there is a measure of competition and this is provided by intraparty rivalries. Thus, the competition exists in the primary elections as candidates compete for the nomination, which will certainly ensure their election in November.

Open Primary: This is a form of direct primary election in which the voter may cast a ballot for the candidates of either party without having to declare party affiliation. As it is used in a few states in America, the voter may vote only for the candidates of one of the two parties. A more open form of this primary would allow voters to choose candidates from both parties or to choose a candidate for one office from the Republican and a candidate for another office from the Democratic party. Few states use any form of open primary as politicians of both parties generally dislike the idea of having registered members of another party helping to select their party's candidates.

Opinion Leaders: These are the people who regularly talk about politics, candidates, and issues with their family, friends, and associates. About a quarter of the adult population fit into this category. Public opinion is formed here among these highly motivated and interested people.

Organizational Activists: These are the people who devote a substantial portion of their time to developing political parties and formulating issues. Their role in public opinion is vital. They are frequently the precinct captains, poll watchers, committee persons, and party leaders. They may work through pressure or lobbying groups as well as through organized political parties. No more than 1 percent of the adult population fits into this category.

Organizational Contributors: These are the people who volunteer their services to political parties or who donate money to parties and candidates. About 5 percent of the adult population of the nation fit into this category. Parties are quite dependent on these activists to get their messages across to voters. No candidate for major office can do without these supporters.

Party Column Ballot: In this form of ballot candidates are listed in a column under the party's name. This form of ballot is used in Indiana and thus is sometimes called Indiana ballot. Party operatives generally prefer this form of ballot to the office-block ballot since the latter emphasizes the office rather than the party affiliation.

Party Discipline: In many democratic nations parties maintain very strict discipline over their members. This is not true in this nation, at least not at the national level. Presidents have attempted to purge or cause the defeat of members who vote against their programs. Congressional election committees may withdraw support from maverick members. At times parties have withdrawn their institutional support from candidates. At the most local level political bosses are at times more successful in maintaining party discipline, using such devices as slates. There is no real concept of party discipline in regard to rank and file party members. Since most elected officers are nominated by primary ballot the party cannot easily maintain its discipline over these officers. Presidents, state governors, and others may withhold patronage from officials who incur their disfavor.

Party Identification: Some persons have an inner psychological attitude which disposes them to attach themselves to a given party. We may choose a party because of family association with the party in question. Conversely, we may react away from a party because of rebellion against our parents or others who are associated with that party. A given cause in which we have a personal interest may attract us to a party that is, at least at the moment, espousing our cause. We may choose a party because it is successful at the moment or we may favor the underdog and seek to rebuild the minority party along lines pleasing to us. We may favor a particular leader and choose the leader's party in order to be close to the leader or his or her cause.

Party Orientation: Frequently, elections are conducted on a partisan political basis only, with no discussion of issues. Voters are encouraged to vote a straight ticket for all candidates put on the ballot by their party. This serves the interest of the majority party, but the minority party may seek to convince its members to do likewise while seeking to influence members of the other party to cross over and vote against their own party's candidates. When one of the parties has been disgraced, as in the case of the Watergate Scandal, members of the other party may try to convince voters that all members of the scandal-ridden party should be voted out of office. Thus, party orientation has both positive and negative implications.

Patronage: Politics brings many rewards to the winners and of these few are more important than patronage. This power allows the office holder to appoint, or at least recommend, individuals to jobs. It may also, with less claims to legitimacy, allow an office holder to influence the awarding of contracts for various goods and services. In many areas patronage is a way parties have of rewarding ward heelers, precinct workers, bag persons, and like supporters and activists. State road worker jobs in many states are given for party support and service, as are many other unskilled or semi-skilled positions in state offices, such as janitor and elevator operator.

Petition: In many states a prospective candidate must have a petition signed by a certain number of voters who attest to the desirability of having that person's name placed on the ballot to stand for his or her party's nomination for public office. Frequently, the number of signatures is expressed as a percentage of voters who voted in the last gubernatorial or presidential election in that area. In several states petitions are used in the processes of recall, referendum, or initiative. Petitions are used in elections to try to limit prospective candidates to those few who are seriously interested in holding the office.

Pivotal States: Seven states have 211 electoral votes of the 270 needed for selection of the president and vice-president. These states are most important to the presidential ambitions of any candidate. Thus, the candidates will frequently devote proportionately more of their time and efforts to winning these states' electoral votes than they will to winning in the smaller states where fewer votes are to be found. These states are: California, New York, Pennsylvania, Illinois, Texas, Michigan, and Ohio. Theoretically, a candidate could carry as few as 12 states and still win if those 12 were those with the largest electoral vote.

Platform: In the national conventions of political parties a set of principles and political stands is agreed on. These principles are gathered together in a platform. Generally, party platforms are stated in a very general way so that the individual planks may be interpreted in several ways and so that no faction of the party is offended. In the more recent party conventions some factions have tried to incorporate very controversial planks that deal with issues such as abortion and homosexuality, into the platforms.

Plurality: Excepting the selection of the president and vice-president by the electoral college most elections can be won in the United States will less than a clear majority, even of those who voted, let alone a majority of those eligible to vote. When one candidate wins an election by virtue of receiving more votes than the opponents, but has less than a majority, he or she is said to have secured a plurality. Several candidates for president have received only a plurality of the popular vote, including Lincoln, Kennedy, and Nixon (1968).

Political Action Committee: A number of organizations have been forbidden to engage in political campaigns directly by various laws. For example, the Taft-Hartley Act of 1947 prohibits labor unions from using members' dues for political purposes. To overcome such prohibitions voluntary organizations may be formed where voluntary fees are collected by the organization and distributed to individuals whose campaigns are supported by the main organization. The "Committee on Political Education" of the AFL-CIO and the UMWA's "Compac" are examples of political action committees. Business and fraternal, civic, and trade organizations may also form PACs. The normal way to do this is to form a "political victory fund" that has a title similar to the main organization.

Political Boss: In some area politics are run by a single individual or by a very small elitist group (sometimes called an oligarchy). These persons are commonly known as manipulators, power brokers, or merely as bosses. They may demand money from candidates to "deliver the vote." They may use legitimate devices, but few bosses are truly reluctant to use illegitimate means such as vote buying, chain ballots, and even terrorism and violence. Some monies may be used for licit purposes, such as paying poll workers or car drivers, but more frequently monies are used to buy votes. Bosses are frequently found in cities. A recent book refers to the late mayor of Chicago, Richard Daley as "Boss Daley." In the past (and perhaps in the present) bosses delivered the vote in New York, Philadelphia, and other cities. A boss and his followers and enforcers may be called a "ring" as in the New York City "Tweed Ring" of the 19th century. This was headed by "Boss" Tweed who allegedly extorted monies from contractors and others who provided services to the city.

Political Party: A political party is formed when significant numbers of persons have interests in common and they then decide to formalize these interests by nominating and running candidates for office.

Parties have names (Democrats, Republicans), symbols (Republican elephant, Democratic donkey), members (workers, supporters, contributors), staffs, and goals. They are recognized as legitimate organizations that run candidates for office. They work to win elections and to promote ideas, ideologies, and causes.

Poll: The measurement of public opinion is useful in many areas of politics, from planning election strategy and campaigns to deciding how to vote on an issue according to the measure of support shown by the voting public. Polls are generally taken among miniature reconstructions of the political universe, such as the constituents of a congressional district, a state, or the nation. One must be able to distinguish between such a valid poll and one that has no valid or scientific base.

Poll Tax: This is a direct per capita tax levied on prospective voters. It really was a device to prevent the poor, especially blacks, from voting. It was seldom a revenue raising device and failure to pay resulted only in the removal of one's name from registration lists for the most part. Somewhat belatedly, the poll tax as a device to limit the vote was rendered useless by the Twenty-fourth Amendment.

Poll Watcher: These people are on the bottom rung of the operatives of the major political parties. They spend election day at the polls doing a variety of jobs. They may look for election law violations. They keep a list of registered voters of their party, checking off the names of those who have voted. They may secure the aid of others, including drivers, in locating those who have not voted and bringing them to the polls.

Popular Vote: This term must be understood in comparison to the vote of the electoral college. In the popular vote one counts all votes cast in the general election for a given presidential–vice-presidential ticket. The electoral college actually elects these officers. In the Hayes-Tilden election Tilden received more popular votes than did Hayes but lost in the electoral college.

Position Papers: Occasionally elections are run by candidates who choose to discuss the issues in the election and take stands on those issues in the hope that the voters will cast their votes on the basis of the development of these issues rather than on the basis of candidate appeal or party identification. In order to exploit his or her stand on an issue the candidate will prepare, or have prepared, a set of papers that outline in some detail why the candidate feels the way he or she does about the issues. These papers are often individualized for each issue in which the candidate has an interest.

Precinct: See Chapter 13, p. 240.

Preferential Ballot: This is sometimes called advisory ballot. The results of an election are not binding on anyone. This ballot merely instructs the representatives, most often to a political convention, what preferences the voters have. Many primary elections for state or national nominees are merely preferential.

Pressure Group: Individuals who share common sentiments, feelings, ideologies, political philosophies, or social outlooks may create formal groups that then seek to influence the political system, and probably their fellow citizens. Such groups are called pressure groups. Those pressure groups who try to influence legislators directly, as by hiring lobbyists, are subject to certain regulations. However, those who do their work in a less formal manner are subjected to few controls, because their work is clearly protected under the First Amendment.

Primary Election: In the United States candidates for political office are given the party's nomination in a primary election. Some states require that candidates for office be members of the same party whose nomination they seek. In an open primary one may vote in a primary election irrespective of one's party of registration. In a closed primary one may vote only in the election of one's own party. Crossing over is a practice of voting in the primary of the opposing party.

Propaganda: This is the art of influencing the ways others think by subtle or direct manipulation. Today propaganda cannot be separated from the mass media, because the use of radio, television, newspapers, magazines, and journals is vital to propaganda efforts. Those seeking to influence public opinion may use their own materials, such as handouts or flyers. When the government tells us that Social Security programs benefit us it is propagandizing its point of view. Most democratic societies insist that government propaganda efforts be directed at other nations and not used internally. Otherwise, interest and pressure groups, and political parties and movements are generally free to use propaganda.

Property Qualificiations to Vote: In the colonial period of American history it was common practice to require voters to own property in order to enjoy that right. The basic assumption was that property ownership ensured voter responsibility. Various actions of government, including fiscal policies, are or may be restrictions on property. Therefore, only those owning property should be permitted to vote. This qualification was dropped before the Civil War.

Protest Vote: This device has been used increasingly in America as a result of political alienation felt by some individuals and groups. A vote is cast for a candidate not because of any merit attached to the candidacy—indeed, the voter expects the candidate to lose—but as a form of protest against the political system. The individual at least votes, but he or she is just showing disgust with the regular parties and what he or she views as nonchoice among candidates.

Public Opinion: Various individuals and groups within society hold views on a variety of issues. It is the function of polls to determine what views are held by the population. Public opinion is expressed in referenda, elections, lobbying activities, and pressure group publications and materials. Public opinion may support the existing political regime or it may oppose the regime.

Registration: This is a process whereby prospective voters are required to establish their identities and residences prior to an election so that they may be declared eligible to vote. In most areas voter registration may be accomplished by mail or in person. Some states allow immediate voter registration on election day by merely presenting some form of identification such as a driver's license.

Runoff Election: Generally, a plurality of votes is sufficient to nominate or elect a candidate. In some states, the state law requires selection by a majority of those who voted. If no one receives a clear majority of votes in the first election a runoff election may be ordered between those two candidates who received the largest number of votes cast. Runoff elections are used only in primaries in this nation. Under certain conditions a reelection may be ordered (usually by the courts) in a general election race, for instance, if a tie exists after a recount, but this is not really a runoff.

Short Ballot: Rather than have the electorate fill every state or local office by democratic process, the ballot may be shortened by allowing the voters to choose only a very few officers, usually legislative representatives, president/vice-president, and governor. Thus, the voter comes to know the candidates since there are only a few to be considered. Since the Jacksonian era we have thought of it as our natural right to select as many officers as possible. Many offices are now staffed professionally rather than as a result of popular vote, as, for example, state superintendent of schools, once an elected office in some states.

Single Member Legislative District: Since the "one man, one vote" rulings from the Supreme Court, the members of the House of Representatives must be all elected from single member districts or all elected from the state as a whole. In some states that have but one representative, the district is coextensive with the state. In other states, members must be selected from districts of approximately equal population (within each state), each district having one member, or the entire delegation must be elected by the entire population of the state. Few congresspersons like the latter alternative so nearly all use their influence to have single member districts created. Rarely, in states, there may be multiple-member legislative districts and single member legislative districts coexisting.

Slate: Slates are used primarily in primary elections. It is a list of candidates agreed on by some group before an election. Individual candidates may create a slate to pool their advertising costs. Individuals may try to add their names to a slate in order to have more popular members draw voters to the lesser known candidates. A slate may be used to allow individuals with regional appeal to use the regional strength of other candidates in a pool. Interest groups may create slates of candidates which run across party lines in order to ensure the election of candidates who favor their positions on issues.

Social and Economic Status (SES): Much has been written in recent years on the importance of social and economic status in voting behavior. The fundamental assumption made here is that the more affluent voters vote one way and the economically disadvantaged vote in another way. Presumably, lower SES classes vote Democratic while more wealthy classes vote Republican. Studies have suggested that there is some validity to this claim, and supporting data have been found in studies of political party associations in other democratic nations such as England and Japan.

Special Election: Although some vacancies may be filled by appointment and others are filled by special provision of the law, many others must be filled by voters. If a regular election is not available for such purposes because the vacancy must be filled before such an election, a special election may be called. Occasionally, an irregularity may occur in a regular election which must be reconciled through some special election.

Split Ticket: Political scientists ideally would like to see voters cast their votes for the best candidates. Presumably, neither party has a monopoly of good talent. Thus, voters may choose some candidates from each party or split their tickets (ballots).

Straight Ticket Voting: If one chooses to vote for all candidates from one political party one is said to be voting a straight ticket. Obviously, political parties would prefer voters to cast a straight party ballot. Some states have a single lever to pull or box to check which enables one to vote only for all candidates from one's party.

Suffrage: The Constitution and statutory law confers on individuals the right to participate in the election of their officers and legislators. In states the population or some portion thereof may be permitted to vote on referenda on many issues, including ratification of state constitutional amendments. The Constitution forbids the discrimination against individuals because of race, religion, national origin, or sex. Suffrage was once limited by qualifying clauses such as the requirement of property ownership.

Third Party: In our two party system we refer to any party other than the Democratic or Republican party as a "third" party. Americans tend to favor the two party system to such a degree that third parties receive little or no popular support. Many attempts have been made to reorient American politics toward more ideological parties, but there has been no tangible success here. In a few states third parties also nominate the candidates from the two major parties. For example, in New York, the Liberal Party usually nominates the Democratic candidate while the Conservative Party may nominate the Republican candidate. Most third parties are ideological (American Nazi, Communist, Socialist) or are oriented toward a single issue (Prohibitionist, Vegeterian). Occasionally, in a single election, such a party will have some success as in the case of the Wallace campaign in 1968.

Two Party System: Although many democratic nations have several, even many, major political parties, the United States has existed with only two powerful and mainstream parties. Third political parties have had only brief moments of success, usually when tied to a single, strong personality, as for example, when the American Independent party ran George Wallace in 1968. States within the union likewise have been dominated by the two party system, although some have been controlled by one party generally. Americans regard the two party system as permanent and the only possible way to provide popular but stable government.

Unit Rule: According to the 1970 rules of the Republican and Democratic parties, delegates may cast their votes irrespective of the actions of the rest of the state's delegation. In prior years the Democratic party allowed the state delegation to cast its vote in its entirety irrespective of the minority wishes of some delegates. Thus, candidates sought to win the majority of a state's delegation in the hope that the state would invoke the unit rule, thus allowing the head of the delegation to cast the vote for the entire bloc of votes.

Vital Majority: In America the majority of the citizens prefer a center position on the political spectrum, avoiding the extremes of the political right or the political left. This center position is generally quite protective of basic institutions and ways of doing things. Although fundamentally conservative, Americans tend to support the entrenched and established liberal state.

Voting Rights Acts of 1965, 1970, and 1975: The first act authorized the use of federal registrars in areas where 50 percent of the eligible voters were registered to vote. The states affected included parts of North Carolina, South Carolina, Alabama, Georgia, Louisiana, Mississippi, and Virginia. The 1970 act extended the 1965 act and allows the 18 year old vote. It also suspended the use of literary costs and provided more uniform rules for absentee ballots. The 1975 act again extended the 1965 act and required bilingual ballots in certain areas. The impact of the first two acts had been on black voters. The 1975 act was designed to increase participation by other minorities, including Spanish-speaking and native American persons.

CASES

Avery v. Midland County (390 US 474, 1968):   In this case the Supreme Court applied the "one man, one vote" principle to county government. Where county commissioners or like officials are elected within the county in single or multiple member districts, the obligation is the same as for legislative districts, that is, to provide equal representation. The case involved a county in which commissioners were elected from single member districts, but where some were elected from underpopulated rural areas whereas others were elected from a large metropolitan area where the commissioners represented many times as many people as those elected from rural areas represented.

Baker v. Carr (369 US 186, 1962):   In this case the Supreme Court held that there is no due process when the legislature of a state is apportioned so that a substantial majority of the voters is denied the opportunity to elect members of that body. The Supreme Court ordinarily refuses to consider "political" matters, but here it found jurisdiction and considered this appeal to be justifiable in the federal courts. The state had failed for over 60 years to reapportion as the state constitution had required. The court held that each person was entitled to one vote which had the same weight as that of his or her neighbor in selecting state legislative representatives. This is the "one man, one vote" rule.

Columbia Broadcasting System v. Democratic National Committee (412 US 94, 1973):   In defining the "fairness doctrine" wherein responsible opinions must be aired free of charge in response to the endorsement of candidacies and positions on social, economic, and political issues by broadcasting stations, the Supreme Court held that the fairness doctrine need not be applied to editorial advertising. Stations need only provide balanced presentation of information on issues of public importance. Access to all persons who wish to speak out on public issues does not have to be provided.

Cousins v. Wigoda (319 US 477, 1975):   The Supreme Court held that a state court cannot intefere with the selection of delegates to a national political party convention in this case. National political parties enjoy a constitutionally guaranteed right of association. The interest of states in ensuring the integrity of the electoral process is not compelling in this case and thus states may not interfere with the process of selection of delegates to national conventions.

Ex parte Siebold (100 US 371, 1880):   The Supreme Court found that Article I, section 4, of the Constitution gave the Congress sufficient powers to legislate in matters concerning elections for federal offices. This power was granted here only in regard to general, but not primary, elections. In *Newberry v. United State* (256 US 232, 1921) the Supreme Court denied such powers to the Congress over primary elections, but reversed this decision later in *United States v. Classic* (313 US 299, 1941).

Guinn v. United States (238 US 347, 1915):   In this case the Supreme Court overturned "grandfather's clause" laws in the states. States had restricted the right of blacks and foreigners to vote by requiring that before an individual could vote, the individual had to show that he or she had an ancestor who voted or was eligible to vote.

Lane v. Wilson (307 US 268, 1939):   To avoid voter registration of blacks after the Civil War states came up with a wide variety of strange laws which were aimed at restricting the vote to whites. One such type of law was the "grandfather's clause" which held that one could vote only if one's ancestors were eligible to vote. The Oklahoma Constitution, which restricted voters to those whose ancestors could vote in 1861, was invalidated by the Supreme Court in this case. The court reasoned that the legislature in creating this requirement was seeking only to disenfanchise citizens who were otherwise eligible to vote. This requirement did not protect the integrity of the voting and electoral process.

Mahan v. Powell (412 US 735, 1973):   Since the "one man, one vote" rule was adopted in *Baker v. Carr* (1962) the Burger court has allowed greater variance in state legislative districts in population size than it has permitted in congressional district size. In this case the Supreme Court permitted a 10 percent maximum variation in state legislative districts, primarily in order to preserve, insofar as possible, the historic and meaningful units of local elections. The courts may allow such considerable variance if the courts can be convinced of the legislative intent to construct districts that are meaningful to the populations involved while attempting to maintain equal representation.

Newberry v. United States (256 US 232, 1921):   Although the Supreme Court had recognized the power of the Congress to regulate state elections so long as there were federal officers to be elected (in *Ex parte Siebold*, 100 US 371, 1880), it applied this power exclusively to the general elections. In this case the court refused to grant the power to Congress to regulate primary elections. Only 20 years later the court discovered that the Constitution did grant powers to Congress to regulate primaries (*United States v. Classic*, 313 US 299, 1941) and thus overturned the *Newberry* precedent.

O'Brien v. Brown (409 US 1, 1972): The Supreme Court held that federal courts may not intervene in the deliberations of national political party conventions. The courts were not permitted to assume jurisdiction here because of the necessity of having political processes wherein free and open freedom of choice could be allowed without fear of governmental intervention. The political processes of a free state must be allowed to run without judicial interference.

Red Lion Broadcasting Co. v. FCC (412 US 94, 1973): Radio and television stations may endorse political candidates or express views on political, social, or economic topics. However, they must provide free time to those whose candidacies or views they oppose. The Supreme Court in this case upheld an order issued by the Federal Communications Commission which required the allocation of free time to the opponents of those the radio station endorsed. The court reasoned that a limited number of frequencies are available for radio/TV broadcasting and so those holding licenses have a special responsibility to provide balanced presentations. This can be accomplished by reserving time for responses to endorsements and to editorials given on behalf of the station management.

Smith v. Allwright (321 US 649, 1944): In this case the Supreme Court overturned a previous ruling (*Grovey v. Townsend*, 294 US 45, 1935) wherein the courts had permitted political parties, as voluntary associations, to practice racial discrimination in the selection of their nominees for office. Here the courts held that blacks were entitled, under the Fifteenth Amendment, to participate in primary elections, and their right to do so could not be abridged by the states in any way.

South Carolina v. Katzenbach (383 US 301, 1966): In this case the Supreme Court sustained the Voting Rights Act of 1965 as a lawful exercise of federal powers. The courts have been proven to be unequal to the task of examining voter registration records and of determining whether an individual had been unlawfully deprived of his or her right to vote. The attorney general of the United States was not charged with this and there existed within the Constitution, especially in the Fifteenth

Amendment, a plentitude of power to allow such federal registration of voters within the states.

U.S. Civil Service Commission v. Letter Carriers (413 US 548, 1973): The Supreme Court upheld provisions of the Hatch Act against challenges based on overbreadth and vagueness in this case. The statute proscribes only partisan political activities, and this is justified in the opinion of the Court in terms of the objectives set out in the law.

United States v. Classic (313 US 299, 1941): This Supreme Court ruling gave the Congress (and the federal government) powers to regulate primary elections in the states. The Court found that Article I, section 4 of the Constitution gave Congress the power to regulate the entire election process, including primary elections, so long as the election involved the selection of federal officers.

United States v. Rumely (345 US 41, 1953): While avoiding basic constitutional questions, the Supreme Court did hold that the House Lobbying Committee lacked statutory authority to investigate all lobbying activities intended to influence or retard legislative activities. If a congressional committee wishes to ask questions or obtain documentary information it must have proper statutory authority prior to making inquiries or the witnesses may legitimately refuse to answer questions or otherwise supply information.

Williams v. Rhodes (393 US 23, 1968): An Ohio law required that third parties, in order to place presidential electors in the ballot, had to gather petitions signed by 15 percent of the number of voters in the last gubernatorial elections as opposed to only 10 percent for the two major political parties. The Supreme Court could not find a compelling reason to allow this requirement to stand and thus invalidated the state law. However, in the case of *American Political Party v. White* (415 US 767, 1974) the high court sustained a Texas law requiring a petition of 5 percent of eligible voters to be gathered within 30 days in order to place candidates on the ballot for new political parties or for third parties which had won less than 2 percent of the vote in the preceding gubernatorial election.

5

The Presidency

Above the Law: President Nixon argued in his television interviews with David Frost that in some ways the presidency was above the law and not responsible under it. Some have viewed this as a revolutionary theory of presidential power and operation. Nixon created extralegal investigative and "dirty tricks" agencies unknown to Congress but funded out of public monies. He thought that such instruments of the presidency were permissible because the president was not subject to the law as were others.[1]

Actor in the Environment: The president is restrained by a number of factors. He must obey the Constitution, live within agreements legitimately made with foreign nations, and live with precedents established by previous presidents. The president must also honor commitments made in campaigning, and bargains struck with congresspersons. The Congress has in recent years added greatly to restraints on the presidency in acts such as the War Powers Resolution. The president is swept under at times by world or domestic events not of his making. All these things contribute toward making him an actor who must operate within a given environment.

---

[1] The generic "he" has been used when referring to officials such as the president and vice-president for clarity. Bias is not intended.

Amnesty: This is a general removal of penalties or other legal disabilities incurred as a result of some crime. Amnesty may be granted by the president or by the Congress. The term is most often applied to larger groups, such as the amnesty granted to former soldiers of the Confederate army by Lincoln and Andrew Johnson.

Appointment: The process whereby the president names certain public officers, ambassadors, Supreme Court justices, and heads of agencies is called appointment. Actually the process is subject to the approval of the United States in its "advise and consent" function. In short, the president is really nominating individuals for offices subject to the approval of the Senate. In the vacation of Congress the president may make temporary appointments. To become permanent the appointment must be approved by the Senate.

Assassination: Assassination is the taking of the life of a public official or prominent leader of a nation or group. Four American presidents have been assassinated: Lincoln, Garfield, McKinley, and Kennedy. Attempts have been made on the lives of other presidents, including Truman, Jackson, and Ford.

Bricker Amendment: Introduced as a proposed amendment to the Constitution by Republican Senator John Bricker of Ohio, this would have required additional Congressional approval of treaties. Under this proposal, no treaty could have been made which would give the federal government new powers. It would have negated the effect of the *Missouri v. Holland* (1920) decision of the Supreme Court which allowed the federal government to acquire by treaty powers it did not formerly possess. It would also have prevented a treaty or other international act from becoming effective internally (within the United States) without the direct consent, by law, of Congress. The proposed amendment failed by only one vote in the Senate in 1954. It might have checked to some degree, the imperial presidency and federal powers generally. The War Powers Act of 1973 is one result of the spirit of the sponsors of the Bricket Amendment.

Cabinet: By custom the Cabinet is composed of the heads of the principal agencies of government. George Washington began the practice of meeting regularly with his vice-president and four principal officers. Such sessions may be informal and secret and no minutes are kept and formal votes are rare. However, some presidents required formal agendas and had the minutes of the meetings recorded. Eisenhower had a military man's preference for very formal Cabinet meetings. The president ultimately must decide policy although he may value the advice of his Cabinet highly.

Carter Doctrine on Human Rights: Since coming to the presidency in 1977 Mr. Carter has emphasized his concern for human rights all over the world. He favors freedom to emigrate as a right of all persons from all nations. He favors the guarantee of the basic freedoms of conscience noted in the Atlantic Charter signed by the allied powers during World War II. He has expressed his dismay at the lack of human rights in many nations including the Soviet Union, Uganda, South Africa, and Rhodesia. He refused to meet with Prime Minister Ian Smith of Rhodesia, in part, because of the repression of blacks in that nation. He has undoubtedly been influenced by reports from groups such as Amnesty International and by Congresspersons such as Senator Henry Jackson. Some feel that he has jeopardized detente with the USSR because of his public statements of Soviet human rights issues, something the USSR considers to be of its own internal concern and not the concern of other nations.

Cases Act: In 1972 Congress required that the president file with the two Houses copies of all executive agreements entered into by the president. The act does little because (1) it fails to define clearly what an executive agreement is and (2) it has no real power to compel presidents to follow the provisions of the act.

Character: In his book, *The Presidential Character*, Dr. James David Barber creates a typology of the presidency based on two sets of criteria: active-passive and positive-negative. Rather than judging a presidential candidate on the candidate's specific stands on specific issues, Barber would have us judge him or her on character. We ought to be concerned with the candidate's activism and enjoyment of public services.

Chief Legislator: The president is not a member of Congress and thus cannot introduce legislation. He can, however, cause legislation to be introduced in Congress by friendly Congresspersons. He causes scores of bills to be drawn up by his executive offices. He promotes these bills by advocating their adoption in his State of the Union address and in other public appearances. He may trade off favors with Congresspersons to get his bills passed. He meets with leaders at informal meetings, frequently at breakfasts at the White House, to press for passage of his bills.

Chief of State: Since we have no titular head of state such as a king in the United States the president is called upon to do various things which really detract from his time to do other, more important things. He nominally heads many organizations, including some American Indian tribes, the American Red Cross, Scouting, and the like. He accepts foreign heads of state and hosts state banquets. In short he fulfills the physical and psychological need for a king. The president acts out a role in these ceremonial roles and in ceremonial functions, a role not assigned to him directly by the Constitution.

Cold War: A term used to describe Soviet-American relations since the end of World War II. The war has not actually been fought along battle-lines (that is, "hot") but it has been real. Historians speak of a "thaw" coming in the cold war. Some have argued that the present era of detente with the Soviets marks an end to the cold war.

Commander-in-chief: Article III, section 2 of the Constitution says that "the president shall be commander-in-chief of the army and the navy of the United States and of the militia of the several states when called into the actual service of the United States." As commander-in-chief the president may order the nation's military forces into service, may nationalize the state National Guard units, and may dismiss military commanders who disobey his orders. In the nuclear age it would be the president who would have to make any decision to use nuclear weapons if we were attacked by the nuclear forces of a foreign power. Because of the time factor Congress could not be consulted.

Constituencies (presidential):   Richard Neustadt identifies four presidential constituencies: governmental offices; the leadership and congressional delegation of the president's own political party; the American people who look to the president for inspiration and leadership; and those abroad, including heads of other states, who look to the president for leadership. Each of these have distinctive expectations of the presidency. The first three categories are not mutually exclusive.

Cult of Personality: The president is necessarily identified in the public mind with the American system of government. Hence one finds Nixon's Watergate, Franklin Roosevelt's New Deal, or Harry Truman's Fair Deal. By his actions the president can inspire confidence in the system or distrust of it. He can instill a sense of honor and pride or a sense of shame.

The public may see him as an energetic leader or a pathetic figure who is unable to cope with realities of office. If the public sees him to be a fine and good fellow of virtue and wisdom he may be said to have established a cult of his personality. This is a popular measurement of the individual who holds the presidential office and has little to do with his actual accomplishments.

Deadline: A president must perform certain of his functions with a certain amount of time. The time limit may be set by the Constitution as in the case of vetoing bills (10 days) or by custom as in sending annual messages to Congress. He must also observe election deadlines if he is to stand for re-election. International events may also establish informal deadlines within which he must act.

Declaration of War: See Chapter 11, p. 218.

Diplomatic Recognition: Ordinarily the United States "recognizes" the existence of foreign governments. This is formalized by the exchange of diplomatic personnel. In modern presidential history Woodrow Wilson refused to recognize the revoluntionary government of Herta in Mexico. Other presidents have followed Wilson's lead, most recently when John Kennedy withdrew recognition of Castro's Cuba. Other nations have not been recognized because of their violations of human rights. Still other governments are not recognized because they are occupied by a hostile power. On the other hand, occasionally, the presidents may continue to recognize governments whose nations are occupied by an alien power. In effect, the official American policy may be to honor governments that do not actually control the national territory of the state they are presumed to represent.

Director of Foreign Policy: This is a term coined some half a century ago by then Supreme Court Justice Sutherland who referred to the president as the sole functionary in the field of foreign affairs in the American system. The president alone establishes diplomatic relations with foreign nations or severs such ties. He alone deals "at the summit" in foreign affairs with other heads of state and chooses what the course of foreign policy will be. The president causes treaties to be negotiated by diplomatic personnel or special envoys. In short, while the Senate must approve treaties and the appointment of diplomatic personnel, it is the president alone who can show initiative in these areas.

Doctrine: This term describes the very special pronouncement of major policy by a president. It is ordinarily a unilateral declaration by the president although it might involve a bipartite or multipartite announcement by heads of several states. Among the major doctrines are the Truman Doctrine, the Monroe Doctrine, and the Nixon Doctrine (See separate entries for each of these doctrines).

Domestic Council: This advisory body was established in 1970 to coordinate and create domestic policy. Membership includes the president, vice-president, appropriate Cabinet officers, a director of the council's staff, and such other individuals as the president may include. President Nixon used his National Security Council as a model for this office.

Emergency Powers: Beginning with the Franklin Roosevelt administration, the Congress has delegated a number of emergency powers to the president to be used at his discretion. Over 500 such laws give the president wide powers to act in an emergency. He may seize property, production facilities, communications networks and facilities, and commodities. He may assign the armed forces to foreign posts, declare martial law, and order suspension of civil rights. The Congress sought, in the National Emergency Act of 1976, to control such delegations of power.

Enforced Discretion: A term coined by Richard Neustadt, this refers to actions the president refused to take, primarily because of the position he holds. One example of this would be Harry Truman's decision not to respond to the charges leveled at the executive office by Senator Joseph McCarthy who accused Truman of harboring Communists in the executive department. A president may also choose not to respond to personal attacks on himself or his family.

Executive Agreement: Modern executive agreements are often held to have begun with Theodore Roosevelt. Modern presidents have assumed that they have the right to make agreements and memoranda of understanding with their counterparts in foreign nations. Because these agreements are much easier to execute they are used more frequently than treaties, which require the advise and consent of the Senate. The Supreme Court has held that this is an "implied" power under treaty-making powers and thus these agreements have legal standing. An executive agreement binds only the president who has made it. By custom most presidents honor standing executive agreements made by their predecessors.

Executive Office of the President: This is the president's immediate staff, including his Office of Management and Budget, and Council of Economic Advisers. Others included are his legal counsel, secretaries, national security advisers, and other administrative, political, and legislative assistants. Their work is done in six major areas: public relations, foreign policy, domestic policy, economic policy, congressional relations, and administration. The office was established by Franklin Roosevelt under the Reorganization Act of 1939.

Executive Order: This term covers a wide variety of acts, regulations, and pronouncements by the President. These orders are used in implementing and carrying out the legal and constitutional functions of the office. Frequently, the Congress will delegate broad authority to the president to be used as he chooses. To be valid, executive orders must be published in the *Federal Register*.

Executive Privilege: President Washington refused to provide documents to the Congress concerning the defeat of General St. Clair near Fort Jefferson, Ohio. Other presidents, following this precedent, have refused to render up presidential documents for congressional examination. Little was made of this policy in recent years until the Watergate incident when President Nixon invoked the privilege of withholding information in the public interest. In a book on this subject, Dr. Raoul Berger calls executive privilege a myth, without constitutional grounds.

Executive Reorganization of 1977: In July 1977 President Carter streamlined the executive office, eliminating seven units of the office. Most of the functions of those units were transferred to appropriate Cabinet offices. Carter indicated that the executive office organization should closely resemble the work of the president. Those that did not so relate were to be placed seomwhere else more appropriate to their functions. These changes were to result in a 28 percent cut in staff of the executive office.

Expectations about the Presidency: Americans have set unrealistically high standards for presidential performance. They tend to view a president as a miracle worker who can accomplish anything he wishes. Such expectations have tended to weaken the presidential office.

Head of State: See *Chief of State*, p. 78.

Illness and Health: The Twenty-fifth Amendment provides for the temporary transition of power from the president to his vice-president in cases when the president cannot function as chief executive. The fact that the vice-president is serving temporarily automatically limits his power to argue and persuade. Bills that the president might successfully engineer through Congress often fail without his personal touch. Conversely, bills that might be blocked by the president might slip through Congress. President Eisenhower's illness in 1955 came at a crucial time in international relations. Likewise, the School Construction Assistance Bill of 1956 was passed by the Congress at the time Eisenhower was having surgery for ileitis.

Image: The president becomes a king-like image to Americans. All presidents attempt to project a favorable image of themselves and their families and immediate followers. Such images fulfill basic psychological needs of Americans. The image of the presidency simplifies government for most people, that is, the president becomes the whole of government for them. He is the symbol of national unity and of social stability.

Impeachment: Generally, this is a quasijudicial process that allows the removal from office of public officials who have committed high crimes or misdemeanors. There is a special process outlined in the Constitution for the impeachment of a president. The House of Representatives must bring the charges, the Senate tries him, and the Chief Justice of the United States presides. The only president to be impeached was Andrew Johnson and he was acquitted by the Senate by a one vote margin. The Senate is required to vote for impeachment by a two-thirds margin. It may only remove the president from office, but a president who is impeached may not be pardoned or hold office. He may still be tried in the courts for his crimes. Officers other than president may also be impeached and in such cases the president may not use his power of pardon.

Imperial Presidency: This is a term coined by Arthur M. Schlesinger, Jr., in his book *The Imperial Presidency*. Schlesinger argued that by 1972 presidential power was so great and misused that it threatened the separation of powers doctrine and the whole of the constitutional system. The powers had accumulated as a result of emergency powers granted to or assumed by the presidency in wars or national emergencies since 1932. Presumably, the presidential office has assumed autocratic proportions and none of the traditional legal, moral, or political restraints on the presidency are effective in checking its power.

Jacksonian Theory of the Presidency: Jackson conceived of the presidency as a power co-equal to the Supreme Court in determining the constitutionality of laws. If a law had been passed by Congress and signed into law by one's predecessor, one still might be bound to carry it out although one had no way to veto it, and thought that the law was wrong. Jackson felt this way about the national bank created by Congress on the recommendation of Monroe. Thus, he reviewed the law and found it to be counter to the Constitution. He then felt free to violate the law, since in his opinion, that law was unconstitutional.

Jawboning: The power to persuade is thought by Richard Neustadt to be among the president's greatest powers. Certainly, it is his strongest informal power. It refers to the power of the president to try to use the presidential office to persuade others, without benefit of formal powers or legislation, to do what the chief executive believes to be in the national interest. He may try to mediate a strike or convince industries to lower prices or negate price increases.

Jay Treaty: As concerns presidential powers and operations, the executive-congressional relations in the matter of the treaty negotiated with England by John Jay in 1895 is most instructive. Washington refused to render up to the House of Representatives the documents associated with the negotiation of this treaty. The House was unwilling then to appropriate monies wherewith the treaty could be effected. While the House has no formal role in the treaty making (or approving) process its cooperation is frequently needed in order to ensure success in foreign policy, especially when money must be appropriated for carrying treaty provisions into execution.

Kitchen Cabinet: This term was applied to a loose group of advisors who were not part of the regular Cabinet during Andrew Jackson's administration. Presidents frequently prefer the advice of such advisors to that of Cabinet officials. President Franklin Roosevelt use his "brain trust" and President Nixon used his foreign policy advisor Dr. Henry Kissinger in preference to his Secretary of State William Rogers.

Leadership Responsibility: The president has, since Jackson's presidency, been responsible for the leadership of three constituencies: executive, partisan, and national. The president, along with the vice-president, is the sole national executive office. He alone has a national constituency. He also is the leader of his political party and he is leader of the executive office.

Marshall Plan: In June of 1947 Secretary of State George Marshall addressed Harvard University. He advocated an economic plan that would revitalize the economy of Western Europe, which had been all but been destroyed by the Second World War. Some 17 European states received aid from the United States between 1948 and 1952. The aid was in excess of $21 billion. The initial authorization was for $5 billion under the European Recovery Act of 1948.

Minority President: Several presidents have received less than 50 percent of the votes cast in the popular election for president. Abraham Lincoln received the smallest percentage of the popular vote ever given to a winner in the Electoral College in the election of 1860. One man, Samuel J. Tilden, actually received a majority of the popular vote but lost in the Electoral College to Rutherford B. Hayes.

Monroe Doctrine: See Chapter 11, p. 223.

National Emergency Act of 1976: The act terminated various emergency powers that had been in effect as a result of prolonged crises. These powers had been granted to the president, beginning with Franklin Roosevelt in the 1930s. It also provided guidelines to be used by future presidents in declaring states of emergency. Regular congressional review of emergency decrees and executive orders is required. The president must now submit to Congress a list of emergency powers he will use and the source, with reference to the law, of such powers. Emergency powers may be used for six months and renewed for a second six months. A majority vote in both houses of Congress can negate such powers. Presumably, what the Congress delegates, it may withdraw.

National Security Council: This agency develops national defense policy and helps prepare the United States for possible future military actions including war and the support of our allies. It advises the president who ultimately is responsible for all national policy development. It consists of the president, the vice-president, secretary of state, secretary of defense, director of the office of emergency preparedness, and whatever other advisers the president may wish to include.

Nixon Doctrine: See Chapter 11, p. 224.

North Atlantic Treaty Organization (NATO):   See Chapter 11, p. 225.

Oath of Office: Persons taking elected office or assuming employment in the government swear (or affirm) that they will uphold the Constitution and faithfully execute the laws of the United States. In *Mississippi v. Johnson* the Supreme Court found that the presidential oath of office was morally, but not legally, binding.

Pardon: Individuals convicted of a federal crime, excepting impeachment, may be released from the punishment or legal consequences of his or her conviction by presidential pardon. This power extends to contempt of Congress or of the federal courts. A *conditional pardon* attaches conditions to the pardon which must be fulfilled before the pardon becomes final. An *unconditional pardon* attaches no conditions (also called absolute pardon). A pardon may cover any and all crimes, and it may come before conviction or trial, as in President Ford's pardon of Richard Nixon.

Party Leadership: The president is necessarily the real leader of his political party. As the standard bearer of his party during his candidacy, he leads his ticket on the ballot. He is elected in a partisan election and is known by his political party association. He is expected to work for the election or re-election of the party's candidates in future elections. Many presidents have effectively increased their power by obtaining help within the party. The president must work with the other leaders of his party, especially in the Congress.

Pocket Veto: The president is granted a full 10 days in which to consider bills before signing them into law or vetoing them. If Congress should adjourn before these ten days expire and the president has not signed the bill into law it is said to be pocket vetoed. Such a bill, of course, does not become law. The president may sign a bill into law after the adjournment of Congress. Pocket veto occurs only when the president does nothing after adjournment.

President Elect: For all intents and purposes the American people elect their president in the general election in early November. He is officially the president-elect when chosen by the Electoral College (or by the House of Representatives if the Electoral College fails to elect him). He remains the president-elect until he is officially inaugurated on January 20.

If the president-elect should die or resign before he is inaugurated the vice-president-elect is sworn in as president.

Presidential Succession Act of 1947: This act provides for presidential succession. If there is no vice-president of the United States, the office goes to the speaker of the House of Representatives followed by the president *pro tempore* of the Senate. If the latter two offices are vacant, temporary succession is provided by moving to the Cabinet, beginning with the secretary of state.

Recess Appointment: When the Senate is not in session the president may make interim appointments to vacancies normally requiring the advise and consent of the Senate. When the Senate again goes into session the interim appointment must be approved by the Senate. Such appointments expire, if advise and consent is not given to full appointment, on the last day of the succeeding session.

Removal: The president generally must have the consent of the Senate to appoint public officers, but the removal of officers from the executive branch generally may be accomplished by the president acting alone. The Tenure of Office Act of 1867 required that the president receive approval of the Senate for removal, and it was because of the violation of this act that Andrew Johnson was impeached. The Supreme Court allowed President Wilson to remove his Postmaster General, then a Cabinet-level position, without Senate approval. The removal of a member of a federal regulatory office is not permitted except for specific crimes, usually malfeasance or misfeasance in office.

Reprieve: A person convicted of a crime may have cause to request postponement of his or her sentence. The person may have new evidence to present or the chief executive may feel that there is some reason to doubt that the conviction was true or just. The president may also grant a reprieve for some humanitarian reason. Presidents may grant reprieves only in federal cases.

Resignation: Any officer who relinquishes his or her post after he or she has qualified for it, has resigned. Resignation is done in the manner prescribed by law, frequently to the officer's immediate superior. One president, Richard Nixon, and two vice-presidents, John Calhoun and Spiro Agnew, have resigned.

Secret Service: As a result of assassinations and attempts on the life of several presidents, a branch of the Treasury Department, the Secret Service, was established to protect the president and his family. These officers also protect major contenders for the presidency since the assassination of Robert Kennedy. They also protect visiting dignitaries from foreign nations. Agents monitor known cranks who might assassinate a president and check out letters and calls threatening the president.

Selling of the President: Today a presidential candidate must be exposed to the general public, much in the same way a new commercial product is marketed. He must be shown to be handsome and charming and he must be paraded before the public clothed in the garb of truth and justice. In short, the campaign staff must try to show that the candidate has the necessary qualities to be the leader the public wants. The truth about the candidate is not to be shown. The term was popularized by Joe McGinniss in his book, *The Selling of the President, 1968.*

State of the Union Message: Article 2, section 3 of the Constitution provides that the president report "from time to time" on the State of the Union. He is to recommend measures to the Congress for its consideration. It has become customary for the president to do this in person and at the beginning of the legislative session. As a result of his recommendations, scores of bills that have been drawn up by executive departments, many months in advance, are introduced into the Congress by Congresspersons who are friendly to the administration. Because of the multimedia coverage of this annual message it has become a major instrument of presidential policy.

Stewardship Theory (Presidency): Although first found in the writings and speeches of the federalist statesman James Wilson, this idea of presidential power was popularized by Theodore Roosevelt. The Constitution is to be viewed only as a means of restraining the presidency. Anything not forbidden to the president must be allowed to him by implied powers. He is thus empowered to take any action not forbidden by the Constitution or by law. The contrary view of severely restricted presidential power was elucidated by William Howard Taft, ironically, Roosevelt's handpicked successor.

Style: Presidential style simply recognizes the individual personalities of the men who have held the office. For example, each president will try to persuade others. How he persuades is a part of his style. The president will appear in public. How and when he will appear is a part of his style. He will make speeches and campaign in partisan elections. How he does so is another part of his style.

Succession: If the president should die or resign he is to be succeeded by the vice-president. After the vice-president, the Constitution allows the Congress to determine the order of succession to the presidency. The Presidential Succession Act of 1947 places the speaker of the House next in line, followed by the president *pro tempore* of the Senate. In the absence of the latter two, the officers of the Cabinet follow temporarily until a speaker or president *pro tempore* would be selected.

Summit Diplomacy: This is a term popularized by Elmer Plischke in his monograph of the same title. It refers to the personal diplomacy of the president of the United States with counterparts in other nations. Subsummit diplomacy might include negotiations involving the vice-president and his foreign counterparts. In rare instances subsummit diplomacy would include a high-ranking special envoy of the president with his equivalent from other nations.

Taft's View of the Presidency: Sometimes viewed as a strict constructionalist view of the Constitution, this theory holds that the president can do only those things or take only those actions that are specifically delegated to the office by the fundamental law of the land. No enlargement of the presidency is possible except through constitutional amendment. There is a certain irony here in that Taft was the handpicked successor of Theodore Roosevelt who expounded the opposite, or stewardship, theory of the presidency.

Temporary Transition of Power: The Twenty-fifth Amendment to the Constitution was designed largely to provide for executive leadership in case the president could not, by reason of health, discharge his duties. If the president notifies the speaker of the House and the president of the Senate that he cannot perform his duties, the vice-president acts as president. If the vice-president and a majority of the Cabinet notify the same officers, the vice-president again may act as president until the president again can perform his duties. This is important because several presidents have been unable for varying periods of time to perform their duties. Woodrow Wilson suffered a disabling stroke and was not able to function as chief executive for several months. James Garfield and William McKinley languished in pain for several days after their fatal wounds were inflicted. Dwight Eisenhower took the first steps toward this transition of power during his illness (September 24, 1955) and his operation (June 9, 1956), when he transferred power to Richard Nixon, his vice-president. Lyndon Johnson made the same arrangement with his vice-president, Hubert Humphrey, when Johnson had his gall bladder removed.

Tenure of Office Act of 1867: This act was passed by Congress to try to prevent Andrew Johnson from removing members of Lincoln's Cabinet whom Johnson did not like, but who were supported by the Congress. It was for alleged violations of this law that Johnson was tried before the Senate on impeachment charges. The act required that the president obtain the Senate's approval before removing an officer appointed with the consent of the Senate. This act was repealed in 1887. A similar act applying to postmasters was passed in 1876 but was found to be unconstitutional in *Myers v. United States.*

Textbook President: Thomas Cronin in *Washington Monthly* (October 1970) charged that texts in American government fail to expose myths created about the presidency and that such texts have perpetuated such myths. Textbook authors have overidealized the presidency, making it an institution no human could possibly live up to. The myth is that the president is a kind of superstar who unifies the political system, creates public policy, guides the people toward the American dream and makes things go well in society. Such claims to super status convince the presidents to make claims and promises they cannot possibly fulfill.

Treaty: This is a form of international act in which two or more sovereign states propose, alter, or terminate mutual rights and obligations. Treaties are negotiated by the president and are said to be ratified when approved by two-thirds of the Senate. Many treaties execute themselves, but others require an act of Congress to become effective. The latter are non-self-executing treaties. No treaty has ever been held to be unconstitutional, although in one case (*Missouri v. Holland,* 252 US 416, 1920) powers not heretofore belonging to the federal government were granted under a treaty.

Truman Doctrine: See Chapter 11, p. 229.

Two Term Tradition: Washington and Jefferson served two terms as president and then chose to leave office, although in both cases it was probable that the men could have been elected to a third term. Grant, after serving two terms and leaving office, sought his party's nomination, saying that the tradition applied only to consecutive terms. Grover Cleveland ran twice successfully and in between lost an election. Theodore Roosevelt attempted to win a third term after serving one full term and a portion of McKinley's unexpired term. Franklin Roosevelt broke the tradition, winning four terms. The Twenty-second Amendment, ratified in 1947, limits a person to two full terms and not more than two years of an unexpired term.

Veto: The Latin term means "I disapprove." Presidents may veto legislation by stating their reasons for doing so and returning the bill to the house of origin. A veto may be over-ridden by a two-thirds affirmative vote of each house. If there are fewer than 10 days left in a legislative session and the president does not sign a bill into law it fails to become law by pocket veto.

Vice-President: According to the Constitution the vice-president presides over the Senate. He may attend cabinet meetings and meetings of special groups such as the National Security Council. He may represent the president (and the nation) abroad. If the president dies or resigns he becomes president. If the vice-president becomes president, or if he dies or resigns, the Twenty-fifth Amendment provides for the selection of a new vice-president. Gerald Ford was the first vice-president to come to office using this special process. He was also the first unelected (by popular vote) vice-president and president.

"Vital Place of Action": This is a term coined by Richard Neustadt to describe the vast powers mandated to the presidential office by presidential "common law" and by statutes such as the Railway Labor Act, Taft-Hartley Act, Employment Act, and National Security Act. In instance after instance, one time acts by presidents in emergency situations have become compelling precedents, dictating future presidential action. Many such emergency actions have been backed by legislation underwriting such actions.

War Powers Act of 1973: To curb the use of American troops abroad in undeclared military actions such as Korea and Vietnam, the Congress required that henceforth the use of troops by the president was to be subject to the following limitations: (1) a declaration of war is needed for prolonged use of troops outside the country; (2) Congress may specifically authorize troop deployments in an appropriate legislative act; (3) in case of attack on the nation or its army the president may act immediately. The president who deploys any combat troops abroad must notify Congress of this within 48 hours. The Congress then must either declare war within 60 days or end the commitment. The president may commit troops for another 30 days after which Congress may, by joint resolution not subject to the veto, order the troops to be returned home. Wherever feasible the president is to confer with Congress before committing American troops.

Watergate: During the 1972 presidential campaign individuals linked with the Committee to Reelect the President broke into Democratic headquarters in the Watergate apartments in Washington, D.C. The various charges aimed against advisers to President Nixon are termed the "Watergate Crimes." The term has been telescoped to include any or all crimes alleged to have happened, or proved to have been committed during Nixon's presidency. It is now used to describe political crimes in general. Many feel that "Watergate Crimes" have undermined confidence in all institutions of government.

Weekly Compilation of Presidential Documents: This is a systematic publication of presidential documents which provides current information and a permanent reference source concerning presidential policies and pronouncements. It contains such items as transcripts of the president's news conferences, his televised speeches, and such other materials as the White House chooses to release. It is a method of informing the general public of presidential happenings.

White House Staff: These men and women are the president's immediate aides and staff. They are there to assist the president in various tasks such as relations with the news media. They are expected to be loyal to the individual holding the presidential office. They often distort the president's views of the outside world and of other advisers, department heads, and congresspersons.

Witch Hunt: When unconfirmed allegations are made by investigators or Congresspersons against groups or individuals it is assumed that guilt is being established by hearsay or innuendo. When broad, sweeping, and unproven allegations are made against individuals and groups we may have a witch hunt.

CASES

Curtiss-Wright Export Corp v. U.S. (299 US 304, 1936):   This case upheld the statute giving the president broad discretion in permitting sales of arms abroad. Because of the prominent role played by the president in foreign relations the Court allowed this delegation of broad and discretionary powers to the president. Such a broad delegation of power of the domestic front might not have been permitted. The court referred to the "exclusive power of the President as the sole organ of the Federal Government in the field of international relations—a power which does not require as a basis for its exercise an act of Congress, but which, of course, like every other governmental power, must be exercised in subordination to the applicable provisions of the Constitution."

Ex Parte Grossman (267 US 87, 1925):   The president had pardoned a person who had been held in contempt of Congress. Only impeachment of a public official is beyond the pardoning power of a president. The Court rejected the argument that contempt proceedings were beyond the power of other divisions of power to interfere with.

Field v. Clark (143 US 649, 1892):   The Supreme Court held that the legislative power of the Congress cannot be delegated. However, such legislative power is not unconstitutionally delegated when the president is given discretionary powers.

Kendall v. United States (12 Peters 524, 1838):   Under the separation of powers doctrine in the Constitution, the president is not answerable to either of the other two branches of the federal government. Except in cases of impeachment the president is exempted from compulsory processes against him. It also held that when the Congress imposes a function or duty or a mission on a public minister he must carry out his orders from Congress even if the President orders him to do otherwise.

Mississippi v. Johnson (4 Wall 475, 1867):   The Supreme Court held that the enforcement of laws by the president was a political, not a ministerial, duty of office. The presidential oath was morally, but not legally, binding on the president. Courts could not enjoin a president from enforcing laws that were allegedly unconstitutional. The laws themselves could be tested in the courts, but not the action of the president enforcing the laws.

Myers v. United States (272 US 52, 1926): The Supreme Court upheld, in this case, the power of the president to remove at his will and pleasure, any person appointed to a job by the president, even though the consent of the Senate had to be given to the appointment. This doctrine has since been mitigated in *Rathburn v. United States* (295 US 602) where in 1935 the Court limited the president's power to remove officers in the independent regulatory agencies and those not performing "executive functions."

Prize Cases (2 Black 635, 1863): This was a group of four cases that upheld President Lincoln's rule by executive decree and order during the Civil War. Specifically, Lincoln's use of naval blockade, accomplished under executive order, was sustained. It is doubtful whether the courts today would sustain such rule by decree except in wartime.

Rathburn (Humphrey's Executor) v. United States (205 US 602, 1935): This case mitigated the earlier *Myers v. United States* (272 US 52) decision relating to the removal of officers appointed by the president with the advise of the Senate. In the *Rathburn* decision the president was restricted from removing officers from independent regulatory agencies and officers not performing "executive functions."

United States v. Nixon (418 US 683, 1974): This case involving former President Nixon clarified a portion of the claim to executive privilege by the president. Under executive privilege a president may not withhold transcripts of conversations held *in camera* with his advisers or others, if such transcriptions are to be used in criminal proceedings. The Court recognized the basic principle of executive privilege as vital in the division of powers system, but the Court found the rule of law and the integrity of the judicial process to be of a higher order.

United States v. Pink (315 US 203, 1942): The courts recognized the power of presidents to make executive agreements, thus giving these legal status. The Court reasoned that the power to make executive agreements was a latent power under the treaty-making power granted to the president.

Youngstown Sheet & Tube Co. v. Sawyer (343 US 579, 1952): President Truman, threatened with slowdown in production of steel by a strike during the Korean War, had seized the Youngstown Sheet & Tube Company. The Supreme Court held that, in the absence of specific authority, the president could not seize or operate private property, even if the strike threat might handicap our troops in the field.

6

The Bureaucracy

Ad Interim: This term refers to an official who serves in an office for a brief period of time after the death, resignation, or removal of his or her predecessor, and until such time as a permanent replacement can be elected or appointed.

Administration: In the public sector, administration means the enforcement of laws and rules made to ensure that public policy is carried out. Laws are made by the Congress and orders are issued by the executive. It is the function of the bureaucracy to see that the letter and spirit of such acts are followed. Without administration, public policy would not be translated into action. The science of public administration studies the actions of the bureaucracy and trains individuals for administration in the public sector.

Administrative Law: There are two groups of administrative law: (1) the body of law created by administrative agencies pursuant to authorization given by legislation (such administrative rules are published in the Federal Register); (2) law limiting public officials and giving certain rights to those citizens dealing with those officials.

Administrative Law Judges: This is the new title for hearing examiners. These persons hear cases within regulatory and administrative agencies concerning the applications of administrative rules and regulations made by bureaucrats pursuant to laws made by the Congress.

These judges are appointed under civil service rules. The judges have a measure of independence not existing heretofore, when the hearing examiners were both judge and prosecutor in applying the administrative law to individuals and corporations. The judges may also advise administrative and regulatory agency heads on proposed changes in administrative laws.

Administrative Order: Administrative agencies are empowered by laws made by Congress to issue directives that carry the force of law. An order is usually applied to a particular case, thus distinguishing it from rules and regulations that are general in intent. Administrative orders are frequently directed at correcting an infraction of a rule or regulation. Orders are often issued after a hearing on a particular matter has been held. These hearings are similar to formal court proceedings. With the growth of government, most businesses and many individuals are subject to a wide variety of administrative orders and hearings.

Administrative Procedure Act of 1946: This act requires that all administrative laws prepared by administrative agencies be promulgated by publication in the Federal Register. The act requires that public hearings be held on such rules when proposed by an agency. It also requires that a statement of appeals procedure be made public. Additionally, it sets standards for judicial review of administrative determinations by regulatory agencies. (See *Railroad Commission of Texas v. Rowan & Nichols Oil Co.,* 311 US 570, 1941.)

Administrative Reorganization: Administrative organizations, departments, and bureaus are constantly being created by the Congress to deal with a wide variety of problems. Far too frequently little forethought is given to overlapping jurisdictions and parallel functions of agencies. At times the president may seek to improve services and eliminate duplication, thus making government more responsible to the citizenry. The process is called administrative reorganization. A number of commissions and reports have suggested ways government can be reorganized, beginning with the First Hoover Commission in 1947. The Reorganization Act of 1949 allows a president to propose reorganization, which becomes effective unless vetoed by the Congress in either house within 60 days.

American Federation of Government Employees: Founded in 1932, it is associated with the AFL-CIO and is one of the principal labor unions representing federal governmental employees.

American Society for Public Administration: This is the professional organization for teachers and practitioners of public administration. It publishes the *Public Administration Review*, the definitive journal in the field. It has student rates available.

Auxiliary Agency: Certain services are provided by centralized agencies to other agencies of the government. An agency that has as its clientele group other governmental agencies is called an auxiliary agency. Certain accounting, purchasing, and personnel functions are performed regularly by auxiliary agencies.

Board: This term is frequently used interchangeably with commission. It consists of a group which is charged with directing some governmental function, such as paroles for those serving time in prison. The use of a board allows bipartisan membership, something not possible with a single head. To head an agency or bureau with a commission or board instead of with a single administrator is one of the most controversial decisions made by legislatures.

Bond: This is a certificate of indebtedness which is given by the person borrowing money to the person lending that money. Ordinarily it requires the borrower to pay interest to the lender at times and in ways specified on the bond. Private corporations and governments may issue bonds as may quasigovernmental and special government agencies. Some bonds pledge the use of the general taxing power of government and are called *general obligation bonds*. Other bonds finance facilities such as toll roads or parking lots and pledge merely the revenue accumulated from the use of the facility to retire the bonds and pay the interest. These are revenue bonds. Some bonds are paid off at the end of the specified period of time out of a special sinking fund and others are paid off in a series, with the first of the series perhaps maturing in as little time as six months or a year.

Borrowing Power: See Chapter 10, p. 195.

Budget and Accounting Act of 1921: See Chapter 10, p. 195.

Bureau: Correctly, a bureau is a subdivision of an agency. Not all subdivisions are called bureaus. Terms like "office" or "service" may be substituted. The Bureau of Indian Affairs, for example, is a subdepartment of the Interior Department. The Internal Revenue Service is a unit of the Treasury Department.

Bureaucracy: This term refers to an administrative system wherein the operatives of government are housed in specific bureaus and agencies. These operational units of government are responsible for carrying out the laws of the land and for making administrative laws following legislative mandates. They are the units of government most frequently encountered by the general public as they deal with the public in providing governmental services. Without the bureaucracy government would be impossible.

Career Service: Governments are dependent on the bureaucracy to carry out policies coming from the legislative and executive branches. We have become increasingly aware of the fact that policies ought to be implemented by trained and qualified professionals who are removed from politics and changeover caused by changes in politics. The various levels of government in the nation have been seeking to staff agencies with persons chosen on a merit basis to serve in government as a career.

Cease and Desist Order: Administrative agencies are empowered by the Congress to prevent certain acts that the legislature has made illegal. Orders given to individuals, businesses, and labor unions to refrain from doing something in violation of the law are called cease and desist orders. These orders are issued frequently after an administrative hearing, which resembles a court trial. This power was first granted to the Interstate Commerce Commission, but has been given since to other regulatory and administrative units of government.

Centralized Purchasing: See Chapter 10, p. 196.

Certification (Civil Service): Modern civil service systems require placement to be made on the basis of merit. By evaluating credentials and by grading standardized examinations, the civil service commissions provide lists of candidates eligible to serve in various positions in government. The commission will certify various individuals who have qualified for consideration for positions, allowing agencies to select from among the most qualified candidates, often three top candidates. If a person is not hired, his or her name is returned to the list of certified eligibles.

Chain of Command: This is a firm line of authority running from top to bottom within an agency or bureau, which makes the decision-making process known to all employees. It creates the mutual responsibility and obligation that marks proper bureaucratic organization.

Civil Service: In an attempt to end government appointment that had been based on partisan "spoils system" politics, the federal government created the Civil Service System. It placed persons in most government jobs according to merit as established in competitive examinations, assessments of skills, and according to educational background. The system began here in 1883 with the Pendleton Act. About 90 percent of federal employees are covered by civil service. These persons encompass lower and middle range bureaucrats. Jobs are classified generally in the federal government by civil service classifications.

Civil Service Act of 1883: This act created the Civil Service System. Although it has been amended many times it is still the basis for the Civil Service System today. It established open and competitive examinations as the merit basis for appointment to federal jobs. It originally covered less than 10 percent of all federal employees, but today, it and adjunct systems cover most nondecision and nonpolicy making employees. It was enacted as the direct result of the assassination of President James Garfield by a disgruntled office seeker.

Civil Service Act of 1940: This act extended the Civil Service System, and allowed the president to give coverage to nearly all employees of the federal government whose appointments do not require the advise and consent of the Senate.

Civil Service Commission: Established in 1883, it is composed of three members appointed by the president with the consent of the Senate. It is the central personnel agency of the national government. It is charged with recruiting, examining, and rating potential federal employees. It prepares and maintains a list of potentially eligible persons for various positions. It also determines eligibility for veteran's preference. It checks on political activity by civil servants and supervises a variety of services, such as retirement benefits, insurance programs, and the like. It conducts security checks when required and accepts letters of recommendation for prospective employees.

Classified Service: Most positions in the federal government, and many in state governments, come under the jurisdiction of Civil Service Commissions for purposes of filling or helping to fill vacancies. Those positions are filled by the agency itself, under permission granted by Congress, in a manner similar to civil service procedures.

Clientele: Some agencies are designed to serve sectors of the general public. Those whom they serve are their clientele. The Bureau of Indian Affairs was created to serve certain needs of the Amerindians.

Code of Federal Regulations: The Federal Register is published daily, listing rules and proposed rule changes for various governmental agencies. Annually, these rules are collected and published in book version known as the *Code*, which is divided into 50 titles. This is the general and permanent compilation of federal regulations.

Comptroller General: The comptroller general prescribes accounting standards that executive agencies must follow and helps federal agencies develop proper accounting systems. In accounting procedures review, he works with the Office of Management and Budget (OMB) and with the Secretary of the Treasury. He makes the final administrative decisions regarding the spending of allocated money and decisions involving the propriety of an expense. He oversees the allocation of government contracts and makes certain that proper procedures have been followed in bidding on and awarding of government contracts. Within the bureaucracy his decisions are final and binding, although other determinations may subsequently be made in the courts or in the Congress. He may settle any claim against the United States as the final bureaucratic authority. He also has certain functions under the Energy and Policy Conservation Act of 1975 in the allocation of energy.

Consolidation: When agencies are created by Congress to solve crises as they occur, or to do things when Congress wishes to have such things done, duplication of services sometimes occurs. To avoid duplication and to promote greater efficiency, agencies are often rearranged so that several departments or independent administrative units are consolidated into one agency. One major department thus does all the work needed in one field. The tendency of legislatures is to create too many agencies in a given field of operation. Functional consolidation overcomes this diffusion of power and responsibility. When President Carter was elected to office, he promised to consolidate governmental offices into a handful of hopefully more responsive departments.

Consumer Product Safety Commission: Created by Congress as a result of lobbying efforts by consumer groups, the agency has as its responsibility the protection of the general public from dangerous and unsafe products. It is a regulatory agency headed by a five-member board whose members are appointed by the president with the consent of Congress. It has been criticized by many, including President Carter, for failing in some of its principal missions, while harrassing small businesses by issuing conflicting, unnecessary, or absurd rules and regulations. The commission checks products for abuses of such laws as Hazardous Substances Act, Poison Prevention Packaging Act, and Flammable Fabrics Act. It also carries on a program of consumer awareness and education.

Decentralization: This administrative concept is applied within large organizations and departments, allowing much decision-making to be done by subunits.The assignment of authority may be made according to subject areas or on a geographical basis. It is very difficult for an agency head or commission to review all areas where decisions must be made. Consequently, decentralization allows greater specialization by lower levels of responsible officials. Still, major decisions are made centrally.

Delegation of Authority: Major authority resides with department heads or boards charged with responsibility for agency behavior and accomplishment. To allow greater specialization of expertise and to allow agency heads to concentrate on major decisions, some authority is given over or delegated to other responsible officials at the lower levels of the chain of command. Most successful public administrators learn how to delegate appropriate kinds of responsibilities to lower levels of administration. They must also learn how to choose a responsible person who can handle the authority they wish to delegate, because the commission or agency head still must accept responsibility for things done with the delegated authority.

Department: Major governmental administration is accomplished through large administrative units which concentrate on the broad areas of governmental responsibility. Such major areas of administration are called departments. Many departments are included in the President's Cabinet. A few departments, which have been absorbed by new departments, have retained their titles, such as the Department of the Navy, which was absorbed by the Defense Department, but the title is misused here.

Dollar-a-year man: When private enterprise provides a person to the government to head a special project or to prepare a special report or perform some other specialized function, the person's salary is often provided by that enterprise. He or she is thus paid one dollar for the year's services, the minimum allowed by law. Some very wealthy persons may also work for government at this minimum salary. Presidents who are independently wealthy traditionally receive their salaries and donate the full amount to a favorite charity.

Energy Policy and Conservation Act of 1975: The comptroller general is empowered to verify by examination information on energy as provided by private enterprise to the government. He may perform quasijudicial duties, such as subpoenaing witnesses, or examining appropriate documents in carrying out this inspection. The office of this branch of the General Accounting Office is located in Houston and it has certain powers to assess penalties for noncompliance with provisions of the act.

Ex Officio: This term defines powers that come inherently with a certain office or position. Hence, the comptroller of the currency is *ex officio* a member of the Federal Deposit Insurance Corporation Board.

Federal Register: This daily publication contains public federal regulations and other legal documents from the executive department. It also contains a list of public meetings to be held under the "Government in the Sunshine" law. It has the text of proposed changes in federal administration law. The Office of the Federal Register conducts periodic educational workshops on using the Register.

Federal Report Act of 1973: The comptroller general and his General Accounting Office may review the information-gathering practices of the independent regulatory agencies. Information that is gathered by these agencies must usually be cleared with the GAO before it may be released, as must the forms to be used to acquire the base information. The purpose of the act was to reduce the number of forms distributed to the private sector and to avoid duplication of information gathered. It was also designed to protect certain basic rights of employers and corporations.

Field Office: Many persons believe that government is concentrated in capital cities, whether on the federal or state level. In fact, only about 10 percent of federal employees are actually located in Washington, D.C. The other 90 percent are in field or regional offices located throughout the United States and in its territories and possessions. These offices allow the government to serve its various clientele groups better since the offices are located near the bases of operation of those the agency must serve or regulate.

Fiscal Year: See Chapter 10, p. 201.

Freedom of Information Act: This amendment to the 1966 Administrative Procedure Act was to make information maintained by the executive branch more available to the general public. The *Code of Federal Regulations* contains information concerning the Freedom of Information Act and how the private citizen may obtain this information. Agencies who refuse to provide information may be ordered to do so by the courts. Most information requested under this act will be provided, but it does allow certain exemptions, such as for protection of national security.

General Accounting Office: See Chapter 8, p. 119.

General Schedule (GS): The Civil Service System requires classification of positions according to the demands of various jobs. These general ratings range from GS 1, the lowest level of government appointments and pay schedules to GS 18, the highest level of appointment and pay covered by civil service. Ratings are given according to education, scores on standardized examinations, prior experience, and rating by superiors. Pay schedules are thus similar for given jobs among the many agencies of the federal government. College graduates ordinarily begin at GS 5, while those with specialized and graduate education begin at GS 7 or GS 9.

General Services Administration: This agency, founded in 1949, buys and maintains, and, when necessary, disposes of all government properties. It is a central clearing house for most government purchases. It is an auxiliary agency that performs services for other federal agencies.

Government Corporations: These are a hybrid mixture of government and business. The government owns and operates some business enterprises such as the electric generating systems of the Tennessee Valley Authority. The government basically controls most of their activities.

Governmental Reorganization Act of 1949: Following recommendations for needed reorganization offered by the First Hoover Commission, the Congress authorized the president to consolidate and reorganize agencies as he saw fit. Plans for changes in the bureaucratic system must be provided to Congress. Either house may vote to suspend the consolidation or reorganization, thus exercising a legislative veto over presidential activity. If neither house of Congress disapproves the proposed changes within 60 days of receipt of notice, the changes are considered acceptable and the president may proceed. The power has been extended and President Carter has used this power to some extent in the first phases of his promised thorough reorganization and consolidation of federal bureaucracy.

Government Printing Office: This is a publications operation wholly owned and operated by the federal government. It prints a wide variety of books, pamphlets, and documents. The variety of publications includes translations of foreign publications, magazines of popular interest, "how to" books, consumer guides, and treaties.

Hatch Act: In 1939 Congress passed legislation to forbid the firing of most government employees for reasons of partisan politics. It also prohibited federal employees from engaging in partisan politics, although they may, of course, vote. Federal employees cannot be asked for donations to partisan political campaigns. State employees whose salaries are paid with federal money are also covered.

Hearing: Hearings are an instrument used by the bureaucracy for several purposes. First, public hearings may be set wherein interested parties may appear to provide evidence and testimony regarding proposed rules and regulations made by the bureaucracy pursuant to laws made by Congress. Hearings are also held as quasijudicial proceedings wherein administrative or regulatory agencies examine alleged violations of their rules and regulations. These hearings are held by a hearing examiner (also called administrative law judge) whose judgments may be overturned by either an agency head or the federal courts. Hearings also give hearing examiners (or administrative law judges) the opportunity to review newly proposed administrative law or review changes in existing rules before making final recommendations to the agency head.

Hoover Commission (First): Created in 1947, this bipartisan committee of experts from many fields made a number of recommendations for the reorganization and improvement of government. Between 1949 and 1955 over half of its recommendations were implemented by Congress or the president. It found that the federal bureaucracy was ill designed for its tasks and that government was a bewildering mixture of agencies that often worked at counterpurposes.

Incrementalism: This challenge to PPBS budgeting holds that one cannot approach problems with definite objectives in mind. One cannot plan alternative ways to achieve objectives because not enough is known about these alternatives. The problems government faces are too complex to allow for any systematic approach.

Independent Agencies: This is a generic term for those bureaus of government which do not fall directly under the presidential office or under Cabinet level positions. The Veterans Administration is not represented in the Cabinet, for example.

Independent Regulatory Agency: These agencies have considerable quasijudicial power over various aspects of national business and the economy. They establish rules made under general grants of power and legislation from the Congress. They are quite independent of the executive branch. The commissioners are nominated by the president with the consent of the Senate. No more than a simple majority may be from one political party. Most often they have five or seven members. They regulate industries and businesses under administrative law and hold hearings that are similar to court proceedings. Their decisions may, under certain circumstances, be appealed in the federal courts. These agencies include: Consumer Product Safety Commission; Federal Maritime Commission; Federal Reserve Board; Federal Trade Commission; Interstate Commerce Commission; Federal Power Commission; Securities and Exchange Commission; Federal Communications Commission; Civil Aeronautics Board; and the National Labor Relations Boards.

Line: Line operations deal directly with the general public or other clientele groups in carrying out legislative programs. Executive departments such as the Commerce Department are line agencies.

National Archives and Records Service: This is an agency within the General Services Administration which holds and maintains many governmental records. It was created in 1949 to preserve records of historic value. It also publishes the Federal Record and the *United States Government Organization Manual*. It administers some of the libraries of former presidents. One of the most famous documents collections in the National Archives is that concerning the assassination of President Kennedy.

Nepotism: As a part of the spoils system, elected public officials frequently obtained government jobs for relatives. With the advent of the Civil Service System this practice was curbed to some degree. However, legislators sometimes appoint relatives to their office staffs. Non-civil service jobs are sometimes used to employ relatives of elected officers. President John Kennedy was criticized for practicing nepotism when he appointed his brother Robert to the office of attorney general in 1961.

Nuclear Regulatory Commission: Established as an independent regulatory agency under the Energy Reorganization Act of 1974, this department licenses and regulates the uses of nuclear energy. It is headed by a five member board. All of the previous licensing and regulatory functions of the Atomic Energy Commission have been transferred to the NRC. As designated by the Congress it is charged with assuring that all atomic energy is used in a safe manner, especially in regard to the environment and national security.

Planning, Programming, and Budgeting System (PPBS). See Chapter 10, p. 205.

Privacy Act of 1974: This act requires that the public must be informed of the existence and character of all personal information systems kept by the government. An individual has a right to see such records on him or herself and the act permits the individual to control to some extent the transfer of that information to other agencies. An individual has the right to know, under this act, who used his or her personnel records. A compilation of these records systems is published as the *Privacy Act Issuances*.

Professional and Administrative Career Examination (PACE): PACE replaced the Federal Service Entrance Examination (FSEE) as the primary test used to position potential civil servants within the merit system of appointment in the federal government. It includes examinations designed to measure one's protential for a wide variety of governmental positions.

Reprimand: This is an official reproof given by a superior to his or her subordinate. It is given for inefficiency, ignoring or violating established rule or procedure, or for some other misbehavior.

Rule of Three: This term is a generic one covering the selection of civil servants from among the top candidates available for positions open in the bureaucracy. Rather than selecting the top candidate, agencies are permitted to select from among several, often three, potential civil servants. The assumption is that there will often be intangible factors that do not show up on standardized examinations or on lists of educational and job experience which can affect selection.

Span of Control: Various individuals may be able to supervise different numbers of subordinates. Nonetheless there is a finite number an individual can reasonably control. This number represents the ideal span of control. Bureaucracies do not work well if that number is exceeded. Waste is the product of minimizing one's span of control.

Spoils System: Before the Civil Service System came into use, federal and state offices were staffed by choosing supporters of the successful political ticket. Washington staffed his office with federalists and Jefferson fired most of these officers, replacing them with his supporters. The statement, "To the victors go the spoils" is attributed to Andrew Jackson who replaced officials in Washington with his frontier followers. Many presidents were forced to waste time with office seekers who expected to benefit from their alleged support of the party ticket. The civil service merit system was then provided to replace the spoils system.

Staff: These individuals serve in advisory capacities, aiding in such functions as planning, programming, and budgeting. The offices of the executive household such as the Office of Management and Budget (OMB) and the Council of Economic Advisers are staff departments.

Sunset Laws: Many states have enacted such laws and the federal government has been urged by citizen lobbying groups such as Common Cause to consider the idea for all its agencies, departments, or bureaus. Periodically, frequently every seven years, agencies come up for review.

The assumption is made that the agency will not be refunded unless it can justify its continued existence. The idea of course, is that the sun should set on those agencies that have outlived their usefulness.

Supplementary Appropriation: If a department or bureau should deplete its funds before the end of a fiscal year it must ask the legislature to give it additional moneys. This happens most frequently when there have been unexpected or unusual expenses encountered by the agency.

Tenure: This is an essential part of the merit system of employment in government. It guarantees that an individual will not be arbitrarily dismissed from a position. Most public employees and school teachers and college professors are covered by grants of tenure.

United States Government Organization Manual: This is an official publication of the federal government, appearing at about six month intervals, which lists the personnel of agencies, and reports on their activities. It also lists agencies that have been discontinued and those merged into other agencies as a result of reorganization and consolidation. It carries summaries of some major legislation of special concern to citizens.

Veteran's Preference: The civil service merit system of appointment to governmental office allows that honorably discharged veterans be given "bonus points" which are added to their test scores. In the federal system, veterans are given 5 points; disabled veterans are given 10 points. Widows of veterans (if not remarried) are given bonus points and the wives of unemployable disabled veterans are given 10 points. They are generally removed from physical fitness and similar examinations. States may also give veterans similar preferences.

Zero-based Budgeting: Each agency, bureau, department, and commission is required, in this approach to budgeting, to fully justify each of its operations. It creates a hierarchy of jobs to be done and services to be fulfilled and sends these to the executive. If the programs and operations are listed in ranked priority, then weak or useless programs presumably could be spotted easily and eliminated. President Carter used this approach to the state budget of Georgia when he was governor of that state, and he has great faith in it.

CASES

Opp Cotton Mills v. Administrator of Wage and Hour Division (312 US 126, 1971):   This case is one of the more significant ones of a long series of challenges to the delegation of powers to administrative agencies. Because of the complexity of some issues the Court found it to be quite proper for Congress to delegate rule-making powers to administrative experts and specialists. So long as the agency operates within reasonable statutory guidelines it may use such delegated powers.

Railroad Commission of Texas v. Rowan & Nichols Oil Co. (311 US 570, 1941):   In this precedent case and in subsequent decisions the Supreme Court has ruled that it will not contradict the administrative expertise of state or federal regulatory agencies. Unless it can be shown that such rulings are based on "insubstantial evidence" they will be sustained. The Administrative Procedure Act of 1946 limited the Court's jurisdiction in such cases except for the determination of applicable laws and the review of substantial evidence under rules of proper evidence.

United Public Workers v. Mitchell (330 US 75, 1947):   The Supreme Court failed to find any invasion or abridgement of the rights of public employees by prohibiting them from participating in partisan politics. It sustained these prohibitions found in the Hatch Act.

7

Congress

Act of Congress: This term embraces all statutes passed by the Congress in which the words, "Be it enacted" are included. Such statutes are subject to presidential veto, and, if vetoed, may be enacted into law by a two-thirds affirmative vote of both houses of the Congress voting separately. Statutes are incorporated into the federal publication, *Statutes at Large of the United States,* and are included in the *Code of Laws of the United States.*

Advise and Consent: Each year the Senate is asked to consider approximately 200 to 400 executive appointments to agencies and departments of government, the federal judiciary, and federal regulatory agencies. Additionally, the Senate is asked to approve treaties negotiated by the president with foreign nations. The Senate must concur by a two-thirds majority before treaties become effective and before appointees may be confirmed.

Amendment: Alterations may be made to legislation introduced in the Congress. Such changes may be made in committee or in subcommittee, or on the floor of that house of Congress wherein the bill is being considered. Changes may simply clarify the language of the bill or changes may be made in the whole of the bill in such a way as to modify the intention of the bill's sponsor.

Appropriation: Monies are set aside by a legislative body for a specific purpose. All monies spent by public bodies must have first been appropriated by the legislature. Many appropriations are made pursuant to requests made by the executive. The annual budget is really an enlarged and complex appropriation.

Architect of the Capitol: This official is an agent of the Congress who is charged with the mechanical and structural care of the Capitol and adjoining buildings, such as the Library of Congress.

Bill: This is the common title given to a proposed piece of legislation when first introduced into the Congress or other legislative body. In the House of Representatives, bills are entitled, "House Resolution (H.R.)" and are numbered. In the Senate they are simply called "Senate (S.)" and given a number.

Bill Drafting: Because of the complex nature of the law, the art of preparing potential legislation is entrusted frequently to professionals in some sort of bill drafting organization. In the Congress members are assisted by the Office of Legislative Counsel. Many bills are drafted, at least in the first draft, by public interest and lobbying groups.

Black Caucus: Traditionally, caucuses were political meetings held by members of one political party, usually within a certain house of a legislative body. With emerging black awareness, it was quite natural that black legislators would form their own caucus to discuss matters of concern to black communities and to expedite civil rights and voting rights legislation.

Blue Collar Caucus: Although most members of Congress are drawn from professional classes or come from wealthy backgrounds there are increasing numbers of blue collar workers in the Congress. One recent development among these working class congresspersons has been the creation of a caucus wherein common problems of working persons are discussed and appropriate legislation is drafted. Most blue collar caucus members are trade unionists.

Budget and Impoundment Control Act of 1974:   This major legislation was passed in order to prevent the impoundment of monies that had been appropriated by the Congress, but not spent by the president.

The act also encouraged the Congress to make its own budget as an alternative to the executive budget prepared by the Office of Management and Budget. It was designed to encourage Congress to analyze in a most comprehensive way the nation's fiscal and monetary policies and to assign congressional priorities to spending programs. In the House of Representatives there are 25 members, with 5 each being chosen from the Ways and Means and Appropriations Committees, 1 each from the majority and minority leadership offices, and the remaining 13 from other committees. There are 16 Senators, chosen for service in the usual manner of assigning committee service. A Congressional Budget Office (CBO) was created to provide technical assistance in budget analysis.

Bullets: Speeches are frequently printed in the *Congressional Record* although they might not have been actually delivered on the floors of the Congress. Each issue of the *Record* now contains this note: "Statements or insertions which are not spoken by a member on the floor will be identified by the use of the bullet symbol" placed at the beginning and end of such an insertion.

Calendar: In legislative bodies, a calendar is a list of bills and other business scheduled to be considered. The House divides its calendars according to the type of business to be taken up. The Senate merely separates its "advise and consent" functions (placed on the executive calendar) from its normal duties shared with the House of Representatives (placed on the Senate calendar).

Caucus: This is a closed meeting of members of one or another political party or other special group (for example, Black Caucus, Blue Collar Caucus) within one or, possibly, both houses of a legislative body. Policy decisions are made here frequently as are decisions on leaders. Strategy may be worked out in caucus on the passage (or blockage) of legislation.

Censure: Article I, section 5 of the Constitution permits each house of Congress to "punish its members for disorderly behavior." Censure is one device congresspersons can use to punish their disorderly colleagues. In 1954 the late Senator Joseph McCarthy was censured by the Senate for abusing his senatorial privileges in mistreating witnesses while seeking Communists in government. In 1967 the House censured Representative

Adam Clayton Powell, fined him $25,000 and removed his seniority for his conduct in office.

Clerk of the House: This office is chosen by the members of the House of Representatives to perform certain mechanical and clerical duties. The clerk is responsible for the publication of the journal of the proceedings of the House in the *Congressional Record*, makes certain contracts for the House, and oversees some internal expenses.

Closure (Cloture): In the Senate members are permitted to engage in unlimited debate on matters on the floor. This is called filibuster, and it is a means of "talking a bill to death." Filibuster may be circumvented by invoking cloture under a rule adopted on March 17, 1949. Three-fifths of the entire membership (60 in number if there are no vacancies) must agree to cloture before it is allowed. After invoking cloture members may still speak for a maximum of one hour on the matter at hand.

Committee: Most work in legislatures is accomplished in committees. Committees are formed out of portions of the total membership, although there is a Committee of the Whole House in the House of Representatives. *Joint committees* are made up of members of both houses of the Congress. *Standing committees* are permanent bodies, usually designed to review certain types of legislation or legislation in certain specialized areas. *Special committees* are created to investigate some unusual or special area of concern to the Congress (or one house of Congress) at a given time. An *ad hoc committee* is a special committee created to investigate some specified, usually limited, area of legislative concern.

Committee of the Whole: This special device found in the House of Representatives allows the membership, or that portion of the total membership present, to become a committee to expedite legislation. The device is used when there is less than a quorum to conduct regular business (quorum is 218 members) but at least 100 members present. All revenue and appropriations bills are considered by the Committee of the Whole House on the State of the Union. Although it is possible to use this in the Senate, it is generally not used.

Committee on Committees: This special committee assigns members to committees. It is frequently attached to party caucuses in legislative bodies, for committee assignments are made by the majority and minority parties separately. It may be constituted by using members of a party serving on an important committee.

Compacts: States are forbidden under the Constitution to conduct foreign relations or to make treaties. States frequently have good reasons for wanting to make formal arrangements with other states for a wide variety of public purposes. Such agreements might involve mutual assistance pacts for snow emergencies or to allow for reciprocity in recognition of permits or licenses. To become effective compacts must be approved by Congress, although such approval is ordinarily a mere formality.

Concurrent Resolution: Resolutions may express the will and sentiments of one house of Congress on a certain subject. The other house may choose to concur with that statement of principle or sentiment by passing a concurrent resolution. Congress may choose to support the president on a matter by passing a resolution of support. In any event, since this is not a law, the president's concurrence is not required, nor is his signature necessary.

Conference Committee: Frequently, because of the process of amending bills, two versions of the same legislation may be passed by the two houses of Congress. Bills must be identical in every way before they can be sent on to the president for his signature. The normal method of resolving the differences between versions of a bill is to send the bill to conference committee. Members of the committee are chosen separately by the two houses of Congress, and each delegation must separately approve the compromise version of the bill. The conferees return the compromise version to the houses for reconsideration. No amendments may be offered to a bill reported out of conference committee.

Confirmation: The president may nominate persons to fill various public offices, ranging from the federal courts, to federal regulatory agencies, to diplomatic missions. Before these appointments become effective the Senate must concur by a two-thirds vote of its membership. Members of the president's Cabinet must be approved by the Senate as well.

Congressional Budget Office (CBO): This office was created under the Congressional Budget and Impoundment Control Act of 1974 to provide the Congress with technical assistance in the scrutiny and preparation of budgets, and help in a wide variety of other fiscal matters. If the

Congress chooses to create its own budget in contrast with the executive budget prepared by the Office of Management and Budget it would do so with the help of the CBO. It offers Congress a variety of computer facilities.

Congressional Campaign Committee: Members of national political parties are sometimes divided into "presidential party members" and "congressional party members." In 1866 as the split between the presidential Republicans, who supported Andrew Johnson, and the congressional Republicans grew intense, the congressional Republicans formed their own election committee. By 1880 the Democrats had also created congressional reelection committees in the Congress. These committees are most active in "off-year" elections, that is, in elections in which the voters will not choose a president. These committees raise monies, hire staffs, and aid candidates of their own party seeking reelection. Frequently, well-known members of Congress will campaign for, or make commercials for, less well-known colleagues, or for colleagues who are involved in difficult campaigns.

Congressional Record: The Constitution requires that Congress publish a journal of its proceedings from time to time. The *Congressional Record* is that journal and it is normally issued daily when Congress is in session. The Senate and the House of Representatives issue separate copies. In an appendix members may publish remarks on a variety of subjects. Speeches inserted in the main body of the *Record* which are not actually materials offered in floor debate are marked with bullets. Members may expunge portions of their remarks from the *Record* or may copy edit their speeches after actual delivery. Thus, the *Record* is not always an accurate recording of the proceedings of the Congress.

Congressional Directory: Congress publishes each year a directory of its members, listing the committees on which congresspersons and senators serve. The directory also gives brief biographical sketches of the members of Congress.

Congressional Research Service: This agency of Congress was created as the Reference Service of the Library of Congress in 1914. It does basic research on legislative and similar matters for members of Congress or its committees. It was redesigned and strengthened in 1970 under the Legislative Reform Act. One reason for strengthening this agent of Congress was that the Congress had come to distrust some of the expert testimony given by technicians and operatives of the executive branch.

Congressional Veto: Congress may grant certain powers, privileges, or prerogatives to the president. If it wishes to ensure performance of the executive it may allow the president to perform certain acts or exercise certain powers unless the Congress disapproves. For example, the Congress may permit the president to reorganize the bureaucracy, but it may retain the right to over-rule the president if it does not like his reorganization plans. Such a "veto" may require the disapproval of only one house or of both houses of Congress.

Congressperson-at-Large: Most states have more than one congressperson. In such cases congresspersons are generally elected from political subdivisions within the state called single member legislative districts. If, however, one or more congresspersons is elected from the state as a whole that person is a congressperson-at-large. Under Supreme Court rulings (*Wesberry v. Sanders* and others) all congresspersons must either be elected from the state as a whole (at large) or from single member legislative districts of the same population size. In states that have only one congressperson, that individual is for all intents and purposes, a congressperson-at large. When state legislatures are unable to agree on constitutionally acceptable redistricting plans, then all congresspersons must be elected at large.

Consensus Building: This is a bargaining process whereby the diversity of interests found among the American people and their elected representatives is reconciled, hopefully for the profit of all people.

Constituency: The people living within the geographic boundaries of the political unit that elected public officials to office are the constituents of these office holders. A congressperson's constituency exists within his or her single member (or possibly multiple member) legislative district, the unit being commonly called a congressional district. Senators' constituencies are statewide. A president's constituency is national.

Contempt of Congress: This consists in the willful disobedience of an order of either house of the Congress or of a committee of either or both houses of Congress. It could also consist in disorderly behavior in or about the halls of Congress. Contempt citations have been issued against individuals who refuse to testify before Congress on matters under congressional investigation. The courts have been reluctant to curb the use of congressional contempt citations, but some rulings have made it clear that the testimony Congress wishes to obtain must be related to the normal and proper business of Congress.

Discharge Petition: This is a device used to force a bill out of a committee and onto the floor of a legislature for consideration by members of that body. A majority of members must sign this petition in the House of Representatives in order to force a bill out of committee. While it is always a theoretical threat to committee chairpersons, it is little used in practice because members are slow to over-ride chairpersons.

Elastic Clause: Article I, section 8, of the Constitution allows the Congress to make all laws "necessary and proper" to carry out its other functions. It was first expanded in use by the Supreme Court under John Marshall who wrote in *McCulloch v. Maryland,* "In the desire to remove all doubts respecting the right to legislate on that vast mass of incidental powers which must be involved in the Constitution," the elastic clause had been added by the Founding Fathers.

Enacting Clause: In order that a bill become operative after passage (and after being signed into law by the president) it must contain an enacting or enabling clause, as, "be it enacted..."

Engrossment: An engrossed bill is in its final form immediately prior to passage. The same is true for an engrossed resolution. All amendments have been incorporated and the bill or resolution is said to be in perfect condition as it ought to be in order to become enacted.

Enrollment: An enrolled bill has been passed by both houses of Congress and is in its final and permanent form for presentation to the president for his signature.

Executive Session: These are closed sessions of committees, boards, commissions, or other public bodies. Public attendance is not permitted nor are newspeople admitted. In some cases, executive sessions may involve only the leadership of these public bodies. Sunshine laws frequently limit or prohibit executive sessions. One advantage of such sessions is that members may feel free to express their ideas and opinions openly behind closed doors, whereas they would be less candid with one another in open sessions.

Expulsion: Article I, section 5 of the Constitution permits each house of Congress to judge and punish its own members. The ultimate punishment available to Congress is the expulsion of a member from the seat to which the member's constituents elected him or her. A two-thirds vote is required to expel a member. Because of the gravity of the penalty and because the constituents would be deprived of representation in that body, it is a little used device. A member might be expelled if he or she were to be convicted of a felony, had exhausted all appeals, and still refused to resign his or her seat.

Expunge: Members of Congress may correct entries made in the *Congressional Record* if they believe they were misquoted. In the Senate the process is called expunging; in the House it is called recision. A member may also strike an entire entry by writing the proper word across that entry, ("expunge" in Senate; "recision" in the House).

Extension of Remarks: The Constitution requires that each house of Congress publish a journal of its proceedings. Congress has permitted members to add additional materials which are not actually part of the actual debates and discussions of that body. These extraneous materials are published as an appendix, and are preceded by the notation that permission has been granted for a member to "extent" his or her remarks to include additional materials. A wide variety of materials can be found in the appendixes to the *Record*, some of which seems to have little to do with the business of Congress.

False Rising: A congressperson may at times be permitted to insert in the main portion of the *Congressional Record* speeches not actually delivered before Congress. Although these are marked with "bullets" to identify the fact that the speech was not actually delivered before Congress, such a speaker is guilty of false rising for he or she usually says, "I rise to..." when indeed the speaker was probably far away from the Halls of Congress and did not rise as indicated.

Federal Register: This is an official publication, which was begun in 1936 to publish administrative rules and regulations, give notice of public hearings, and provide a ready and immediate source of other official materials relating to governmental bureaus, departments, and agencies.

Filibuster: This is commonly called "talking a bill to death." It is used occasionally in the Senate and involves a senator debating against a bill for a long period ot time in front of the other members. It is a delaying tactic used by one member while other Senators in the same "camp" try to change the votes of some of their colleagues. This tactic is used by those opposing the legislation, when they believe that they lack the votes necessary to block the legislation. One effect of the filibuster is that at times the bill's sponsors may modify some of the more objectionable features of the pending legislation. Filibusters can be countered by invoking closure (cloture).

Five Minute Rule: When the House of Representatives operates as the Committee of the Whole House, this rule is used to limit sponsors of amendments to five minutes on the floor to defend the proposed amendment. The opposition is also limited to five minutes of discussion against the proposed amendment.

Floor: The floor is the place of business of a legislative body. A member who is "holding the floor" is talking before that body. When in session only members may be present on the floor of a legislature, although certain other designated persons may be present, such as pages, clerks, and the like. Many legislatures prohibit anyone but another legislator from attempting to influence a member on the floor.

Franking Privilege: Congresspersons who wish to mail letters or materials to their constituents or to use the mails in any other way pertaining to their official position need only affix their signature (or a facsimile) to the upper right-hand corner instead of regular postage. Congresspersons may mail out newsletters to their constituents using the franking privilege.

Freedom of Information Act of 1966: This law was designed to allow private citizens access to public records. There are few exceptions to this right to obtain documents. Most of these exceptions involve matters of national security. The act also reduced the number of materials withheld from the public by being arbitrarily marked as secret. In 1974 the act was amended to permit easier access to the courts to compel public agencies to comply with the act. Courts generally are permitted to judge the propriety of governmentally sponsored exemptions to the law.

Gag Rule: In order to expedite the passage of legislation, especially controversial matters, legislative bodies will often invoke special rules designed to limit debate on the matters when they arrive on the floor for consideration. The Rules Committee of the House of Representatives may attach "gag rules" to bills sent to it.

General Accounting Office: This office was created under the Budget and Accounting Act of 1921 and its powers have been extended by a variety of laws since, including the Government Corporation Control Act, the Legislative Reorganization Act of 1946, the Accounting and Auditing Act of 1950, the Congressional Budget and Impoundment Control Act of 1974, and the General Accounting Office Act of 1974. The GAO is under the control of the comptroller general, who, along with his chief deputy, is appointed by the president with the advise and consent of the Senate to a 15 year term. He may be removed only with the consent of Congress. The GAO assists Congress and its committees in carrying out the legislative and oversight functions. It is an independent, nonpolitical agency of the legislative branch of government. It carries out functions related to claims settlements, law, accounting, and auditing. It is charged with representing congressional interests in reducing waste and increasing the efficiency of the bureaucracy.

Gerrymandering: This practice was named after colonial statesman Elbridge Gerry who was famous for creating unusual legislative districts in order to increase partisan advantage in elections. Generally, legislative districts that are unusual in size or shape are said to have been gerrymandered.

Grant-in-Aid: Monies have been appropriated by Congress to aid local or state governments consistently since 1933. These may be used to create and maintain programs or for construction. Minimum standards are frequently established by Congress that states must comply with in order to receive these grants. Grants-in-aid may be given by states to substate governments.

Hearing: Public sessions of congressional committees, or even of Congress, may be scheduled at times in order to gather testimony from a wide variety of opinions on legislative matters pending before the Congress. Citizens, pressure groups, public interest groups, and paid lobbyists may be scheduled to give testimony and present evidence on the matter under consideration. Many hearings are held by subcommittees.

House Calendar: General legislative matters before the House of Representatives are considered under time allotted under the House Calendar.

Impoundment Control: In 1974 the Congress passed the Congressional Budget and Impoundment Control Act. It was designed in part to counter the attempts by presidents to withdraw monies appropriated by Congress from programs of many types. The act provides for the monitoring of executive behavior and for the reporting of failures of the president to spend monies allocated by Congress. It authorizes Congress to bring suit in the federal courts if necessary to assure the expenditure of monies.

Intestigative Power of Committees: Committees, whether they are special or standing, are permitted to investigate problems so that appropriate legislation may be enacted by the Congress. They may subpoena witnesses, compel testimony, gather evidence, and produce appropriate reports. There are a number of reasons why committees conduct investigations. Sometimes, they hope to shape public opinion; at other times they are following public opinion and responding to public outrage over some matter. They may be genuinely interested in gathering useful information about some subject they hope to correct by appropriate legislation. They may be looking to uncover misfeasance or malfeasance of office by some public official. At times, they are merely created to focus public attention on congressional activity and on congresspersons.

Joint Committee: In the Congress a joint committee is made up of an equal number of members from both houses. A conference committee that is designed to work out compromises between two versions of the same bill is a joint committee. Congress has also created a few standing committees with joint membership, such as the Atomic Energy Committee. There have been many proposals for creating many joint standing committees so as to remove the duplication that results from one house having many of the same committees as the other house.

Joint Resolution: Amendments to the Constitution are proposed by joint resolution, with two-thirds of the members of both houses of Congress concurring. These joint resolutions are marked "H J Res" in the House of Representatives, and "S J Res" in the Senate. Excepting proposed amendments, joint resolutions are signed by the president. They may be used for limited legislative purposes and they may be used to voice the sentiment of Congress on some issue.

Joint Session: Both houses of the legislature may meet together for a certain purpose. The Congress hears the president's State of the Union address in joint session and declaration of war requests are made by the president to joint sessions.

Lame Duck: A person who is still situated in public office after his or her term of office or after he or she has been defeated for reelection is said to be a lame duck. A president who has served one full term of office and then is reelected is immediately a lame duck for he is not eligible for election to a third term. Before the enactment of the Twentieth Amendment members of Congress served until March 4. A candidate who was defeated for relection in November might still influence legislation for four months. One defeated in a primary (possibly as early as March in some states) might serve a full year as a lame duck. The Twentieth Amendment was designed to remove some objectionable features of the lame duck situation, by having newly elected congresspersons take office in January rather than in March.

Law Making: This is the primary function of any legislature. The executive may propose legislation, but the legislature must dispose of it. The political system is designed to allocate value authoritatively and this authoritative allocation of values is done in the large by making and passing laws. The art of lawmaking involves the creation of rules with a concern for fairness and impartiality.

Legislative Day: This is not an ordinary 24 hour time period, for a legislative day may last indefinitely. It begins with the call to order and ends with adjournment. To expedite matters one or another legislative house may recess at the end of a calendar day and begin anew after a specified period of time, still in the same legislative day.

Legislative Reorganization Act of 1946:   This act (1) reduced the number of legislative committees; (2) reduced the number of special committees; (3) regulated lobbying by requiring lobbyists to register, to tell whom they represented, and reveal their direct expenses in lobbying; (4) increased the professional staff available to committees; and (5) increased the staff of individual congresspersons. The most lasting requirement of the act dealt with the regulation of lobbying.

Legislative Reform Act of 1970:   This act (1) modified the voting system so that as few as 44 members could compel a record vote on issues before the House of Representatives; (2) permitted the use of electronic voting systems in the House so as to avoid the use of the time-consuming roll call; (3) required that record votes in executive sessions be made public; (4) changed the name of the Legislative Reference Service of the Library of Congress to the Congressional Research Service and increased its staff and powers; (5) allowed for televised committee hearings if the witnesses and the majority of the committee agreed; (6) allowed as few as 20 members to compel a record vote in the Committee of the Whole House; and (7) allowed a majority of a committee to schedule committee meetings without the chairpersons's consent.

Library of Congress: This major international depository of books was founded in 1800, based on Jefferson's library collection. Copies of all copyrighted publications produced in this nation and in most foreign nations are housed here. It stores the official letters and documents of the nation. It has about 17 million items.

Logrolling: This is a process whereby legislation is passed smoothly through the Congress. With over 10,000 bills introduced into Congress annually, no items may be permitted to block up the legislative process. Congresspersons may vote to expedite matters not of concern to them personally in order that the system continues to operate and bills more of their own interest will come to the floor. It is sometimes described as "you vote for my bill and I'll vote for yours."

Majority Floor Leader: Since much of the speaker of the House's time is taken up in presiding over the House and its operations he needs an assistant. This assistant, the majority floor leader, helps to plan party strategy and design programs. He meets with others of the party's leadership, with leaders of the opposition party, and with regular members of the House. He acts as liaison with the party whips and may assist them.

Morning Hour: This is a special time set aside in a legislature to deal with such routine matters as the introduction of bills, reception of messages from the other house of the legislature or from the executive, and receipt of committee reports. The Senate ordinarily sets aside two hours in the morning of each legislative (not calendar) day to be the "morning hours." In the House this device is less commonly used than in the Senate.

Motion: This is a specific proposal offered by a member of a legislative body, usually preceded by the words, "Be it moved..."

Nonlegislative Powers of Congress: Most of the powers granted to the Congress in the Constitution are connected with the passage of legislation. However, there are nonlegislative functions. The Senate, for example, must advise and consent to executive appointments and to treaties. The Congress as a whole has a number of other nonlegislative functions such as: proposing amendments to the Constitution; passing rules for the operation of that portion of Congress; overseeing staff; approving interstate compacts; participating in impeachments; and approving presidential powers granted by Congress, such as the use of martial law and emergency powers.

Nonvoting Representatives (Congressional Delegates): There are members of the House of Representatives who sit in on committee meetings and attend sessions of the House but who do not have a vote. Such nonvoting representatives come from the District of Columbia, and three American territories. The nonvoting members from the District of Columbia, Guam, and the Virgin Islands are called delegates. The representative from Puerto Rico is called the resident commissioner. An amendment to the Constitution has been proposed that would give the District of Columbia a voting delegation in Congress. The Senate does not extend such nonvoting memberships to these areas.

Pairing: When two members of the House or the Senate are absent from the legislative body, and they are on opposite sides of a bill to be voted on they may pair. One notes that he or she is paired for; the other is paired against. Their votes are not counted, but pairing does allow these members to go on record in a record vote for or against the bill.

Permanent Appropriation: Monies are collected, often from a specific tax, for a certain, specified purpose. These funds automatically are allocated for the purpose until directly repealed. Gasoline taxes may be permanently allocated for highway maintainence or construction.

Pigeonhole: Bills are generally referred to committees in both houses of the legislature. Bills are ordinarily considered and either tabled or sent out to the floor for consideration. Bills on which no action at all is taken are said to be pigeonholed. Discharge petitions may be used in many legislatures, as in the House of Representatives, to force bills that have been pigeonholed out of committee. Because of the large number of bills introduced into legislatures at all levels each year, pigeonholing is a necessary and inevitable part of the legislative process.

Point of Order: All parliamentary bodies operate under set written rules. When a member of a legislative body believes that a rule needs to be applied or interpreted during house proceedings he or she may rise to call for a point of order. The presiding officer is generally compelled to respond to that call and his ruling is ordinarily subject to appeal to the floor. Many legislators are successful because they know and can invoke the rules of their bodies.

Pork Barrel: Congress annually appropriates monies, frequently in the area of public works, for projects that are unneeded or duplicate other public works or programs. Such appropriations are designed to spend moneys in the home districts of powerful and influential senators and congresspersons. Many pork barrel projects are undertaken in the construction of post offices, veterans' hospitals, and dams.

President of the Senate: According to the Constitution the vice-president of the United States is also president of the Senate, that is, its chief presiding officer. If the Senate deadlocks on a vote he may vote on a measure if he wishes it to pass (if he does not wish it to pass he does not vote and the measure fails for want of a majority).

Previous Question: This is a method of ending debate in a parliamentary body. A call for the previous question requires an immediate vote on the main proposal before that body. If the previous question is called in the House of Representatives before debate has begun, each side is then permitted 20 minutes in which to present its case before a vote is taken. The call for the previous is not itself debatable.

Private Bill: Such bills benefit only one or a few persons. Technically, private bills were not to be permitted after the 1946 reorganization of Congress under the Reorganization Act of that year. Nonetheless, many private bills are introduced annually, falling chiefly into three categories: (1) claims against the government not reconciled elsewhere; (2) clearance of land titles, and; (3) permission for aliens to enter the country without having to wait for ordinary immigration procedures to become operative.

Quorum: This is the minimum number of persons who must be present for a body to conduct business. In the House of Representatives it is 218; in the Senate it is 51. In the Committee of the Whole House it is 100.

Ranking Members: In a committee of the Congress, the ranking member is ordinarily the member of the majority party having the greatest seniority on a committee next to the chairperson. Under ordinary circumstances the ranking member would become committee chairperson on the death or resignation of the chair. Changes in seniority practices may, from time to time, alter these procedures.

Ranking Miniority Member: The member of a committee in Congress having the longest tenure on that committee who is a member of the party having the fewer members in that body of Congress is called the ranking minority member. Should his or her party gain a majority in that house of the Congress he or she ordinarily would become the chairperson of that committee.

Ratification: In order that a treaty become effective it must be accepted by two-thirds of the total membership of the Senate. Approval of treaties by the Senate in its advise and consent function is called ratification. About 99 percent of all treaties submitted to the Senate have been ratified.

Reading: This is a vital step in the passage of a bill in a legislative body. After a piece of legislation has been reported out of committee it is placed on a calendar. When the bill is presented to the members it is "read." Ordinarily it must be read on three consecutive days. In the Senate a bill may be read in its entirety on the third reading; in the House it is read on the second reading.

Recess: This is an intermission in a legislative body. It may be called for a portion of a day or for one or more whole days. Article I, section 5 of the Constitution requires that one house of Congress gain the consent of the other house if it is to recess more than three days. Recesses are called for holidays and to allow members to campaign for office.

Rescission: Members of Congress may withdraw or correct remarks made on the floor of Congress and reported in the *Congressional Records*. In the House of Representatives the members may expunge remarks by using the word rescission, marked across the entry in the record.

Recommittal: If one house of Congress is displeased with the work of a committee it may send the bill back to committee for additional study or work. This process is called recommittal.

Reconsideration: A motion may be made in a house of Congress to open for discussion a matter already voted on by that house. In both houses anyone who voted with the majority may move for reconsideration. In the Senate one who did not vote on the bill initially may also so move. Reconsideration may allow a defeated bill to be passed or it may delay a bill already passed by that house.

Record Vote: This procedure requires that a congressperson or senator record his or her vote for or against a measure to be voted on. As few as 20 members can compel a record vote in the Committee of the Whole House and as few as 44 members may compel a record vote in the House. Record votes are mandatory if Congress attempts to over-ride a presidential veto. In the Senate as few as 20 members may compel a record vote (one-fifth of members).

Referral to Committee: This is a vital step in the passage of a bill. Bills introduced into either house of Congress are sent to an appropriate committee for study, consideration, recommendations, and, perhaps, change. The speaker of the House has some latitude in the selection of committees. Because there are fewer committees in the Senate the selection of committees there is nearly automatic.

Repeal: Legislatures at times decide that legislation passed in a previous session did not have the desired effect and they choose to render it invalid. On one occasion the Constitution was amended and later that amendment was repealed. The Eighteenth Amendment made it illegal to sell alcoholic beverages and the Twenty-first Amendment repealed those provisions.

Report: The purpose of sending a bill to a committee is to have the committee study it and report on the bill to the entire house of that legislature. Ordinarily, only bills considered favorably will be reported out of committee. A bill considered unfavorably will be tabled (killed). The report contains the recommendations of committee.

Representation of Interests: There is a wide diversity of interests within the United States, based on ethnic, political, religious, social, economic, and institutional diversity of the American people. Congress, or any legislative body, must attempt to represent these often conflicting interests. The primary function of the Congress is to make rules applicable to all Americans. Their diverse interests must be taken into account in rule-making.

Resident Commissioner: Voting representation is given only to the 50 states in the Congress. However, nonvoting representation is given to four areas that are not states: Guam, Puerto Rico, District of Columbia, and the Virgin Islands. The nonvoting representative of Puerto Rico in the

House of Representatives is called a resident commissioner. The representatives from the other three areas are called delegates.

Revenue Bills: The Constitution provides that revenue bills originate in the House of Representatives, although such bills must eventually be passed by the Senate and signed by the president (or passed over his veto by a two-thirds majority of both houses.) Revenue bills raise moneys to be spent by the Congress.

Rider: It is sometimes difficult to schedule controversial bills in legislative bodies. One way to bring an unscheduled bill to the attention of the members is to attach it to a bill under consideration. When one bill is added on to another it is commonly called a rider.

Roll Call: A quorum must be present to do business in a legislative body. Quorum is usually a simply majority (for example: 218 in House of Representatives; 51 in Senate). To establish whether a quorum is present the clerk may call the roll of members. One way to record the "yea" and "nay" votes on a matter under consideration before the legislature is to call the roll, recording members' votes. Since legislative reorganization took place in 1970 the House has been permitted to use electronic devices to record members' votes rather than having a formal call of the roll of members. A roll call vote may be required in the House by as few as 44 members; and by as few as 20 members in the Senate.

Rules: All legislative bodies have adopted rules that provide organization, order, and direction to their operations. The Constitution allows each house of the Congress to make its own rules of procedure. Generally, these rules follow standard parliamentary procedure. The House Rules Committee may create special rules under which a bill may be considered.

Rules Committee: Most parliamentary bodies have committees that consider new rules of procedure or changes in existing rules. Their function thus is internal to the legislative body. In the House of Representatives there is a Rules Committee which has a very special function. It is permitted to create special rules under which a particular bill may be considered. Such special rules might limit or wholly eliminate debate on that bill. In the past the Rules Committee was very powerful and was controlled by conservatives who used their powers to block many social and welfare bills. There is no equivalent committee in the Senate. In state legislatures rules committees are frequently made up of committee chairpersons and ranking minority members. Such rules committees serve frequently as steering committees with powers to schedule bills for votes by the whole legislature.

Safe District: There are many districts wherein the elected representative has, by virtue of long service or strong personal appeal, created a situation that virtually guarantees him or her of reelection. Generally, a safe district will have a large registration of voters of the party to which the representative belongs. In some safe districts the opposition party may not even field a candidate in opposition to the incumbent.

Secretary of the Senate: Until a president *pro tempore* is elected in the Senate, the acting presiding officer other than the vice-president (who is constitutionally the Senate's normal presiding officer) is the secretary of the Senate. The secretary is the keeper of the Seal of the Senate and performs other duties such as: distributing Senate paychecks; administering oaths; certifying the Senate portion of the *Congressional Records*: certifying that bills have passed the Senate; and certifying that treaties or executive appointments have been approved by the Senate.

Select Committee on Intelligence: The Senate created a special committee in 1976 to provide oversight to the Central Intelligence Agency (CIA) and other similar agencies. By mid-1977 the House of Representatives had also created a similar committee.

Senatorial Courtesy: In making appointments involving officers to serve in a state, or national officers from a certain state, the president is expected to consider the opinion of the state's senior senator who is a member of the president's party. If there is no senator from that state belonging to the president's party, he is expected to clear the appointment with other party officials from that state. Senatorial courtesy extends even to the appointment of federal judges. Failure to practice senatorial courtesy may cause the president's nominee to be rejected by the Senate.

Seniority: Seniority is a measure of continual service on or in a particular body. It is computed as a base for selection for service on an important committee. For example, an individual may have to have accumulated considerable seniority in the House of Representatives before he or she might be allowed to join the Rules Committee. It is also a mark of continual service on a committee. The member of the majority party with the longest continual service on a committee is generally its chairperson. The member with the next longest service who also belongs to the majority party is called the ranking member. The person belonging to the minority party with the longest continual service becomes the ranking minority member of the committee. Seniority is also an important fact in choosing offices of a legislative body.

Sergeant-at-Arms: In the Congress there is a sergeant-at-arms in each house who acts as the chief law enforcement officer of those bodies. He also assists in bringing absent members to the halls of legislature to vote on matters before them. In Congress he also has certain ceremonial functions to perform.

Session: Congress meets once a year unless called into a special session by the president. Every second year, one-third of the Senate and all members of the House are required to stand for reelection. In the January following such congressional elections there is a new Congress (for example, the 90th Congress). The numbers began with the meeting of Congress following adoption of the Constitution. Each Congress meets in two sessions, the first session following elections. Congress begins a new session ordinarily on January 3. Bills that did not become law in a previous session of Congress die at the end of the session and must be reintroduced anew in the next session.

Sine Die: This Latin term means that a public body has concluded its business and its session has ended.

Slip Laws: These are pamphlet-like reprints of laws enacted by Congress. They are ordinarily issued within a few days after passage by Congress and after the president's signature has been obtained (although they are also issued for bills that become law after 10 days without his signature and for laws passed over his veto). Listings of such laws are found in several places, including the *Weekly Compilation of Presidential Documents* and the *Federal Register.* The United States *Statutes at Large* is essentially a collection of slip laws.

Speaker of the House: This person is the presiding officer of the House of Representatives and is elected by its members. While he need not be a member of the House constitutionally, he is traditionally a senior member of the majority party. He has great powers in controlling the passage of legislation. He has considerable influence in the selection of members of the majority party to serve on committees. His support can aid a presidential program and his opposition can kill such programs. He is first in line to become president after the vice-president of the United States.

Special Representation: In his book, *The Legislative Process in Congress*, George Galloway argues that Congress is required each year to spend ever more of its time in oversight and special representation functions and less time on legislation. Congresspersons are forced to spend a significant portion of their time attempting to mediate disputes between bureaucracies and their constituents. Congresspersons have become the public's special representatives against a complex and often bewildering bureaucratic structure they now seek to control.

Standing Committee: The work of legislative bodies is primarily done in committees which consider the substance of legislation proposed by the executive, the bureaucracy, the members themselves, and, occasionally, by the general public or interest groups. These committees are created at the beginning of a legislative session or they may be automatically carried over from previous sessions. Generally, membership is reconstituted after each election. There are 21 standing committees in the House of Representatives plus a special rules committee. There are 15 standing committees in the Senate. The House Committees are: Agriculture; Appropriations; Armed Services; Banking; Budget; District of Columbia; Finance and Urban Affairs; Interior and Insular Affairs; International Relations; Interstate and Foreign Affairs; Judiciary; Labor and Education; Merchant Marine and Fisheries; Post Office and Civil Service; Public Works and Transportation; Science and Technology; Small Business; Standards of Official Conduct; Veterans Affairs; and Ways and Means. In the Senate the standing committees are: Agriculture; Forestry and Nutrition; Appropriations; Armed Services; Banking, Housing, and Urban Affairs; Budget; Commerce; Science, and Transportation; Energy and Natural Resources; Environment and Public Works; Finance; Foreign Relations; Governmental Affairs; Human Resources; Judiciary; Rules and Administration; and Veterans Affairs.

Statute: The formal expression of the law is called a statute. It is distinguished from the unwritten, or common, law.

Statutes at Large: At the end of each legislative session all acts and resolutions that have become law are gathered together in a collection called *Statutes at Large*. There are two parts. The first contains public bills and joint resolutions. The second contains private acts and laws, concurrent resolutions, treaties, presidential proclamations, and treaties.

Steering Committee: This is an executive committee, usually contained within a caucus. It frequently decides the official party or caucus position on bills pending before the legislature. Steering committees such as the Democratic Steering and Policy Committee in the House of Representatives, are frequently used to make committee asignments.

Straw Vote: A preliminary head count is often made within a public body before a formal vote is taken to determine the sentiment of that body on an issue or bill before it. Straw votes are generally taken on an informal basis. They aid the leadership, the opposition, or the sponsors in planning strategy. In common usage, straw votes are used by newspaper frequently to try to project, in the absence of more scientific testing, winners in an election.

Subcommittee: In legislatures most work is done in committee. Special smaller units of a committee may be created out of the committee membership to conduct partial or whole studies of bills or other matters. Subcommittees then report their findings to the whole committee. Subcommittees often have greater expertise in specialized matters and the members frequently deal directly with bureaucrats. In 1975 the Congress had 268 subcommittees; in 1978 that number had grown to 299. Of the 299 subcommittees, 268 were attached to standing congressional committees and 31 were attached to special or *ad hoc* committees.

Subsidiary Motion: This is a parliamentary procedure used by the Congress and other legislatures. This motion is made to adopt a particular way of considering or disposing of a matter before that legislative body.

Sunshine Law: This is a generic name given to a number of legislative proposals which are designed to make meetings of various public bodies open to the general public. There is an assumption made here that in democratic systems, the people have a right to know how their governmental bodies operate. The federal law opens nearly all meetings to the public except for the few that concern national security. The *Federal Register* contains a list of all public meetings and hearings conducted by bureaucracies, giving the meeting time and place and a list of subjects to be discussed, and the telephone number of the officer in charge in case additional information is required. Transcripts of meetings must be maintained and these must be made available within a short time to interested parties. Many states and local governments have similar requirements for public meetings.

Suspension of the Rules: Legislative bodies, such as Congress, are generally permitted to make their own rules of procedure. One rule may allow a member to vote to suspend part or all of the other rules. In the House of Representatives a two-thirds vote may allow that body to suspend its rules and vote immediately on a bill under consideration. This is a time-saving device designed to hasten a bill's passage.

Trustee: When a legislator acts on behalf of constituents without asking for their direct inputs he or she may be said to be acting as their trustee. This is a way of stating Edmund Burke's (1729–1797) theory of virtual representation. Burke believed that voters should choose the best and most virtuous of their number to represent them without subsequently telling the individual how to vote. Their job is to select the best person and it is then his or her job to determine how to vote.

Unanimous Consent: This is a parliamentary device used to speed up the handling of routine matters so that time can be allocated to more important matters. It is sometimes known as recording the passage of a measure "without objection." One use of the device is the granting of unanimous consent to a congressperson to read materials into the appendix of the *Congressional Record.*

Union Calendar: In the House of Representatives money bills are placed on special time slots known as the union calendar. Bills that appropriate money or levy taxes or those public bills that are primarily associated with raising or spending moneys are placed on this calendar. This is the common abbreviation for "Calendar of the Committee of the Whole House on the State of the Union."

Viva Voca Voting: This term is used to cover oral voting in a legislative body. It avoids the time consuming process of record voting. Members are asked to call out "yea" or "nay" on a matter brought to a vote.

Whips: These persons are party officials who attempt to mobilize the members of their party in a legislature so that votes on matters on which the party has taken a stand are kept within party lines. They act as liaison persons between the party leadership and the rank-and-file members. They are charged with convincing party members of the value of supporting party stands and with mustering the members for votes on important matters. There is a majority and a minority whip in each house of Congress.

CASES

McGrain v. Daugherty (273 US 135, 1927): The Supreme Court held in this case that the Congress may compel individual citizens to give testimony before the Congress and its committees and subcommittees, provided such testimony is required or useful for framing the laws of the land. Congressional investigations into a wide variety of subjects is dependent on such testimony. The court thus protected the right of the Congress to obtain information, provided it is related to the rightful work of that body.

Marbury v. Madison (1 Cranch 137, 1803): John Marshall wrote this famous opinion for the Supreme Court. It is perhaps the most significant decision ever rendered by the high court, for it established the doctrine of judicial review. Marshal held that the Constitution is the "precise, unchanging and paramount" law of the land. It is designed to limit the powers of government, especially of the legislature. Although the high federal court had previously invalidated state laws, it had never attempted to invalidate a law passed by the Congress before. Marshall held that all acts of all legislatures in the United States were subject to review by the Supreme Court, and any act repugnant to the Constitution could be, and would be, rendered null and void. Although few laws were struck down by the federal courts in the first 100 years of the Republic, many laws have been invalidated in the last 70 years, following this precedent case.

United States v. Harris (347 US 612, 1954): In 1946 the Congress passed the first major law designed to regulate, to some degree, the activities of professional and paid lobbyists. The act required lobbyists to register and to report income and expenditures. The Supreme Court in this case sustained the major provisions of the Federal Regulation of Lobbying Act. It cautioned the Congress that such legislation could be directed only at those who professionally attempted to directly influence legislation. Regulation generally was not permitted of those whose efforts were indirect, aimed at molding public opinion, nor of private citizens seeking to influence their congresspersons. The Court agreed that the Congress had a right to know who was spending how much money to influence legislation.

United States v. Johnson (383 US 169, 1966):   In order that full freedom of discussion and debate on legislative and other matters pending before Congress be guaranteed, Article I, section 6 of the Constitution permits congresspersons to consider these matters and discuss them freely without the possibility of being involved in court litigation. The Supreme Court noted that constitutional provision but held that such immunity from prosecution was valid only in Congress. It did not extend to congresspersons' remarks made outside formal or informal sessions of Congress and its committees.

Watkins v. United States (354 US 178, 1957):   In attempting to define the powers of the Congress in compelling testimony from witnesses before Congress or its committees, the Supreme Court found, in this case, that Congress must be able to demonstrate that questions put to witnesses bear on some legal and constitutional function of the Congress. It cautioned Congress about "fishing trips" in which the Congress or its staff would question witnesses in an abstract way in the hope that something of value might accidentally be found.

Wesberry v. Sanders (376 US 1, 1964):   In this landmark case the Supreme Court ordered that Congressional districts within a state must contain substantially equal numbers of voters. Failure to redistrict to follow population trends may result in court ordered redistricting or in the courts requiring that congresspersons be elected at large rather than from single member legislative districts. This is the "one man, one vote principle" applied to congressional elections.

8

The Court System

Acquittal: This is a formed certification by a court that an individual has been found "not guilty" of a crime with which he or she was charged. An individual may be acquitted because of insufficient or faulty evidence or because the prosecutor has failed to establish guilt either before a judge or a jury. An individual who is acquitted of a crime cannot, under our prohibition against double jeopardy, be tried again for the same crime in the same level of jurisdiction.

Administrative law: See Chapter 6, p. 95.

Administrative Office of United States Courts: Created in 1939, it deals with courts inferior to the United States Supreme Court. It prepares the budgets, allocates expenditures, supervises clerical staffs, and compiles statistical information, and a variety of other mundane and routine but necessary functions.

Admiralty Law: This body of law deals with shipping and commerce on the high seas, and on the navigable waters of the nation. More than most law, it draws on the practices of nations, international acts and customs, and on tradition, although the Congress has provided considerable code law to supplement these other sources. Federal courts have exclusive jurisdiction in this area of the law under Article III, section 2 of the Constitution.

Adversary System: The courts are neutral bodies that arbitrate disputes between two or more individuals or between the state and one or more persons. The court cannot act until a case is brought before it. When two lawyers argue the rights of persons before a court, each presenting testimony and evidence, we have the adversary system in operation. Attorneys from each side are expected to present their arguments with full force and vigor.

Affidavit: This is a statement given under oath in which an individual provides information he or she believes to be true. In certain circumstances an affidavit may be used in courts.

Amicus Curiae: Literally this means a "friend of the court." The person is not associated with either party in litigation. He or she is heard primarily to assist the court in some matter of the law.

Appellate Court: This a higher court which has the power to review the cases decided in lower or inferior levels of the court system. The United States Circuit Courts of Appeals is a wholly appellate court system. The United States Supreme Court receives most of its cases on appeals. The opposite of an appellate court is a court of original jurisdiction in which cases are first tried. Many courts have both functions. The United States Supreme Court has some original jurisdiction functions.

Arbitration: Some disputes between conflicting parties can be settled without recourse to the courts by using independent and uninvolved arbitrators. Under certain circumstances binding arbitration may take place. Here the parties agree in advance to accept the facts and/or the settlements in the case as discovered by the arbitrator. A professional organization, the American Arbitration Association, maintains a list of professional arbitrators in many areas. Arbitration obviously saves time and expense for the courts.

Arraignment: Individuals accused of crimes must be brought before a magistrate or other proper authority to plead "guilty" or "not guilty" to a set of specific charges. The charges prepared against the accused may be prepared either by a prosecutor or a grand jury.

Arrest Warrant: A law enforcement officer who personally witnesses a crime may arrest the person who committed it without a warrant. In nearly all other cases the individual may be arrested only after a warrant has been issued by the court or other judicial figure having the power to issue warrants. The Fourth Amendment prohibits arbitrary arrests. Warrants are issued only if there is probable cause of a crime and reasonable relationship between the incident of crime and the individual arrested.

Attorney General: The attorney general is head of the Department of Justice and holds Cabinet rank. He is the principal legal adviser to the president. He is also the principal law enforcement officer of the nation and heads a staff of attorneys and other professionals who enforce federal law and court decisions. He heads up the federal jail system, directs federal attorneys, and administers the federal marshall system.

Bail: In medieval codes a vassal king was required to make himself available to substitute for his lord if that king were held for ransom or required to appear in a court. Today, bail is posted in money or property as a guarantee that the person accused of a crime will appear in court. It is a method of freeing an individual until the trial comes up on the court docket. This allows the individual to assist in gathering testimony and evidence on his or her own behalf. The Eighth Amendment to the Constitution forbids the levying of excessive bail. The courts determine bail by assessing the person's standing in the community, wealth, and the nature of the crime of which he or she is accused. Some individuals are permitted to remain free until a trial when there is near certainty that they will appear in court. The latter is called release on one's own recognition.

Brief: Attorneys for each side of an adversary proceeding, and especially for cases presented on appeal, outline their principal contentions and note what they believe to be the applicable law in a written summary called a brief. A *Brandeis brief*, named after the late Supreme Court justice, is one which contains sociological and essentially nonlegal arguments. Despite the term, many briefs are quite long.

Challenge: An individual is guaranteed, by the Bill of Rights, a fair and just trial by a jury of peers. To create a jury out of a list of prospective jurors, defense and prosecuting attorneys may ordinarily reject some. If challenged for cause, the attorney must show that the juror is somehow incapable of being objective and that he or she cannot be expected to render a fair and impartial judgment. A limited number of *preempted challenges*, rejections of a prospective juror without giving a reason, is permitted.

Charge: After all evidence has been presented in a trial and the attorneys have made their closing arguments and statements, the judge may instruct the jury on certain points of law or on the proper way to consider evidence. Federal judges have generally wide latitude in charging a jury, whereas the latitude given to state judges may very from one state to another. The charge to the jury sets the law they are bound to follow according to the judge's interpretations and definitions. Generally, they may not apply other law. The charge may refresh the minds of jurors, especially after a lengthy trial, but it may also create prejudices.

Chief Justice: In the United States Supreme Court system this refers to the principal of the nine judges. He performs administrative tasks such as assigning the writing of the court's opinions. He presides over the Senate during the impeachment of a president or vice-president. (He is also chairperson of the Judicial Conference of the United States). For the most part he is merely one of the nine members of the court and has the same one vote that the other eight have in deciding cases. Obviously, the chief justice may vote in the minority on any given decision as his vote is not meant to influence the votes of the other eight. Courts are frequently referred to by the name of the chief justice; for example, the Warren Court was named after Earl Warren, its chief justice. Some other notable chief justices include John Marshall (1803–1835), Roger B. Taney (1835–1864), and Charles E. Hughes (1930–1941). Only one president ever served also as chief justice, William Howard Taft (1921–1931).

Circuit Executive of the Courts of Appeals: In 1971 Congress authorized the appointment of a circuit executive for each circuit court council. The circuit executive summons on an annual basis all circuit and district judges in his circuit. These meetings may involve members of the bar as well. He also administers the nonjudicial business of the courts within his circuit. He may call other meetings of the district and appeals judges within his circuit.

Civil Law: Individuals have certain rights in society which their fellows may not violate. If one individual commits a noncriminal act, that is, an act not against the public order, against another person, the latter may seek civil remedy. Thus, one's right to a good name may not be violated by an individual's slander. One may sue the individual in the courts for damage of reputation under civil law.

Class or Representative Action: This is ordinarily a kind of civil action in which one or more individuals in a similar legal situation sue either for themselves or for all members of that class. The individual may choose to terminate his or her action at any time. Class actions have been limited in federal courts to those whose individual claims are at least $10,000, the minimum required for a federal suit (*Zahn v. International Paper Co.* 414 US 291, 1973). The courts have also required that all potential litigants must be notified of the class action suit at the expense of those suing under class action (*Eisen v. Carlisle & Jacquelin*, 417 US 156, 1974).

Code Law: Each state and federal government publishes a compilation of the standing law in a code. The federal law as passed by Congress, and including all changes and amendments is published in the *United States Code*. Each year the *Code* is updated with supplements and new volumes. Codes may be annotated to expand and clarify the meanings of the laws.

Common Law: The United States Constitution recognizes the common law especially as developed early on in England. Common law arose from the application of reason by individual judges to concrete circumstances. When the common law was seen to be internally inconsistent, it was replaced by code law, which consists of the acts of the legislature. The common law tradition, that of using prior cases as precedents in current actions, created the system wherein decisions of courts, especially the Supreme Court, became precedents used to decide current cases. The common law is frequently called "Judge made law."

Concurrent Jurisdiction: The Constitution forbids the government to try an individual twice for the same offense in the same jurisdiction. The states and the federal government represent two levels of jurisdiction. When there is authority in the law vested in two levels of courts to hear cases involving the same offense, we have concurrent jurisdiction. Thus, bank robbery may be both a federal offense and an offense against the law of the state wherein the robbery took place.

Concurring Opinion: When a member of a judicial body, such as the Supreme Court, agrees with the conclusions of the majority in their decision in a case, but disagrees with all or part of their reasoning, he or she may write an opinion, given in addition to the opinion of the court, which sets forth his or her own personal ideas on the subject and explains how he or she arrived at the same conclusion. Justices often will concur in order to issue a call to further action or to suggest ways in which a doctrine may be extended or further developed.

Confession: An individual who admits to committing a crime is said to have confessed. Confessions must be voluntary and must be closely tied (within six hours) to arraignment according to a provision of the Omnibus Crime Bill of 1968. Confessions may not be extracted by force or under duress. A confession must be corroborated by evidence that a crime actually took place.

Constitutional Law: The highest law of the land is the Constitution of the United States. Laws made by the Congress may not violate the Constitution. If laws do violate the Constitution, the Supreme Court as the highest level of authority in the land may strike down such laws, thus declaring these laws to be null and void. This authority of the Supreme Court was discovered in *Marbury v. Madison* (1 Cranch 138, 1803).

Contempt of Court: This would be a willful act of disobedience to a legal order of a judicial body. If committed in the presence of the court it would be *direct contempt*. If action was taken to avert the consequences of court it would be *constructive contempt*. *Criminal contempt* is action taken against the court itself. Failure to carry out the court's orders for the benefit of another person would be *civil contempt*.

Criminal Law: This kind of law applies to crimes against the public order. It is based almost exclusively on statutory law. Although most criminal cases are handled within state courts, there are a number of federal criminal offenses with which the federal courts must deal. Additionally, the federal courts handle certain appeals of criminal convictions from the states, especially those involving claims that due process of the law was violated.

Dissenting Opinion: When a judge disagrees with the opinion rendered by a majority of the judges on a court he or she may write a dissenting opinion, which provides his or her reasoning and arguments. While such opinions have no technical legal standing, many dissenting opinions of yesteryear have become the basis of current court positions. The most valuable dissenting opinions are generally those provided by members of the Supreme Court. More than one judge may dissent, and thus more than one dissenting opinion may be provided as an appendage to the opinion of the court. Two or more justices may choose to join in a dissenting opinion or such an opinion may be written by only one judge.

District Court: The federal courts having original jurisdiction in most cases are the district courts. There are 88 in the 50 states. All states have at least one district court and some have several. There are also federal district courts in American territories and in the District of Columbia. Each court has at least one full-time judge and some have as many as 24 judges. Judges in the state districts are appointed for life with the advise and consent of the Senate.

Docket: This is a list of cases or other proceedings to be heard by a certain court. Brief minutes of these proceedings are included.

En Banc: Certain courts, such as the United States Court of Appeals have or may have a large number of justices. There are as many as 15 members on some appeals courts. Ordinarily, on one of the larger courts, a three-judge panel hears cases. When all of the judges choose to hear a case they are said to sit *en banc*.

Equity: This is a form of "judge made" law. It had its origins in early English courts where the statutory law was found to be inadequate to deal with certain cases. Judges then rendered decisions according to principles of equity and justice.

Evidence: Every court has rules under which information related to the alleged incident or crime may be admitted. Such information may be helpful or harmful to the accused. Information that has been illegally obtained, such as by illegal wiretapping, illegal entry, or forced confession, is not used in criminal proceedings.

Ex Parte: Occasionally a judicial proceeding is introduced into the courts where there is no adverse party as is traditional in our adversary system of law. The terms *ex parte*, meaning "in regard to the party of," and *in re*, meaning "in the matter of," are used to describe judicial proceedings instituted for or by a party without an adversary.

Federalist View of the Supreme Court: Alexander Hamilton provided the Federalist view of the Supreme Court's functions in what became a classic description. He said that it had neither sword nor purse, but relied only on its place in the hearts of its countrymen, and on the law abiding habits.

Federal Magistrate: These officials were appointed under the Federal Magistrates Act of 1968 to replace the United States Commissioners. Federal magistrates are appointed for eight-year terms by federal district judges. They are the lowest level of federal judicial authority. They may arraign prisoners in federal custody, issue arrest warrants, set bail, and hold preliminary hearings. If a defendant charged with a minor federal crime waives the right to a trial he or she may be tried before a federal magistrate.

Felony: Major offenses against the law are called felonies. These crimes are usually punished by large fines, imprisonment for a year or more, or by death. The federal district courts are ordinarily the court of original jurisdiction for crimes considered to be felonies against the United States. County or circuit courts try such cases in the states. The opposite of a felony is a misdemeanor and such cases are usually heard before federal district magistrates or justices of the peace in the states.

Grand Jury: This is the principal instrument used in the federal courts to obtain an indictment. It generally consists of from 12 to 23 members who consider evidence presented by state or federal prosecuting attorneys and determine if there is sufficient evidence available to the prosecution to proceed with a trial. If indicted, the defendant is bound over for trial; if not indicted, he or she may go free. Normally indictment requires only a majority vote, but not a unanimous one. The Supreme Court has found that states are not required to have grand jury indictments under the Constitution.

Habeas Corpus: This is an order to "present the body" to be charged with a specific crime or be released. It is designed to prevent arbitrary imprisonment and to prevent the state from holding a prisoner without communication to the outside world. The writ may be suspended only in times of war or invasion. Presumably the suspension of this writ requires congressional authorization, although President Lincoln suspended it several times during the Civil War without such authorization.

Hearing: In criminal cases a hearing is held to decide if the accused should be bound over for trial. This is often called a "preliminary hearing" or "preliminary examination." In cases decided under the rule of equity, an *interlocutory examination* or hearing is the trial.

Indictment: A formal accusation charging a person with a crime is an indictment. It is frequently drafted by the prosecutor and accepted by a grand jury. The indictment informs an accused person of the precise charges laid against him or her. Some indictments are prepared by judges on hearing the information given, and indictment prepared, by prosecutors.

Information: When a grand jury is not used, either in the federal or in the state courts, an accusation is made under oath by the prosecutor before the court, which charges the individual with a crime. The materials and allegations presented by prosecutors are weighed by the judge, who then decides if the information is sufficient to warrant binding the defendant over for trial.

Injunction: Courts frequently are asked to stop an act or restrain individuals or organizations from doing something. If the court agrees, it issues an order called an injunction. These injunctions are issued under equity law. The term *mandatory injunction* means that the court has issued a formal notice that something must be done. Injunctions are frequently sought by management to stop labor from striking.

International Law: See Chapter 11, p. 221.

Judicial Activism: This is the opposite of strict constructionism and of judicial restraint. It presumes that the courts ought to play a major role in the development of American public policy; indeed, some justices believe that the courts should lead the legislative and executive branches in many areas of human concern such as the elimination of racial discrimination. The Constitution thus becomes a call to action, an elastic document whose beauty lies in its flexibility. It is never static and no interpretation of any part of it is designed to remain forever. Thus, the Constitution is "amended" by court interpretation and application.

Judicial Conference of the United States: The chief justice of the Supreme Court serves as chairperson of this conference, which includes as members: the chief judge of each circuit; a federal district judge from each circuit who is elected by circuit and district judges of the circuit at their annual judicial conference; the chief judge of the Court of Claims; and the chief judge of the Courts of Customs and Patent Appeals. This conference constitutes the governing body of the whole federal judicial system.

Judicial Review: The Constitution was specific in defining the functions of the federal court system. In the case of *Marbury v. Madison* John Marshall held that laws passed by Congress may be reviewed against the Constitution. Laws that are unconstitutional may be struck down by the courts and thus rendered null and void. Using that precedent the Supreme Court today regularly reviews legislation to determine if it is constitutional. We could not conceive of our system of checks and balances working without judicial review.

Judicial Restraint: This is a conservative approach to the understanding of the Constitution which denies that the courts have any special role to play in the creation or formulation of public policy. When principles of law are discovered and when the Constitution is properly interpreted, there is little room left for changes in the future. The Document is then viewed statically. It is opposed to judicial activism and to sociologically based jurisprudence.

Jurisdiction: Every court in the land has certain tasks assigned to it. Before a case may be heard in a court, the court's jurisdiction to hear the case must be established. The term means "to say the law." A court having proper jurisdiction may then "say the law" in the case before it. Jurisdiction is generally either that of hearing certain types of cases as original jurisdiction or on appeal from a lower court having proper jurisdiction.

Jurisprudence: The law constitutes an exact science. The study of the law as an exact body of knowledge is called jurisprudence.

Jury: The Constitution guarantees a trial by jury of one's peers. A jury is a group of laymen chosen at large by a random selection subject to final approval of attorneys in the case. A *grand jury* is asked to decide if there is sufficient evidence to warrant a trial. If there is such evidence an indictment is rendered. A *petit jury* is the trial jury, which decides guilt or innocence. The jury is empaneled and sworn to render a true, just, honest, and impartial answer to question of fact presented to it.

Justifiable Question: Courts hear only cases involving the law. They are not required to assume jurisdiction in political questions. Thus, it must be established that a case is proper for the court to hear before the court will assume jurisdiction. The case must involve a true situation and not an artificially contrived situation. The persons bringing suit must have a real interest in the case, and not merely be curious about their outcome in such litigation. The court must be satisifed that the case should be considered by the court and not by other authorities. If these questions are answered to the satisfaction of the court then it may assume jurisdiction, provided that the court petitioned is the proper one to hear the case.

Least Means: In framing laws, legislatures are compelled to cause the least difficulty and to do the least harm possible to the citizenry. If a situation can be remedied by minimal interference in the private lives of citizens, then this method must be chosen over more elaborate and complex methods that cause greater injury to innocent persons. The courts may feel compelled to invalidate legislation that clearly violates the "least means" rule.

Mandamus, Writ of: This is an order by a court having proper jurisdiction to a public official requiring him or her to perform his or her legal or constitutional functions or duties. It is applied to ministerial but not discretionary duties.

Marshal: The federal courts require officials to serve official papers, hold persons accused of crimes, make arrests, and like functions. Such law officers, corresponding to county sheriffs in the states, are United States Marshals. They are appointed for four-year terms by the president with the consent of the Senate. Although they do the work of the courts they are part of the executive, not the judicial, branch of government, for they are officers of the Department of Justice.

Misdemeanor: A minor offense against the law is called a misdemeanor. Such minor offenses constitute the bulk of the work of the court systems at both the federal and state level. Most misdemeanors are handled by federal magistrates for the federal government or by justices of the peace (or district magistrates) for state government. Most do not involve the use of indictment or jury trial.

Original Jurisdiction: Courts may have two kinds of jurisdiction: original and appellate. In original jurisdiction the court is the first or primary point at which a case is heard. Even the Supreme Court has original jurisdiction in certain areas, such as cases involving two states.

Overbreadth: Statutes may be created to regulate certain activities. When a statute is too broad in its coverage, so that it regulates both protected and unprotected activities, the statute may be struck down by the courts. Many laws, especially with respect to First Amendment freedoms, are so broad that they cover protected areas of individual lives as well as the unprotected areas wherein governmental regulation is permitted.

Parole: Under certain conditions an individual may be released from prison before the expiration of his or her sentence. The person is granted release for good behavior and with reasonable anticipation that he or she will lead a good and productive life afterward. The person will be supervised by a probation officer. Federal paroles are granted by a board created under the Justice Department. There are eight members of the board who are appointed by the president with the consent of the Senate.

Petition: This is a generally inoperative guarantee of community right which allows a person to present grievances to a legislative or executive body. The First Amendment grants the right of petition to the citizenry. A petition may also be addressed to a court and here its use is common.

Plea Bargaining: The costs of a formal trial are high and a trial requires the use of already overcrowded courts and understaffed prosecutors' offices. For the accused a trial means humiliation and he or she cannot predict the outcome. Thus, attorneys for both sides may negotiate. Most often the accused will then plead guilty to a lesser crime than that with which he or she was charged early on in the proceedings.

Political Questions: The courts were established to settle criminal and civil matters, not political ones. The courts themselves must decide when a dispute brought before them is political and when it is judicial. The constitutional guarantee of a republican form of government to the states, for example, has been held to be a political question and thus the question must be settled elsewhere. Many presidential activities in the field of foreign affairs, such as the recognition of foreign governments, are political matters not to be settled by the courts.

Precedent: In our system of justice, the rulings made by prior courts in previous decisions of like nature are held to be of great importance in present decisions. Judges are frequently asked to decide between apparently conflicting precedents. The Supreme Court occasionally overturns precedents, but generally it is a conservative creature which is bound by precedents of the past. Lawyers who argue constitutional cases rely heavily on precedents. The common law is largely precedent law.

Privileged Communication: Information is frequently provided to legal counsel by the client. The lawyer generally may not be questioned about such information because of the unique relationship that exists here. Evidence that seeks to break down this relationship is generally not admitted into the courts. Other special or privileged communication exists between a clergyman and those in his spiritual care, husband and wife, and physician and patient. Some newspersons have claimed that privileged communication exists between informant and reporter.

Probation: Sentence may be suspended for persons convicted of crimes, thus permitting them to be free provided their behavior is satisfactory. Such persons are supervised by probation personnel. The assumption made here is that in some cases, especially involving juveniles, prison will do more harm than good. Some persons are presumed to be able to rehabilitate themselves, or be rehabilitated by others, outside prison walls. Failure to maintain good citizenship may result in imprisonment.

Public Defender: Since the Supreme Court's ruling (*Gideon v. Wainwright*, 372 US 335) in 1963, the courts have been required to provide legal counsel free of charge to those who cannot afford to hire a private attorney. Such attorneys are called public defenders. In 1970 Congress authorized public defenders in the federal courts. The creation of specially trained and selected, generally full-time public defenders is held to be superior to the older system which relied on the good will of public spirited attorneys who voluntarily gave their time, the system of arbitrarily court appointed attorneys, or the defense of indigents by legal aid associations.

Referee: In certain cases, ordinarily those involving bankruptcy, civil rights, and voting rights, the courts may appoint a person, frequently an attorney, to conduct hearings on matters connected with the case and then report to the courts. The referee then does much of the mundane and basic work for the courts.

Rule Making: Congress has occasionally conferred on the Supreme Court the power to prescribe rules of procedures to be followed by the lower levels of the federal judiciary. The Supreme Court has made rules covering civil and criminal cases in the federal courts, bankruptcy proceedings, admiralty cases, copyrights, and procedures in minor criminal matters before U.S. magistrates.

Sociological Jurisprudence: Nominally, this approach to the law applies the findings of sociology to the law. One then looks not for the actual veriage of the Constitution or the law, but for its effects on society or some community or subgroup within society. One can find this approach in the court decision that overturned racial segregation laws, ordered desegregation, and then mandated integration. These decisions had as their sociological base a study of the black community in America by Gunnar Myrdal called the *American Dilemma* wherein Myrdal and his associates found that the segregation of the races had "quarantined" blacks from the mainstream of American life.

Solicitor General: An official of the Justice Department, the solicitor general represents the federal government before the Supreme Court or before any other federal, or even state, court. Before the federal government may appeal a case, his approval must be given. He is the chief legal council of the nation.

Stare Decisis: This is a principle of English law accepted in this nation which recognizes that legal principles once discovered by the courts are of great value in deciding future cases of like nature. One then stands by the previous decisions. Our system places emphasis on the keeping of records so that prior decisions are available for the use of attorneys in preparing their briefs and for courts in preparing their decisions.

Statute of Limitations: Most cases must be litigated before the expiration of a certain period of time or the case may not be tried at all. Some major crimes, such as murder, are not limited, but most other offenses, especially minor transgressions against the law, must be prosecuted within limited periods of time.

Statutory Construction: Legislatures make laws, but those laws are not always as clear as one might wish. In such cases the court must attempt to find meaning in the law. To discover such meaning the courts may consider the history of the legislation, the debates over the proposed legislation in legislatures, and the nature of the problem the legislation seeks to correct. The search for such meaning expands the powers of the courts as they create meaning. If legislation lacks clarity the courts may choose to void the law rather than seek the legislative intent.

Statutory Law: Laws made by the Congress, state legislatures, executive orders from the president or a state's governor, and treaties are the basic forms of statutory law. Most law considered by the courts today is of this type. It is law that eminates from specific, constitutionally authorized sources. Laws are found in codes, such as the *United States Code.*

Strict Construction: One who holds that the Constitution should be interpreted very narrowly is said to be a strict constructionist. Advocates of this doctrine hold that there are no implied powers in the Constitution. All grants of power have to be given clearly and directly or the power does not exist. Strict construction was to be found in early cases that overturned original child labor or minimum wage laws, for example. The opposite is sometimes called "judicial activism." Strict construction is basically the same as judicial restraint, and, practically, the two terms may be used interchangably.

Subpoena: The courts, the Congress, certain juries, and administrative bodies and legislative committees may compel witnesses to appear to provide information and give testimony. The written notice that compels the witness to come forth is called a subpoena. A *subpoena duces tecum* requires the witness to provide specified documents and materials.

Supreme Court of the United States: Generally, the Constitution is not specific about the number of courts to be created, the number of judges to sit on a court, and the exact functions of a court. The United States Supreme Court is the only one named in the text of the Constitution. It is the highest court of appeals in the nation. It receives appeals from lower federal courts and it also has some original jurisdiction, as in cases between states. It has nine members, but the number of judges could be changed by law. The court is in session from October to May.

Taxpayer's Suit: Most states permit a taxpayer, irrespective of personal stake in the situation, to bring suit against public officials to stop illegal or illicit payments. Such suits are not permitted against the federal government.

Temporary Emergency Court of Appeals: Created in 1971 to deal with cases and controversies that may arise under economic stabilization laws, this court has been operational since February 1972. Its principal place of operation is Washington, D.C. It has exclusive jurisdiction over cases that may arise out of economic control laws. It has eight members chosen from among district and circuit judges by the chief justice of the Supreme Court.

Test Case: For a case to be justiciable a real issue involving a true situation must be presented to the court. The courts do not give advisory opinions in the United States. To determine the application of a law or executive act, or to determine whether a law or executive order can be applied to a given situation, a true test of the matter in question must be presented in a lawsuit. A test case must then be a true case, even if an individual willfully violates the law for the sole purpose of determining the status of a law or executive act. Major decisions of the courts, especially the Supreme Court, which decide important issues, or rule on major laws or executive actions are generally called test cases, even though the term itself implies preplanned action.

Tort: This is a wrongful act, but does not include breach of contract, for which an individual may bring civil suit in the courts of law.

United States Attorney: This is the title given to government lawyers who prosecute criminal cases in the lower echelons of the federal court system. These are usually younger lawyers whose appointment is often political. When Jimmy Carter became president he pledged to remove politics from consideration when appointing federal attorneys. Then, he cause U.S. Attorney David Marston to be removed from office in a blatantly political move.

United States Courts of Appeals: These judicial bodies were created by Congress in 1891 to relieve some pressure on the Supreme Court in matters of appeals of cases that originated in the federal courts. They may review all final decisions of the federal district courts, except in a few cases where direct review by the Supreme Court is mandated by law. They also review and enforce orders of administrative bodies such as the Interstate Commerce Commission.

United States Court of Claims: Established in 1855, this court has original jurisdiction in matters of claims against the United States provided such claims are based on the Constitution, act of Congress, presidential or executive department order, or contracts to which the United States is a party. Its jurisdiction is nationwide and it becomes involved when the attorney general is served with the appropriate papers. The seven members usually sit in panels of three, but may set *en banc*. It also has 16 trial judges, one of whom is chief of the Trial Division. Litigation is heard by one of the trial judges and the facts are then presented to the panel.

United States Court of Customs and Patent Appeals: This court was established in 1929 to replace a previous customs court. It receives appeals from the United States Customs Court, the United States Patent and Trademark Office, and the United States International Trade Commission. It also reviews decisions of the secretary of commerce made under the Education, Scientific, and Cultural Materials Importation Act and decisions of the secretary of agriculture made under the Plant Variety Protection Act. It also reviews petitions for extraordinary writs issued under the All Writs Act. Its judgments are final unless reviewed by the Supreme Court on writ of certiorari.

United States Customs Court. Established in 1890 and given altered jurisdiction and status several times, most recently in 1956, this court has exclusive jurisdiction for civil actions arising out of tariff laws. It also hears complaints from manufacturers and wholesalers pursuant to the application of such laws as the Anti-Dumping Act of 1921 and the Tariff Act of 1930 in regard to imports. It has a chief judge and eight other judges, any of whom may be designated by the chief justice of the Supreme Court to sit as a district court judge. Cases are ordinarily heard before a single judge, although in certain cases, such as constitutional challenges, it may sit with three-judge panels or even *en banc*. It generally sits in New York City.

United States Reports: Supreme Court cases are reported in these volumes. In the beginning they were cited according to the court reporter's name: Dallas (1790–1800); Cranch (1801–1815); Wheaton (1816–1827); Peters (1827–1843); Howard (1843–1860); Black (1861–1862); and Wallace (1863–1874). They are now cited as "US" or United States Reports. The first 90 volumes are cited by the reporter's name. The first number means volume and the second number means that the case begins on that page. Hence, 232 US 419, means that the case is found in volume 232 of the US Reports and it begins on page 419. The precise location of a quote is given as: 232 US 419 at 423. Earlier volumes are cited as: 1 Cr (Cranch) 137.

United States Tax Court: Created in 1969 under the Tax Reform Act of that year, the court succeeded a series of earlier tax appeals courts. It hears controversies involving the payment of income, gift, estate, and similar taxes. Under the 1974 Retirement Income and Security Act it has certain duties related to institutions dealing with tax-sheltered retirement funds. Under the Tax Reform Act of 1976 it has certain duties related to the tax status of charitable institutions and donations made to such tax-exempt institutions by private persons. Since the Tax Reform of 1969 it may simplify claims made before the court in matters dealing with personal income underpayments of less than $1500. It has 16 member judges, but cases are ordinarily heard before a single judge.

Vagueness: Laws must be clear and concise. In 1939 the Supreme Court ruled that any law is unconstitutional if it "either forbids or requires the doing of an act in terms so vague that men of common intelligence must necessarily guess at its meaning and differ as to its application." (*Lanzetta v. New Jersey*, 306 US 451). Laws cannot be so framed that they can easily be applied differently to various groups within society, or interpreted in varying ways by bureaucrats to protect some and prosecute others who have done the same act.

Venue: Each court operates within a specified geographical area. That area may be as broad as the nation or as narrow as a portion of a county. Venue is the area wherein the courts operate and from which jurors are chosen. Trials are ordinarily held in the same area in which the crime is alleged to have been committed. If the defendant has reason to believe that his or her case has been prejudiced in that area, as by adverse publicity, the defendant may have his or her lawyer petition the court for a change of venue. The defendant will be tried, if venue is changed, in a similar court in a different geographical area.

Writ: Courts may issue a variety of written orders called writs, which require an individual to do something or perform a duty, or which prohibit an individual from doing something. Writs must be followed or the individual who fails to perform may be held in contempt of court.

Writ of Certiorari: This is a court order sent by a higher court to a lower court requiring that records of a case be sent up for review. Under the Judiciary Act of 1925 most cases reviewed by the Supreme Court arrive through the issuance of this writ. Four of the justices of the highest court of the land must agree to issue the writ before it is ordered. Ordinarily, on appeal, an attorney will request that the appellate court issue the writ of certiorari. If the court refuses, the record carries the entry "certiorari denied."

Writ of Error: This is an order that is issued by a higher court to a lower court to send up the records of a trial for purposes of examining these records to determine if errors were made in the trial. The appellate court may find that errors have taken place, usually by finding that objections made by defense attorneys to rulings by the judge should have been sustained. If errors have taken place a new trial may be ordered.

Writ of Prohibition: A higher court may order a lower court to refrain from hearing a case or otherwise exercising judgment in a matter pending before it. This court order is called a writ of prohibition.

CASES

Abelman v. Booth (21 Howard 506, 1859): The states and the federal government are separate levels of jurisdiction. Basically, each is wholly separated from the other in its processes even though the federal courts may review certain state cases, such as cases involving constitutional issues. In this case the Supreme Court invalidated a state court writ of habeas corpus, ordering the federal courts to deliver up a prisoner who was being held in federal custody.

Ashwander v. Tennessee (297 US 288, 1936): Although the case itself deal with the sale of electricity generated at the Tennessee Valley Authority, the importance of the case is to be found in Justice Brandeis' listing of the criteria to be used to pass on the constitutionality of laws. The courts should judge the constitutionality only when absolutely necessary to dispose of the case, and the constitutionality should not be ruled more broadly than necessary to dispose of the case at hand. Even if the law or executive act is of doubtful constitutionality, the courts, under statutory construction powers, should try to rule on the case without reference to constitutional questions.

Chisolm v. Georgia (2 Dallas 419, 1793): The Eleventh amendment to the Constitution was adopted because of the Courts' decision in this case which allowed citizens of one state to sue another state in the federal courts. Despite the Eleventh Amendment, and following this decision interpreting Article III of the Constitution, citizens of one state may still sue individual public officers of another state in the federal courts.

Cohens v. Virginia (6 Wheaton 264, 1821): In this case the Supreme Court affirmed its power to review state court decisions if the state courts have dealt with, or if the case seems to involve, the Constitution, treaties, or federal law. This power extends to cover even cases where a state is a party to a dispute.

Eakin v. Raub (12 S & R 330, 1825): The assertion of the Supreme Court's right to strike down laws made by Congress which were considered to be repugnant to the Constitution (*Marbury v. Madison*, 1803) was widely rejected by Jeffersonians, liberals, and the remnants of the Antifederalists. The latter groups argued that this was an artificial contrivance of the Federalists who had lost the election of 1800 and that it was their last, dying act of revenge against Jeffersonian liberalism. The most eloquent argument against judicial review, a doctrine not clearly established in the text of the federal Constitution, is to be found in the opinion of Judge John B. Gibson of this case.

Erie Railroad v. Tompkins (304 US 64, 1938): For nearly a century the federal courts had applied the common law, and the judges had fabricated such law, in areas such as a diversity of citizenship, where no federal statutory law was to be found. In this case the federal courts were told by the Supreme Court that there was no federal common law. In an earlier case, *Swift v. Tyson* (16 Peters 1, 1842), the federal courts had permitted the federal judges to make law, presumably following the common law tradition, particularly in commercial cases. The *Erie* case overturned this, holding that there was no federal common law.

Ex parte McCardle (7 Wallace 506, 1869): Article III, section 2 of the Constitution allows the Congress to make exceptions and to regulate the appellate jurisdiction of the Supreme Court. The Congress does not grant the court its appellate power but it may make certain specific exceptions to its exercise. In this case the Congress had limited the powers of the court to review certain acts involving Reconstruction, which it feared would be invalidated by the Court. The Court accepted this limitation on its powers.

Kent State Case (413 US 1, 1973): The Supreme Court found little if any judicial control over the state militias or over the armed forces. The complex and professional decisions in regard to the composition, training, or control of these forces are necessarily and essentially military judgments which must be made by the executive and the legislature.

Marbury v. Madison (1 Cr. 137, 1803):   See Chapter 7, p. 134.

Martin v. Hunter' Lesee (1 Wheaton 304, 1816):   See Chapter 3, p. 42.

Powell v. McCormack (395 US 486, 1969):   The federal courts are constitutionally obligated to interpret the basic document of American government, the Constitution, without regard to any inconvenience that such an interpretation may cause the coordinate departments. In this case the Supreme Court found that a member of Congress cannot be refused membership by the House or the Senate if that representative meets the constitutional requirements of that office, provided the member is elected by his or her constituents.

Schick v. Reed (419 US 256, 1974):   The Supreme Court upheld an act of the presidency in which Richard Nixon commuted a death sentence to life imprisonment. This presidential power derives from the power to issue pardons and grant reprieves. It flows from the Constitution alone and thus the Court held that it cannot be modified, abridged, or diminished by Congress.

Scott v. Sanford (19 Howard 393, 1857):   In this, the infamous "Dred Scott Decision," the Supreme Court held that slaves had no legal standing under the Constitution as it was then written. Its real importance is to be found in the fact that it was the second case to be decided by the Supreme Court in which a federal law was invalidated by court action. Some thought that the *Marbury* case was a fluke. It had been 54 years since the Supreme Court had found a federal law to be unconstitutional. This case helped to establish judicial review as a major tool in our separation of powers system.

Sierra Club v. Morton (406 US 727, 1972):   The Sierra Club is an organization that has had a strong historic commitment to the cause of protecting wilderness areas and wild animals. The club's expertise and standing as an expert on such matters was not challenged by the courts. The Supreme Court did dismiss a case brought by the club which attempted to prevent the exploitation of the Sierra Mountains by commercial interests. The Court found that a mere interest in the problem no matter how well-founded in motives or expertise, was insufficient to challenge a federal or state decision. There was no injury that was provable in court which accrued to any member of the club that was over or above alleged injury to all citizens. The "interest" that was violated by the exploitation of the wildlife area was not an interest the courts could recognize or protect.

U.S. v. Richardson (418 US 466, 1974):   In this case a taxpayer claimed that the president in his refusal to reveal the budget of the Central Intelligence Agency, had violated the "statement and account" clause of the Constitution. He claimed that he had a right to know how much money the CIA was given and how it was spent. The Supreme Court ruled that a taxpayer cannot raise generalized grievances about the conduct of government in the federal courts.

9

Civil Liberties and Civil Rights

Affirmative Action: Federal and state law prohibit discrimination against persons because of race, religion, creed, or national origin. Laws further mitigate discrimination to some degree against persons on the basis of sex or age. Plans that have been drawn up to ensure selection for jobs or admission to educational or similar programs on a merit basis while encouraging minority groups to apply are called affirmative action programs. The Bakke decision mitigates the effect of some affirmative action programs and prohibits "reverse discrimination" against majority groups. Where merit employment is hard to establish on a rational basis, racial quota systems such as the "Philadelphia Plan" may be established to correct racial imbalance in employment. Corporations that discriminate against groups on the basis of age, sex, race, religion, creed, national origin, or like areas, may be fined or forced to pay back wages to the victims of such discrimination.

Alien: This is a person who lives in a nation of which he or she is not a citizen. Aliens in the United States enjoy most rights enjoyed by citizens. They may be drafted into U.S. military service. Some states prohibit aliens from owning property. An alien may be deported without a trial as deportation is not a criminal punishment.

Alien and Sedition Laws: This law sponsored by the administration of John Adams was never tested in the federal courts, but it stands as one of the most glaring abuses of civil rights ever seen in the United States in peacetime. The sedition laws made it a crime to criticize the government, a throwback to laws of England against which the colonists had rebelled. About two dozen persons were jailed under the provisions. Adams had hoped to silence his critics, but the passage of these laws led to the defeat of the Federalists in the elections of 1800. The alien laws allowed the president to deport undesirable aliens. This portion of the law was probably constitutional as the Supreme Court has consistently ruled that there are no rights to American citizenship and that deportation is not a criminal proceeding.

Alien Registration Act: See *Smith Act of 1940*, Chapter 9, p. 176.

Antiracketeering Act of 1934: Amended several times, the act makes it a federal offense to interfere with interstate or foreign commerce by acts of violence or coercion.

Antitrust Acts: The Congress beginning in 1890 with the Sherman Antitrust Act, began to try to regulate trusts, monopolies, cartels, and other combinations of business which restrain trade. Antitrust acts are designed to sustain the capitalist system of competition by forcing businesses that control the bulk of a market to break up in order to allow free competition among several or many sellers.

Arms, Right To Keep and Bear: One of the few amendments to the Constitution granting substantive rights to individuals that has not been incorporated under the Fourteenth Amendment, the Second Amendment provides that "the right of the people to keep and bear arms shall not be infringed." The rationale for the amendment is given in its first words, "a well regulated militia being necessary for the common defense." The Supreme Court has not heard a case involving this right since 1939, but it did note then that the states and the federal government may regulate the keeping and carrying of arms provided they did not deprive the government of its reservoir of trained manpower for the army. (*United States v. Miller*, 307 US 174, 1939)

Assembly: The Founding Fathers considered that the right of the people to peacefully gather to discuss public issues of the day was one of the most important rights one could guarantee in a democratic republic. Thus, it was included among the very first freedoms included in the Bill of Rights. The right is guaranteed basically in all cases where the meeting is not held for unlawful purposes, even when an organization obnoxious to the general public, such as the American Nazi party, is involved.

Association, Right of: This involves the right of persons to act in common toward some general or specific purpose, without or with a formal charter or constitution, whether for an indefinite time or for a very limited time. This right is protected against undue or unusual regulation by the First Amendment to the Constitution. Although this right is not specifically guaranteed in the First Amendment (or elsewhere in the Constitution), it is implied in the First Amendment rights to assemble, write and speak, and form religious association, without governmental interference.

Attainder, Bill of: The body of the Constitution guarantees certain rights to individuals by prohibiting the exercise of such powers by government. One such prohibition is bill of attainder. As used in the Constitution, it means a legislative act that at once declares an individual to be guilty of a crime without the formality of a judicial proceeding. It may also cause injury to one's family and forfeiture of one's property.

Bad Tendency Doctrine: A rule of law first discovered in *Gitlow v. New York,* this doctrine holds that legislatures may suppress acts of speech or the written word when such words tend to incite acts of civil disorder or spread revolutionary ideas. Such suppression may occur even if the actual danger is not present. It suffices that such words may have a "bad tendency."

Balancing: One of the great problems within the area of public policy development is that of resolving conflicting interests and rights. An individual may have certain rights, such as being secure in person and property, while society at large has other rights, such as being free of criminals who use their persons and residences to sell illegal drugs. One must then balance freedom and order in such a way as to protect basic personal and property rights while protecting society from those who would abuse its protections.

Bill of Rights: This refers to the first 10 amendments to the federal Constitution, although state constitutions generally contain such provisions as well. These amendments were drafted by James Madison after the adoption of the Constitution in fulfillment of a promise to do so after the new government's apparently unlimited powers. Madison had originally proposed 12 amendments and 10 were ratified. The first eight list specific rights while the ninth gives general protection to "unenumerated rights." The tenth is generally held to be meaningless in legal use.

Capital Punishment: This means that the state may take a person's life as punishment for a crime. The Supreme Court has held that "the death penalty may be properly imposed only as to crimes resulting in the death of the victim" (*Coker v. Georgia*, 1977). The Supreme Court has not found that capital punishment is cruel and unusual punishment in and of itself. The Court also indicated that evidence may be introduced to show mitigating circumstances of the offense or of the offender, making laws unconstitutional which automatically require the death penalty for certain offenses.

Censorship: This is an examination of written, printed, or spoken word, or other form or communication by a public body with an eye to removal of some portions of that material if they are found to be offensive to public security, morals, health, or safety. Censorship is generally rejected in America except in wartime. The First Amendment to the Constitution prohibits most censorship.

Church and State, Separation of: Americans objected strongly to the establishment of a state religion, a practice followed by Great Britain. The nation was founded in large part as a haven for a wide variety of religious dissenter groups and others whose religious practices had been circumscribed in their home nations. Thus, the First Amendment was ratified to prevent such a tie being made between church and state in the new nation. To ensure that no tie would exist between church and state, the Supreme Court has generally prohibited state and federal governments from giving direct and most indirect aid to religious institutions, including parochial schools.

Citizenship: A citizen is a member of his or her community (nation) with full standing before the law. Citizenship is that invisible but very real tie between individual and nation. A citizen is guaranteed certain rights and he or she owes certain obligations to the state. One may be a citizen of the United States and of his or her home state, but since the Fourteenth Amendment, a citizen is guaranteed full national citizenship rights over and against his or her state. Citizenship is granted by birth (law of soil) or by parentage (law of blood). Thus, one born in the United States, or born in a foreign nation of American parents may become a citizen of this nation.

Civil Disobedience: Rooted in the Transcendentalist thought of early 19th-century America and popularized in India by Gandhi, this became the primary tactic of the civil rights movements in the 1960s in

America. It assumes that laws may be unjust and that the just person must, by necessity of conscience, disobey such unjust laws. Thus, it calls for mass disobedience of these questionable laws on the assumption that if all or many citizens disobey the law the political system will change the law. If one person were to be jailed unjustly under such laws, all people ought to be jailed. Dr. M. L. King used this tactic successfully in Alabama to break down various public segregation laws.

Civil Liberty: Operationally, there is no reasonable distinction that ought to be made between "civil liberties" and "civil rights." The term refers to those rights claimed by citizens and guaranteed by the state. The Bill of Rights is the embodiment of civil rights in America. States may also include bills of rights in their state constitution. There are personal, procedural, and property rights that are included within our conception of civil rights.

Civil Rights Acts of 1870, 1871 and 1875: These laws were passed after the Civil War to implement the Thirteenth, Fourteenth, and Fifteenth Amendments. Most of the major provisions of these laws were invalidated by the Supreme Court in the Civil Rights cases of 1883. The Court held that the government could not prohibit private acts of discrimination. Still other provisions of these acts were invalidated by congressional action. Some provisions of the acts still valid make it illegal for state officials to deprive American citizens of their constitutional rights, and make it illegal to deprive citizens of their rights by concerted or group action. The latter provisions were designed to curtail activities of the Ku Klux Klan. In 1968 the Court found meaning in the 1866 law that barred discrimination against individuals on the basis of race in the sale or rental of housing (*Jones v. Mayer*, 392 US 409, 1968).

Civil Rights Act of 1957: In the first civil rights act passed since Reconstruction, the Congress sought to ensure blacks the right to vote in elections, assuming that they could achieve some equality by using the ballot. The Justice Department was empowered to seek out violations of voting rights and present evidence obtained to the attorney general for appropriate action, including criminal prosecution. It also created the Civil Rights Commission.

Civil Rights Act of 1960: This act strengthened the 1957 Civil Rights Act by allowing federal courts to appoint referees to help blacks register to vote after convictions were obtained in the courts related to denial of the vote. It authorized punishment for violations of court school desegregation orders, authorized criminal prosecution at the federal level for transporting explosives in interstate commerce for purposes of destroying property, and required the preservation of voting records for 22 months after an election. The Congress still assumed, in framing this act, that if blacks were given the right to vote, and this right was ensured by the federal government, they could, by voting, ensure for themselves other civil rights.

Civil Rights Act of 1964:   Passed after long and bitter debate in the Congress, this bill reversed the pattern of previous post-Reconstruction legislation which had assumed that black voters, could, of themselves, and without further aid, vote civil rights guarantees in the states. It barred discrimination based on race in public accommodations. It provided for withholding federal funds from programs administered in discriminatory ways. It authorized the federal government to initiate suits in courts to bring about desegretation of public schools and facilities. It extended the Civil Rights Commission and expanded its powers, and created a Community Relations Service. It strengthened existing laws designed to grant the right to vote and provided for speedy resolution of voters' rights cases in the courts.

Civil Rights Act of 1968:   This law prohibits discrimination in the sale and rental of private homes and housing. The act covers about 80 percent of all housing sold or rented, excluding the sale without the services of a realtor of private homes, and the rental of units having four apartments or less. It also makes it a federal crime to travel in interstate commerce to incite riot. In *Jones v. Mayer*, the Court used an 1866 civil rights law to cover most housing, prohibiting discrimination in the sale or rental of these additional units. Between the 1866 act and that of 1968 nearly all housing sold or rented in the nation is freed from racially based discrimination.

Civil Rights Commission: This body was established by the Civil Rights Act of 1957 to investigate into the broad areas of civil liberties and civil rights, such as racial discrimination, discrimination in voting registration, discrimination based on sex, discrimination in housing, job, or educational opportunities, and in the administration of justice. It has acted as a national coordination center for information on civil rights matters. The findings and recommendations of the bipartisan commission have led to civil rights legislation, such as the 1964 Civil Rights Act.

Clear and Present Danger Doctrine: This constitutional doctrine stems from the Supreme Court's decision of *Schenck v. United States* in which the criterion for limiting speech and press was established by Justice Holmes. Speech and press were to be censored only when they were intimately related to a "clear and present danger." The more restrictive interpretation of this right is found in the "bad tendency" doctrine.

Community Relations Service: Created by the 1964 Civil Rights Act, this department serves to help communities mitigate civil rights problems. It is part of the Department of Justice and its director is responsible to the attorney general of the United States. It is directed to cooperate with state and local agencies working in like areas and it may either come in to help by local request or on its own initiative.

Confrontation: The Sixth Amendment to the Constitution requires that a defendant has the right to "be confronted with the witnesses against him." The Supreme Court has required this of states, applying the Sixth Amendment through the Fourteenth Amendment. (*Pointer v. Texas*, 380 US 400, 1965). This is a vital right to safeguard a defendant against nameless informants. Those providing testimony in criminal cases must be prepared to withstand the cross-examination by the defense attorney in open court.

Conscientious Objector: When the Second Amendment to the Constitution was originally drafted, James Madison sought to protect those who had moral and religious objections to bearing arms. Although the final draft contained no such provision, the government has permitted those morally opposed to war to perform alternate services when inducted into the armed services of the nation. In *Girouard v. United States* (328 US 61, 1948), *United States v. Seeger* (380 US 128, 1965), and *Welsh v. United States* (398 US 333, 1970) the Supreme Court has interpreted the meaning of conscientious objector quite liberally so as to include personal moral beliefs as well as religious teachings. In *Gilette v. United States* (401 US 437, 1971) the Supreme Court refused to recognize moral objections to a specific war rather than war as an institution as a valid reason for refusing to serve in the armed forces.

Conspiracy: This consists in a combination or confederacy involving two or more persons formed for purposes of committing by joint effort some illegal or unlawful act. Some acts that are not unlawful in and of themselves become unlawful when done by concerted action of conspirators. To be tried for conspiracy one need not have committed an act; one might be found guilty for planning or discussing ways to perform an unlawful act.

Corruption of Blood: An archaic concept used in Europe, this means that if one member of a family is accused of a crime, his entire family may be punished. No member of his family could inherit his title, property, rights or privileges. It was often done by attainder or by order of the king, and was thereby removed from the normal judicial process. The Constitution specifically forbids laws working corruption of blood.

Counsel, Right: In order to guarantee a fair trial, one who is accused of a crime is now given the right to have a defense attorney. If he or she cannot afford one, one will be appointed at public expense. The Supreme Court first required this for all federal cases under the Sixth Amendment in *Johnson v. Zerbst* (304 US 458, 1938) and subsequently required it of the states under the Fourteenth Amendment (*Gideon v. Wainwright*, 372 US 335, 1963). Previously, the courts had either not required counsel at all, or required that counsel be provided only in cases in which the death penalty might be invoked.

Cruel and Unusual Punishment: The Eight Amendment of the Constitution prevents the use of cruel and unusual punishment. This right is now guaranteed to citizens of the states against state encroachment under the Fourteenth Amendment. The definition of what constitutes cruel or unusual punishment has changed over the last two centuries. Whipping was a common colonial punishment for many crimes, but today it is considered to be excessively cruel. Any form of disfigurement would also be considered to be excessively cruel. The Supreme Court to date has rejected arguments that capital punishment is cruel and unusual despite many claims to the contrary.

De Facto Segregation: If a state or local law in opposition to the federal law and ruling of the federal courts creates segregation of races it is known as *de jure* segregation. If segregation of races is accomplished by virtue of living or habitation arrangements it is called *de facto* segregation. Black neighborhoods may not be legally separated from nonblack neighborhoods, but they may, in fact, be separated because of settlement patterns. To break down such de facto segregation "busing" of school children may be implemented. The Supreme Court dealt with defacto segregation of public school children in *Swann v. Charlotte-Mecklenburg Board of Education* (402 US 1, 1971).

Department of Justice: Headed by the United States attorney general, this department, through its Federal Bureau of Investigation, may investigate abridgements of civil rights in states or in local communities, with or without local assistance, provided federal law has been broken. Its Civil Rights Division enforces civil rights laws. The Department of Justice also oversees the work of the Community Relations Service.

Deportation: An alien has no right to live in this nation. When an alien must be removed from this nation, presumably to return to land of origin, he or she is said to be deported. This is not a criminal proceeding and the alien has very limited rights in regard to this process. Aliens who have acquired American citizenship may be deported and stripped of that citizenship if they falsified their papers or lied about their origins or occupations prior to obtaining citizenship.

District of Columbia Court Reorginization and Criminal Procedure Act of 1970: This is a model crime control package that Congress has created for Washington, D.C., but is offering to the states for adoption locally. It provides for certain "no knock" searches of private property and it allows for pretrial detention of dangerous criminals. It increases the penalties for certain crimes and allows the police greater latitude in the use of electronic surveillance (wiretapping). In 1974 charges were made that the "no knock" provision, designed to prevent the destruction of vital evidence, such as drugs, was being abused and it was repealed by Congress. The law is controversial and it has invited, and will continue to invite, challenges in the courts.

Double Jeopardy: The Constitution prohibits an individual from being twice placed on trial for the same offense. An individual may be tried by different jurisdictions, for example, federal and state for what may amount to the same crime if there are applicable laws at both levels of government. The prohibition against double jeopardy does not apply to trials in which the jury cannot agree on a verdict or to a trial that has ended because of some other impropriety or irregularity. It also does not apply to a retrial ordered by an appeals court.

Dual Citizenship: While Americans enjoy a kind of dual citizenship, having citizenship in their states of residence and United States citizenship, the term generally defines citizenship in two sovereign nations. It is possible for a person to acquire, because of the complexity and diversity of citizenship laws, citizenship in two nations.

Due Process: This is commonly understood to mean procedural rights that a citizen enjoys when he or she is accused of a crime. The individual is entitled to basic protections of the law, and the state, in the process of attempting to prove guilt, must follow certain procedural guidelines. These rights are guaranteed under the Bill of Rights and under court mandated procedures. The body of the Constitution guarantees certain procedural rights and statutory law may require other facets of due process.

Eminent Domain: Although individuals enjoy broad property rights in this nation, the state has a residual right to appropriate private property for a public purpose. One receives or is entitled to receive just compensation for property condemned under eminent domain proceedings. An example of a public purpose for which property may be condemned would be rights of way given over to utilities.

Equal Employment Opportunity Commission: This agency was established by the Civil Rights Act of 1964 to investigate and conciliate disputes involving discrimination in unions, employment agencies, or private enterprise because of race, religion, creed, national origin, or sex. Its board consists of five members appointed by the president with the consent of the Senate. Since 1972 it has had the power to initiate legal actions.

Equal Protection: The Fourteenth Amendment to the Constitution requires that the states not "deny to any person within its jurisdiction the equal protection of the laws." The same amendment also makes all persons citizens of the United States and forbids states to deny the rights of such citizenship. This provision has come to mean that there is a base level of civil liberties enjoyed by all citizens equally. It disallows discrimination based on the color of skin, race, religion, and national origin. It also prohibits discrimination that is irrationally based on sex. It may allow some distinctions to be made and classes created if these are rational, and if these are related to public health, safety, or morality.

Exclusionary Rule: Evidence that has been illegally seized may not be introduced into trial courts. Such exclusion ordinarily does not apply to state grand juries.

Establishment Clause: In the First Amendment to the Constitution we find the statement "Congress shall make no laws respecting the establishment of religion." Some argue that this means merely that one religious sect shall not be favored over another, but the majority argument holds that the federal and state governments cannot aid religion in general, whether or not such aid favors one religion over another. Only when government policies aid religion accidentally or indirectly will such aid be sustained in and by the courts under the First Amendment. The establishment clause creates a wall of separation between church and state.

Ex Post Facto: When such laws were permitted, a legislature, or, historically, a king, could make a law and apply it retroactively. Thus, in effect, an expost facto law makes what was done yesterday a crime today. The United States Constitution specifically forbids such laws.

Extradition: Among sovereign nations, the rendering of fugitives by one nation to another nation wherein a crime was allegedly committed is called extradition. The word is commonly used for the delivery of prisoners by one state to another within the United States, although the proper term for this is rendition. A prisoner may waive his or her right to an extradition or rendition hearing or he or she may go into court to try to block such delivery.

Fair Labor Standards Act of 1938: This is the basic law providing for regulation of child labor and of minimum wage and maximum hour standards for industries manufacturing and shipping goods in interstate commerce. In 1936 the Congress had set such standards for corporations providing services under federal contracts, but this was the first act to attempt general regulation of industry in regard to child labor and minimum wages and maximum hours.

Fifth Amendment: This part of the Bill of Rights imposes a number of significant restrictions on the federal government, and through the Fourteenth Amendment, on the states with regard to the rights of persons accused of crimes. It provides for indictment by grand jury (not wholly applicable to the states), protection against double jeopardy, protection against self-incrimination, and forbids government to deprive a person of life, liberty, or property without due process of law. It restricts the power of eminent domain, forbidding the taking of property without just compensation.

Fourteenth Amendment: Originally, the Fourteenth Amendment was designed to make the former slaves citizens who would be entitled to a full participation in all the blessings of liberty heretofore enjoyed by nonslaves only. In recent reinterpretation this amendment has been used to apply all the basic guarantees of liberties and due process of the law found in the Bill of Rights to the states, thus protecting individuals not only from federal, but from state, encroachment. It had other specific provisions dealing with the post-Civil War South, but these are archaic.

Guilt by Association: This is the practical legal application of the popularly held belief that one who lies down with dogs will get up with fleas. If one associates with known criminals or subversives, one is assumed to be crooked or subversive also. The concept attacks the root of American jurisprudence, which holds that an individual is not guilty of a crime until he or she has been tried and found to be guilty, or has admitted guilt. Americans have sought to ostracize individuals who had been associated with unpopular causes or with Communist or Facist organizations for no reason other than that association.

Immigration: Individuals who leave their native lands and who move to another nation in hopes of obtaining employment and/or citizenship are called immigrants. Immigration is the act of abandoning one's native land and taking up residence in a new land. America has been properly called the land of immigrants because, except for the American Indians, all of the nation's population either immigrated to this nation or are descended from immigrants.

Immigration Appeals, Board of: Created with the Department of Justice, this panel was created to review actions concerning the deportation or exclusion of aliens from the United States. It also hears appeals from companies penalized for transporting aliens into the country illegally.

Immunity: In our jurisprudential system we assume that anyone who has committed a crime should suffer punishment for transgressing the law. In order to obtain testimony needed to convict greater criminals who are higher up in an organization, a prosecutor may choose to exempt an individual from prosecution by granting him or her immunity, in order to obtain testimony against others whose crimes are greater. In the Organized Crime Act of 1970, immunity from prosecution may be granted for those crimes that might be prosecuted under information given by a witness, but the witness still may be prosecuted for crimes that are proven under extraneous information obtained elsewhere.

Inalienable Right: Jefferson, following John Locke, spoke of the various inalienable rights that man should enjoy, placed in or about him by Nature or Nature's God. Presumably these are rights that cannot be taken away or transferred. Specific inalienable rights, according to natural rights thinkings, include life, liberty, pursuit of happiness, and property.

Jim Crow Law: This term refers to laws created sometime after the Reconstruction following the Civil War, and found throughout the nation, which forbade the intermixing of the races. Not only did these laws segregate public facilities and accommodations, but they also prevented interracial marriages. Jim Crow laws were found in the North as well as in the South.

Jus Sanguinis (Law of Blood): Citizenship is determined by the citizenship of parents in most of Europe. This is the law of blood.

Jus Soli: In the United States, following the English tradition, one acquires citizenship by virtue of birth. Thus, one who is born in a nation, on its soil, acquires that citizenship.

Landrum-Griffin Act of 1959: Sometimes called the Labor Reform Act of 1959, it is correctly called the Labor-Management Reporting and Disclosure Act of 1959. The purpose of the act is to provide labor union members with a "bill of rights." Unions must report their finances and operations and file a copy of their constitutions with the Secretary of Labor. Certain classes of individuals, such as gangster and subversives, are barred from holding union office. Misuse of union funds was made a federal crime. Union elections are to be held by use of the secret ballot. Basic First Amendment freedoms are to be guaranteed in union meetings and in union activities. Members may see their records and may sue the union for unfair practices. They have the right to fair and impartial hearings in disciplinary cases.

Libel: This consists of defamatory material, written or published without legal justification. Under certain circumstances, such as when malice is shown, the publisher may be liable for criminal action; ordinarily, it is the subject of civil suits. Much broader latitude is given in libel cases to materials relating to public figures than to private ones. With public persons, one must normally show malice of intent and deliberate disregard to known truth to sustain libel charges.

McCarran Act of 1950: Properly known as the Internal Security Act of 1950, this legislation was designed to control as much as the law would allow the activities of Communist and other subversive political organizations. The Subversive Activities Control Board, created by the act, was abolished in 1973. The courts have invalidated some of its other provisions, such as restricting foreign travel by members of allegedly subversive groups. The Supreme Court also found that certain disclosures required under the act violated the protection of the Fifth Amendment against self-incrimination. The act allows Communist aliens to be deported. It strengthens antisabotage and espionage laws and strengthens the laws controlling sedition. Unions coming under Communist control lose their rights under labor acts.

Martial Law: In ordinary times civilians must be tried in civilian courts, subject to limitations of due process of the law. In wartime, many civil liberties may be suspended and the civilian population may be subjected to military law and military governance. Martial law was used during the Civil War. The Lincoln conspirators were tried, convicted, and condemned under martial law.

National: An individual who has some tie to a state is its national. All citizens are nationals, but not all nationals are citizens. Territorial natives may be, and historically were, nationals of the United States, but not citizens. The rights of nationals who are not citizens may be somewhat less than those of citizens. For examples. only citizens may ordinarily vote in elections.

National Labor Relations Act of 1935: This act created the National Labor Relations Board to allow workers to organize labor unions and practice collective bargaining. This independent establishment has a five-member board which examines allegations of unfair labor practices in interstate commerce. The board oversees elections and certifies the results in determining which unions will represent employees and who union officers will be.

Naturalization: A person who did not acquire American citizenship by birth may acquire it through the process of naturalization. Persons who are of good moral character and who are not members of proscribed organizations or political beliefs may be naturalized after having resided in this country at least five years. A public hearing and a citizenship examination are required.

Natural Law: In the 18th century, political philosophers revived the idea of a set of laws that one could discover in nature. Such laws were placed there by God. These higher laws should form the basis for most human or civil law. Laws contrary to nature need not be obeyed. Natural law gave one natural rights and immunities from government. In a more modern sense, natural law is seen as the base out of which community laws are developed, thus accounting for certain universal laws practiced by all civilized nations. One supposedly can discern natural law by reason alone.

Ninth Amendment: Only a decade ago this amendment was found to be meaningless and forgotten. In the last few years the Supreme Court has found inalienable rights not listed in the body of the Constitution or in its amendments, which are nonetheless basic to a concept of ordered liberty. The original purpose of the Ninth Amendment was to remind the federal government that the rights enumerated in the Bill of Rights did not comprise all rights held by the people. The Supreme Court has guaranteed some rights of privacy under the Ninth Amendment.

Omnibus Crime Control and Safe Streets Act of 1968:   This model crime control bill was designed to provide federal grants to states to strengthen police departments and provide better training and equipment. It increased the powers of police to use wiretapping and electronic surveillance in attempting to obtain evidence. It limited the Miranda and like decisions by allowing the use of voluntary confessions made under most conditions.

Organized Crime Act of 1970:   As Congress investigated organized crime in America, it concluded that special, federal steps would have to be taken, as the states and local governments were unable to deal with crime syndicates adequately. The law enpowered special grand juries to investigate organized crime. It standardized immunity grants given to special witnesses. It limited challenges to evidence used in criminal investigations and it increased federal jurisdiction over interstate transportation of explosives and over gambling operations. It created a "dangerous offenders" class, permitting prison sentences to be given of up to 25 years to these persons on conviction. Some of the provisions of this act will undoubtedly be challenged in the courts for years to come.

Peonage :   Persons who incur debts were often compelled to perform services until the debt was discharged. Such involuntary service is prohibited by the Thirteenth Amendment. This broad interpretation to the antipeonage clause was given by the Supreme Court in *Pollock v. Williams* (1944).

Personna Non Grata: This is a Latin phrase meaning that a person, ordinarily of diplomatic standing, is not welcome in the country where he or she is or was to be stationed.

Petition: The First Amendment guarantees the citizenry the right to petition government to correct problems or deficiencies in governmental services or practices. The process of calling the attention of public officials to wrongs that government may or should correct is basic to the democratic process.

Preferred Position (Free Speech):   There has always been a strong minority position on the Supreme Court which has held that the right of free speech (and often of press) is absolute. Thus, Congress shall make no law of any kind abridging free speech. The same applies to the state legislatures. Only in civil areas, such as libel and slander, would there be any restrictions on free speech. Even here, a private person would have to seek civil remedy for lies stated or published about him or her, but no prior restraint would be permitted.

Press, Freedom of: The right of the "fourth estate" to tell the people about government is one of the most basic rights to be found in any constitutional republic. The right to a free press implies a responsible press, and its publications may be regulated in the interests of public decency. It may not engage in libel or slander. In recent years "press" has been defined so as to include motion pictures. In defining the operations of a free press, there have been problems related to rights of defendants against unfavorable pretrial publicity, and problems related to national security.

Procedural Rights: In the American system of justice, we consider the rights citizens enjoy in the process of being arrested and tried for a crime to be among our most basic rights. These rights are to be distinguished from those substantive rights that are fundamentally grounded in property, and include rights such as the following: trial by jury of one's peers; fair and impartial administration of justice; speedy and just trial and arraignment; and representation by legal counsel. An individual must be informed of his or her rights upon arrest. The individual has the right to have his or her case heard in courts sitting in fixed places and to have a copy of all charges brought against him or her.

Quartering: Just prior to the revolt against England, the king had stationed troops in the private homes of Americans against the wishes of the homeowners. To protect against such an event in the future, the Third Amendment was incorporated specifically to prohibit the stationing of troops in private homes in peacetime. The amendment remains in force today, but it has been little used or defined in the courts. Presumably, if an occasion arose that involved national guard troops of the states, the Third Amendment might be incorporated under the Fourteenth Amendment, thereby limiting state quartering of troops.

Public Person: The courts have defined a public person as one who asks for and desires public recognition, such as a statesman, artist, or performer. A private individual may suddenly, and without knowledge or consent, be thrust into the public eye by virtue of being somewhere at some time when a great or significant event has taken place. A police officer or other public servant may, by virtue of his or her position in the public trust, become a public person because he or she has become involved in a controversial public act, such as an arrest of a prominent gangster. Much greater latitude is permitted in speaking or writing about public persons that about private persons (*New York Times v. Sullivan* (376 US 254, 1964).

Religion, Freedom of: The wall of separation between church and state was established both to protect the church and the state. No established religion is permitted. Neither is the state to interfere with religious practices, save to curb the most basic abuses of safety, as in laws prohibiting handling of snakes, or majoritarian morality, as in laws suppressing polygamy. Even the most bizarre religious practices are tolerated, provided they do not violate health, safety, or ethical laws.

Search and Seizure: The Fourth Amendment prohibits unreasonable searches and seizures. The police may obtain a search warrant in which are listed items that they reasonably expect to find. Such a warrant may be issued only on reasonable evidence that illegal materials are to be found on the premises to be searched. Illegally seized evidence may no longer be introduced in state courts (*Mapp v. Ohio*, 367 US 643, 1971). Materials obtained following due process as specified on the search warrant, and found on the premises to be examined, may of course be used as evidence in a criminal trial. Illegally obtained materials may be used in certain grand jury proceedings (*United States v. Calandra*, 410 US 925, 1974).

Search Warrant: The Constitution protects individuals from unreasonable searches and seizures. In order for the state, using its police powers, to enter a home to search for illegal materials, it must prove that there is good reason to suspect that such materials, fugitives from justice, or persons to be taken into custody are on the premises. A document is then issued by the appropriate court which describes the materials to be searched for or the person who is sought. The search warrant then enables the police to search on the premises named.

Sedition: This includes any act against the government, including public utterances, but short of actual acts of treason. Such acts might include counseling or encouraging others to ignore laws or disobey public officials in the performance of their duties.

Segregation: After the Civil War, the South began to pass laws designed to cut off the non-white population from the mainstream of society. The non-whites were quarantined from society by having "separate but equal" schools and other public facilities. The Supreme Court found this practice to be quite permissible (*Plessy v. Ferguson*, 163 US 537, 1896). In the 1950s a study financed by the Ford Foundation and coordinated by Gunnar Myrdal, a Swede, found that the non-white population has been isolated in many areas of the nation, North and South. The *Plessy* decision was overturned in the decision of *Brown v. Board of Education of Topeka, Kansas* (347 US 483, 1954 *et seq.*).

Selective Incorporation, Doctrine of: In the case of *Palko v. Connecticut* (302 US 319, 1937) Justice Bejamin Cardozo spoke of the incorporation of parts of the Bill of Rights under the Fourteenth Amendment in order to guarantee such liberties not only over and against federal encroachment, but against state abridgement as well. Those rights that would be protected by the federal courts would be those of a fundamental nature; those whose denial would be shocking to the sense of justice and morality of the civilized world; and those that are part and parcel of civilized behavior.

Self-Incrimination: This term means that an individual has disclosed information about him or herself directly, thereby leaving him or herself open to criminal charges. The Fifth Amendment specifically protects an individual from being forced to testify against self in criminal cases. An individual may choose to provide such information, as in a confession, by voluntarily waiving the right against self-incrimination. No unfavorable inference may be made by the refusal of an individual to testify in a case wherein he or she is the defendent.

Seventh Amendment: This is one of the least invoked amendments contained within the Bill of Rights. Common law is used but sparsely in the United States, statutory law and equity having taken the place of common law. Thus, the right to trial by the special six-person jury in cases where Congress allows the common law to be used is a little litigated right. It has not been incorporated under the Fourteenth Amendment and thus made applicable to the states.

Smith Act of 1940:   Properly called the Alien Registration Act of 1940, this law required annual registration of aliens living in the United States. It also made it a crime to advocate the violent overthrow of the American government. The provisions of the act which make it a crime to teach, advocate, or distribute information teaching or advocating the violent overthrow of our government have been sustained by the courts. The act makes it a crime to assassinate public officials or to spead disloyalty in the armed forces. In 1940, the act was designed to curb Nazi and Fascist activities, but it has been used primarily against Communist groups.

Social Security Act of 1935:   Under the provision of providing for the general welfare, the Congress, backed subsequently by the courts, found the power to attack the problem of basic retirement, illness, and accident insurance as a national problem. Little by little most Americans have come under Social Security coverage, excepting federal and most railway employees. The system is optional for state and local governments, most of which have accepted the system. The tax paid by both employers and employees has gradually risen and the long-range prognosis is that the system is in an unhealthy condition financially. Congress and the president will have to decide whether the system is to be self-funding, and thus continue to raise the tax, or whether the general treasury will have to be used to bail out the system.

Speech, Freedom of: The concept of ordered liberty includes the right to speak one's mind on a variety of subjects. The courts have been prone to give the widest latitude of First Amendment freedoms, especially to the written and spoken word. When one speaks or writes about a public person, a person who seeks publicity, or a person who is cast into the public eye by virtue of circumstance, he or she can be restricted only if he or she "woefully" disregards the truth, and intends to do harm to the person. Generally, the courts have protected "symbolic" speech wherein one's idea is expressed by a symbol or gesture.

Speedy Trial Act of 1974: The Congress ordered that by 1980, trials should take place within 100 days of arrest. The prescription offered by the act is as follows. A person arrested is to be charged within 30 days; he or she is to be arraigned within 10 days of being charged; and he or she is to be tried within 60 days of arraignment. Judges are granted certain latitude in determining when a delay is required as, for example, when a mental examination is needed.

Taft-Hartley Management Relations Act of 1947: This law superseded the National Labor Relations Act. It strengthened the National Labor Relations Board and gave it increased duties. It provided for a cooling-off period in labor-management conflicts of 60 days in most industries and 80 days in essential ones. It allowed unions and management to sue one another for breach of contract. It outlawed the closed shop, but permitted the union shop. It allowed states to forbid union shops in its "right to work" provision.

Treason: Article III, section 3 of the Constitution provides that "Treason against the United States shall consist only in levying war against them, or in adhering to their enemies, giving them aid and comfort. No person shall be convicted of treason unless on the testimony of two witnesses to the same overt act, or on confession in open court." States may also punish treason against their own state constitutions. Mere riot or civil disobedience is not sufficient for treason. However, supplying the enemy with information or materials is not itself treason. Julius and Ethel Rosenberg were executed for allegedly passing atomic secrets to the Soviets.

CASES

Adamson v. California (332 US 46, 1947): This case is famous for Justice Black's dissenting opinion. Black argued that the *Palko v. Connecticut* decision was wrong and that the Constitution, as amended by the Fourteenth Amendment, applied fully to the states, guaranteeing the specific subtantive and procedural right to the citizens of the states against state abridgement. He would have included all Bill of Rights freedoms, guaranteeing these against state encroachment, under the Fourteenth Amendment. The "doctrine of selective incorporation," that of including and excluding bits and pieces of the Bill of Rights liberties, is a matter of doing, on a case to case basis, what Black recommended doing in one broad stroke of judicial pen.

Ashcraft v. Tennessee (322 US 143, 1944): This is a basic civil liberties case wherein the Supreme Court held that confessions obtained from accused persons were invalid if they were obtained by "inherently coercive" methods. In this case a confession was obtained after the suspect was drilled constantly by police for 36 hours. This due process case applied to the extraction of confessions within states.

Barker v. Wingo (407 US 514, 1972): The Sixth Amendment to the Constitution requires a speedy trial for those accused of crimes. The Supreme Court tried to determine what was a speedy trial. It studied the length of delay, the reasons for delay, whether the defendant had sought a speedy trial, and whether the delay was prejudicial to the defendant.

Barron v. Baltimore (7 Peters 243, 1833): Until the ratification of the Fourteenth Amendment, the Supreme Court held that the Bill of Rights in the Constitution limited only the federal government and not the states. This doctrine was the basic law until it was broken by the "Doctrine of Selective Incorporation" under which selected parts of the first 10 amendments were made operational in the states under the Fourteenth Amendment.

Barkus v. Illinois (355 US 281, 1958): The Fifth Amendment guarantees citizens that they cannot be tried twice for the same offense. However, this rule applies only within the same level of jurisdiction. Thus, as was the case here, an individual tried and acquitted in federal court may still be tried in state courts for the same offense. There are, however, only two levels of jurisdiction, federal and state.

Berger v. New York (388 US 41, 1967): In attempting to define personal rights against infringement on privacy made by wiretapping, the Supreme Court in this case held that the secret surveillance of private conversations is prohibited by the Fourth Amendment if the electronic device is secreted inside a defendant's residence or office. Justice Black dissented, following the Olmstead decision, saying that a conversation cannot be seized or "searched." Wiretapping would be legal, the Court said, if a proper warrant was first obtained. The Court further found that statutes authorizing search warrants to be used in connection with wiretapping had "to describe with particularity the conversation sought." Wiretapping would have to end when the particular conversation sought was obtained. The warrant could not be used on a "fishing expedition."

Board of Education v. Allen (392 US 236, 1968): In defining the limits on state educational aid to parochial school students, the Supreme Court has allowed some services to be granted to students in church-related schools. In this case the Court allowed the use of tax dollars to provide textbooks, standardized tests, and medical and diagnostic services to parochial school students. Those schools that exclude students because of race or national origin may not receive such services from taxpayers' moneys (*Norwood v. Harrison*, 413 US 455, 1973).

Brown v. Board of Education of Topeka, Kansas (347 US 483, 1954; 349 US 294, 1955): In the 1954 decision the Supreme Court overturned the "separate but equal" doctrine of *Plessy v. Ferguson* (163 US 537, 1896) and ordered the desegregation of public schools. The 1955 decision ordered the states to desegregate "with all deliberate speed." Federal District Courts were to decide what speed was appropriate for school districts under their respective control. The schools in the District of Columbia were ordered to desegregate in *Bolling v. Sharp* (347 US 497, 1954). The Supreme Court found the segregated schools to be involved in arbitrary denial of "equal protection of the laws."

Burstyn v. Wilson (343 US 495, 1952): For the first time the motion picture was afforded some protections under the First Amendment. Other forms of printed expression enjoy far greater freedom from "prior restraint" than the motion picture industry, but the *Burstyn* decision did recognize the motion picture industry as a legitimate form of expression, and thus entitled to some protection.

Cole v. Richardson (405 US 676, 1972): The Supreme Court in this case upheld the loyalty oath administered to state employees wherein these individuals were required to swear that they were opposed to the idea of violently overthrowing the federal or state governments. This was the first oath of loyalty sustained by the Court in several years.

Committee for Public Education and Religious Liberty v. Nyquist (413 US 756, 1973): The Supreme Court, in maintaining the wall of separation between church and state, struck down New York laws that provided financial support for children enrolled in parochoial schools. These benefits included tuition grants to low-income families and certain tax relief benefits to parents of children in parochial schools.

Dennis v. United States (341 US 494, 1951): In sustaining the conviction of 11 top Communists, the Supreme Court also affirmed the validity of the Smith Act of 1940, a law designed to regulate subversive activities in this country. The Court reread the "clear and present" danger doctrine, holding that the nation need not wait until the Communist conspiracy begins to have effect to curb subversive activities of its exponents. It affirmed the "bad tendency" doctrine of the *Gitlow* decision (268 US 652, 1925), a more restrictive reading of the First Amendment freedoms of the speech, press, and assembly than the "clear and present" danger doctrine.

Elfbrandt v. Russell (384 US 11, 1966): The Supreme Court struck down the state laws requiring loyalty oaths that required individuals to declare that they were not Communist party members. The Court ruled that mere membership in the Communist party was not in and of itself a crime and that such an oath was really punishing through "guilt by association."

Engel v. Vitale (370 US 421, 1962): The New York Board of Regents had written a "nondenominational" prayer to be recited in its public schools. The Supreme Court found this to be an improper function of a school system. As a state agency, the Board of Regents was not empowered to write or prescribe religious services. In the following year the Supreme Court struck down all religious services in the public schools in *School District of Abington Township v. Schempp* (374 US 203, 1963).

Epperson v. Arkansas (393 US 97, 1968): The Supreme Court held that states may not bar the use of scientific materials or theories in the classroom simply because they conflict with religious teachings. In this case the Court invalidated an Arkansas law that prohibited the teaching of the evolutionary theories of Charles Darwin. This culminated the long battle that had raged over that question, beginning with the "Scopes Trial" in Dayton, Tennessee when Clarence Darrow and Dudley Field Malone clashed with William Jennings Bryan.

Everson v. Board of Education of Ewing Township (330 US 1, 1947): In making a rare exception to its policy of excluding parochial schools from public assistance, the Supreme Court held that providing public transportation to parochial school children was not a violation of the First Amendment wall of separation between church and state. The Court reasoned that the primary benefit was to the children, not to the school. Since the *Everson* decision a number of other benefits to the students have been sustained, including providing school textbooks.

Ex Parte Milligan (4 Wall 2, 1866): The Supreme Court held that an individual could not be tried in the military courts if he or she was a civilian living in an area where the civilian courts were operational and their processes were unobstructed. This was a limitation on President Lincoln's use of martial law in areas of the North not threatened during the Civil War. Along with *Ex Parte Merryman,* the *Milligan* case counteracted Lincoln's use of martial law without the consent of the Congress.

Fletcher v. Peck, (6 Cranch 87, 1810): In this fundamental case dealing with the protection of private property rights, the Supreme Court prohibited the states from tampering in any way with the rights conferred by previous charter or agreement on corporations.

Freedman v. Maryland (380 US 51, 1965): In 1952 the *Burstyn v. Wilson* case (343 US 495) had brought motion pictures under the protection of the First Amendment. The *Freedman* case attempted to remove many of the "prior restraint" restrictions on movies. Boards of censorship might still exist, but prompt judicial review or rulings by such boards was guaranteed.

Garner v. Board of Public Works (341 US 716, 1951): This was the first of the modern decisions made by the Supreme Court interpreting loyalty oaths. The Court found that the requirement for public employment of a loyalty oath wherein one swore that he or she was not a Communist was a reasonable requirement for public employment. The precedent was overturned in *Elfbrandt v. Russell* (384 US 11, 1966). Since the *Elfbrandt* decision, the Court has sustained a loyalty oath requirement in public employment in which an individual was required to renounce the idea of the violent overthrow of the government (*Cole v. Richardson,* 405 US 676, 1972).

Gideon v. Wainright (372 US 335, 1963): This case has become legend since the publication of the book, *Gideon's Trumpet,* written by Anthony Lewis. In the case the Court held that poor defendants had to be given legal counsel at public expense if they could not afford to hire an attorney themselves. In *Griffin v. Illinois* (351 US 12, 1963) the Supreme Court guaranteed the poor transcripts of their trials and in *Douglas v. California* (372 US 353, 1963) the Court required states to provide free attorneys to the poor for purposes of appeal.

Gitlow v. New York (268 US 652, 1925):   This case reversed the precedent of *Barron v. Baltimore* (7 Peters 243, 1833) by holding that the Bill of Rights can be applied to ensure certain basic rights to citizens of the states against state encroachment. The Bill of Rights was incorporated, at least in part, under the Fourteenth Amendment. In this case certain First Amendment freedoms were guaranteed to citizens against state abridgement. It opened the door for inclusion of other basic rights. The case also is notable for creating the "bad tendency" doctrine, which narrowed the "clear and present danger" interpretation of the First Amendment.

Griffin v. California (380 US 609, 1965):   Overturning precedents, the Supreme Court ruled here that defendants had the right to refuse to testify against themselves in criminal cases.

Griswold v. Connecticut (381 US 479, 1965):   Until this case was decided, the Supreme Court had not discovered meaning in the Ninth Amendment to the Constitution. Here, the Court over-ruled state laws prohibiting the dissemination of information or devices that would aid in prevention of pregnancy. This information was held to be a private communication between physician and patient and not subject to state regulation without unconstitutional violation of privacy.

Hague v. CIO (307 US 496, 1939):   This is the fundamental decision involving assembly. The Supreme Court found that the right to assembly was not isolated to private places, but it was guaranteed in public places as well. The right to assembly was protected in this case against state encroachment under the Fourteenth Amendment. In the subsequent decisions, the Supreme Court has ruled that parade permits may be required, but the process used in granting such permits must be reasonable and states are not required to allow the use of public property, such as jails, for protests.

Heart of Atlanta Motel v. United States (379 US 241, 1964):   Reversing earlier precedents established in the civil rights cases of the 19th century, the Supreme Court sustained the provisions of the 1964 Civil Rights Act that prohibited certain private acts of discrimination. The 1964 law had made it illegal to discriminate against persons because of race in public accomodations. The police power to prohibit such discrimination was found by the Court under federal powers to regulate interstate commerce.

Home Building & Loan Assn. v. Blaidsdell (290 US 398, 1934): In the earliest decisions, the Federalist court under John Marshall and Roger Taney had expended considerable effort in establishing and protecting property and private property rights. In this decision, culminating a change of judicial practice begun in the late 19th century, the Supreme Court found ample powers for the states to regulate private property to protect public health, safety, morals and, here, society's economic integrity.

Hurtado v. California (110 US 516, 1884): Although this decision was rendered before the incorporation of parts of the Bill of Rights under the Fourteenth Amendment was begun, the major thrust of the case, which was that states need not provide for grand jury indictments in criminal cases, holds true today.

In re Gault (387 US 1, 1967): In this major decision the Supreme Court discovered new law which provided juveniles with most safeguards that adults are protected by in court proceedings.

Jehovah's Witnesses Cases: This series of cases involved the religious dissenters known as Jehovah's Witnesses. The Supreme Court held: in *Cantwell v. Connecticut* (310 US 296, 1940) that states may not require permits to sell religious magazines; in *Murdock v. Pennsylvania* (319 US 105, 1943) that states may not require licenses of religious book sellers; in *Martin v. Struthers* (319 US 141, 1943) that states may not prevent door-to-door distribution of religious books; in *Niemotko v. Maryland* (340 US 268, 1951) that states may not require official approval of worship services conducted in public places; in *West Virginia State Board of Education v. Barnette* (319 US 624, 1943) that states may require religious dissenters to salute the flag in public schools in violation of their religion; in *Prince v. Massachusetts* (321 US 159, 1944) that state welfare laws may be used to protect children, as in curbing their selling of religious materials late at night.

Jones v. Mayer (392 US 409, 1968): The Supreme Court found validity for this recent case in a 1866 law which prohibited the discrimination based on race in the sale or rental of private property. The 1866 law was thought to be null and void after the *Civil Rights Cases* (109 US 3, 1883) and had long gone unenforced. This law brought new meaning to the

Thirteenth Amendment and it served notice that the 1968 Civil Rights Law, which was designed to do much the same thing as the 1866 law in regard to the sale and rental of housing, would be enforced.

Kilbourn v. Thompson (103 US 190, 1880): The Supreme Court limited the investigative powers of the Congress, holding that its powers did not include general authority to inquire into private affairs.

Lemon v. Kurtzman (403 US 602, 1971): The Supreme Court, in maintaining a wall of separation between church and state, struck down laws that allowed the payment of teachers of nonreligious subjects in parochial schools.

Lopez v. United States (373 US 427, 1963): In this case a taxpayer was believed to be prepared to offer a bribe to an Internal Revenue Service agent. The agent was equipped with a taperecorder and met with the man. He did offer a bribe and the Supreme Court allowed the use of the tape recorded information in court. The Court held that the sole reason that the agent could be so equipped was to protect his credibility against an individual who was seeking to corrupt public officials. A similar case involved attempts made by the attorney for labor racketeer James Hoffa to bribe a prospective juror. (*Osborn v. United States*, 385 US 323, 1966)

McGowan v. Maryland (366 US 420, 1961): In this case the Supreme Court held Sunday closing laws to be constitutional. States were not required to have such laws, but if the state chose to create this kind of legislation it could be sustained. While the original purpose of these laws was religious, the Court found the present purpose to be secular, in that these laws provided a day of rest and relaxation.

McNabb v. United States (318 US 332, 1943): The Supreme Court here invalidated a conviction based on a confession obtained while the accused was unlawfully detained. The Supreme Court ruled that a prisoner must be arraigned without delay. The Speedy Trial Act of 1974 attempts to establish guidelines for both arraignment and extraction of confessions within reasonable time limits as related to arraignment.

Malloy v. Hogan (378 US 1, 1964): This case applied the protections against self-incrimination granted to defendants in federal cases to defendants in state courts. It applied the Fifth Amendment to the states through the Fourteenth Amendment.

Mapp v. Ohio (367 US 643, 1961):   In this case the Supreme Court applied the federal standards of evidence admission to the states. The Court held that illegally seized evidence could not be used in a state trial against a defendant. In *Aguilar v. Texas* (378 US 108, 1964) the requirements for obtaining arrest and search warrants were stiffened.

Miami Herald Publishing Co. v. Tornillo (418 US 241, 1971):   A Florida law required that newspapers who criticize candidates for public office must furnish free space to such candidates for replies. The law was invalidated by the Supreme Court in this case. Justice Burger held that while responsible journalism is desirable, it is not within the power of the state to so regulate the free press.

Miller v. California (413 US 5, 1973):   The Supreme Court sustained earlier decisions that held that obscenity was not protected under the First Amendment freedoms. It reversed earlier decisions on the determination of standards to be applied to test whether or not a thing was pornographic. The scope of regulation was limited to materials showing or describing sexual activity. A local jury then must decide if a piece of material is utterly devoid of artistic merit and if it is designed to appeal to purient interests.

Milliken v. Bradley (418 US 717, 1974):   In this case, which limited racial desegregation through busing of school children to achieve racial balance, the Supreme Court held that school districts could not be crossed unless one of two things could be established: (1) that the boundaries had been drawn for such school districts to avoid desegregation, or (2) that the school systems had been practicing racial segregation.

Miranda v. Arizona (384 US 436, 1966):   Miranda was arrested on suspicion of kidnapping and rape. He was not told that he was entitled to an attorney. He was told that what he said might be used against him. He confessed to the crimes and was convicted. The Supreme Court reversed his conviction holding that one accused of a crime must be informed of the right to counsel before questioning. The prosecution may not use as evidence in a minimal case a statement resulting from police interrogation unless the defendant has first been warned of the right not to be questioned, of the danger that any such statement may be used against him or her, and of the right to have an attorney present during questioning. If the defendant cannot afford an attorney, one must be appointed without charge. The defendant may choose to waive any or all of these rights. The decision was designed to ensure the defendant that, irrespective of financial position, he or she was to be guaranteed the basic rights all people were entitled to have under our egalitarian legal system. It was also another check on alleged police brutality. The courts had already reversed a long series of confessions extracted from defendants by torture and under duress.

Moore v. Dempsey (261 US 86, 1923): In this case the Supreme Court held that states must provide a reasonable and fair trial, and that it is not enough to go through the mere motions of a trial. The defendants must not be tried under threats of mobs or by judges whose judgment may be influenced by passion.

NAACP v. Alabama (357 US 449, 1958): In order to protect the rights of individuals to form associations, certain steps must be taken to prevent other individuals or associations from discriminating against or harrassing the individual members. In this case, the Supreme Court ruled that states may not require associations to reveal their membership lists if it seemed likely that such revelation would subject the members to discrimination at the hands of the community.

Nardone v. United States (302 US, 1937): The Supreme Court in this ruling upheld the Federal Communications Act, which said in part, "no person . . . shall intercept any (wire) communication and divulge or publish" its contents or meaning. The decision restricted the interception of wire communications, but left other forms of eavesdropping unrestricted. The decision did not prevent eavesdropping so long as the contents were not made public. The decision applied only to federal officials, not those in states. Any federal conviction based on illegally obtained wiretapping would be reversed under this decision.

National Labor Relations Board v. Jones & Laughlin Steel Corp. (301 US 1, 1937): In this case the Supreme Court upheld the National Labor Relations Act, which gave labor the right to organize and to bargain collectively with management. The case also sustained the National Labor Relations Board (NLRB). The Congress was held to have the power to regulate those activities having a "close and substantial relation to interstate commerce."

Near v. Minnesota (283, US 697, 1931): In this landmark case, the Supreme Court ruled that freedom of the press is vital to a free state. Newspapers and other publications cannot be restrained from publishing.

Even if the paper or its staff have previously exceeded legal standards of conduct, they cannot be restrained in the future from publishing. Any individual breach of the law may be punished, but only after the materials have been oriented. This ruling effectively prevents prior censorship of the press.

Nebraska Press Association v. Stuart (427 US 539, 1976): The courts are often asked to decide between two conflicting rights. In this case, the Supreme Court had to determine the proper law in a conflict between the right of the press to cover controversial trials and the rights of the accused to a fair and impartial trial. The court was unwilling to limit a free press, thus holding the First Amendment freedom of the press above those guaranteeing a fair and impartial trial.

New York Times Company v. United States (403 US 713, 1971): In 1971 several newspapers, including the *New York Times* had received copies of documents stolen from the government relating to the war in Vietnam. These materials have become known as the "Pentagon Papers." The attorney general obtained a restraining order to prevent their publication. Because we reject any concept of prior restraint of the press, save for grave matters of national security, the burden of proof to establish that there was compelling reason to stop publication rested with the government. Three justices argued that no prior restraint was permitted in any case, for any reason. The other six justices found that the government had failed to prove that there was compelling reason to prevent publication.

Olmstead v. United States (277 US 438, 1928): This was the first decision rendered by the Supreme Court in its attempt to reconcile modern electronic surveillance with the Fourth Amendment right against unreasonable searches and seizures. In this case, Chief Justice Taft rejected the concept of applying the Fourth Amendment to wiretapping or "bugging," saying that one's home and possessions are not interfered with by such eavesdropping.

Palko v. Connecticut (302 US 319, 1937): In this landmark decision, the Supreme Court attempted to define the application of the Fourteenth Amendment to the Bill of Rights. Since the *Gitlow* decision, the Supreme Court had begun to protect rights of citizens of states from the state governments. Justice Cardozo, writing for the majority, found that the Constitution did not necessarily guarantee specific procedural rights, such as right to grand jury indictment. Rather, it required that rights on the "different plane of social and moral values" be guaranteed because these were "the very essence of a scheme of ordered liberty." The implied protection of federalism in this case would preclude the federal courts from tampering too much with state procedures.

Pierce v. Society of Sisters (268 US 510, 1925): The Oregon legislature passed a law requiring that children within specified age limits attend public schools. No provision was made for private or parochial school instruction. The Supreme Court found this to be an unconstitutional infringement on the rights of parents to direct the education of the children, protected under the Fourteenth Amendment.

Plessy v. Ferguson (163 US 537, 1896): In the years after the American Civil War, the initial spirit of civil rights was lost and states began to pass laws providing for the segregation of the races in a wide variety of public facilities and accommodations. This case allowed racial segregation in public transportation, and, by inference, elsewhere, as in schools, provided the facilities were "separate but equal."

Pollock v. Williams (322 US 4, 1944): Under the Thirteenth Amendment, the Court found that states may not require individuals to perform certain duties or to work in order to discharge debts. The Thirteenth Amendment's antipeonage provisions prevent enforced servitude even for purposes of paying off debts.

Regents of the University of California v. Bakke (98 S.Ct. 2733, 1978): The University of California had created a minority quota and special minority consideration category related to admissions policy for its professional schools in order to encourage minority admission. Bakke claimed that he was more qualified for entry than minorities who were admitted. The Supreme Court held that special admissions programs that utilized explicit racial classifications in the selection of applicants for admission were impermissible. It also held that a public college or university might consider race or ancestry as a factor in the selection of applicants for admission so long as such factors are not used as explicit or exclusive criteria, but are used along with a number of other criteria designed to guarantee diversity in the student body. The schools must determine that such racial or ancestral data would be used to determine, with other supporting data, if a student might serve a community need. The minority opinion, supported by four justices, argued that minority quotas used to guarantee minimum minority participation in programs can be justified in light of past discrimination practices and to guarantee a number of minority graduates in approximate proportion to the population of the minorities.

Reynolds v. United States (89 US 145, 1879):   As a condition to admission to statehood, Utah was required to pass laws designed to curb the practice of polygamy, a practice common in the Mormon communities there. The Supreme Court upheld these antipolygamy laws as a correct application of state law. Although religious practices are generally ignored by the law, the state does have the power over-ride religion in determining public health, safety, and moral standards. Subsequent decisions have sustained antisnake handling laws and laws designed to limit the use of illegal drugs in religious services.

Roe v. Wade (410 US 113, 1973):   The Supreme Court here found meaning in the Ninth Amendment, protecting the right to privacy. The Court ordered invalidation of laws prohibiting abortion during the first six months of pregnancy. The state may regulate abortions in the last three months; however, it cannot prevent abortions that are required to save the mother's life. The Court's ruling reflects the changing status of women in American life and growing concern for privacy from state regulation of ethical conduct.

Roth v. United States (354 US 476, 1957):   The Supreme Court sustained the traditional argument that obscene materials receive no protection under the First Amendment. However, the Court broadened the rights of publishers to print materials of a sexual nature by narrowing the definition of pornography. Those materials that are designed to appeal to "purient interests" are pornographic unless they have "redeeming social or literary value." The standards to be applied under *Roth* are of the greater community, that is, national standards. The *Miller* decision (413 US 5, 1973) changed the standards to the local values held in states or communities.

Rowan v. Post Office Department (397 US 728, 1970):   The Supreme Court upheld a federal law allowing an individual to refuse to accept "erotically arousing" or "sexually provocative" materials. An individual need only ask that his or her name be deleted from such lists. The Court held that it makes no difference what kind of material is involved, and that material may include mail order catalogues advertising such items as undergarments or nightwear.

Scales v. United States (367 US 203, 1961): The Supreme Court narrowed previous decisions defining subversive activities under the Smith Act of 1940 in this decision. It rejected "guilt by association," holding that to prosecute an individual under the Smith and other subversives control acts, one had to show the individual to be an active member who knew and understood the aims of the Communist (or other) party to be the violent overthrow of the American government.

Schenck v. United States (249 US 47, 1919): This decision upheld the conviction of Schenck who had admittedly circulated materials urging young men not to fight in World War I and to resist the draft. This was a legitimate restriction of free speech, the Court found. The case is notable for Justice Holmes' argument that the state can regulate free speech when it finds in such press or speech a "clear and present danger." Holmes argued that the right of free speech does not permit one to yell out "Fire!" in a crowded theater when there is no fire.

School District of Abington Township v. Schempp (374 US 203, 1963): In one of its most controversial decisions ever, the Supreme Court held that the reading of the Bible or the reciting of prayers in the public schools was an unconstitutional violation of the separation of church and state as required by the First Amendment.

Scott v. Sanford (19 Howard 393, 1857) ("Dred Scott Decision"): This decision ruled that slaves were not men; rather, they were property under the Constitution. It had the secondary effect of overturning the Missouri Compromise of 1820. The Thirteenth Amendment to the Constitution made the former slaves citizens, while the Fourteenth and Fifteenth Amendments gave them certain rights and made them United States citizens entitled to all rights enjoyed by all citizens.

Scottsboro Cases: (294 US 587, 1935) Nine black youths were accused of rape in Alabama. What happened to them has become one of the most famous stories in American judicial history. In their first trial, the state failed to give them legal counsel despite the fact that rape was a capital crime in the state. After a new trial was ordered, the Supreme Court also found that blacks had been excluded historically from juries in the county in which the men were tried, and a third trial was ordered. Eventually the defendants were found guilty, although in 1977 the last survivor of the group was given a pardon which was symbolic for the entire group. The cases are important in that they helped to establish due process in the states.

Swann v. Charlotte-Mecklenberg Board of Education (402 US 1, 1971): The Court reaffirmed the Brown decisions (347 US 483, 1954; 349 US 294, 1955), saying that all state-created racial segregation in the public schools must be terminated. It reaffirmed the powers of federal district courts to decide how this was to be done, and strengthened their powers to force desegregation. The Supreme Court underwrote the power of the district courts to order a wide variety of remedies to end desegregation, including busing.

Tilton v. Richardson (403 US 672, 1971): In a series of unusual cases which also included *Hunt v. McNair* (410 US 952, 1973), the Supreme Court, which had disallowed aid to parochial elementary and high schools, now allowed aid and federally insured loans to private and religious colleges and universities. The Supreme Court reasoned that colleges and universities are, by their natures, less religiously oriented and the students are less impressionable than at the lower levels of education.

Torcaso v. Watkins (367 US 488, 1961): In this case the United States Supreme Court invalidated a Maryland law that required public officials to swear that they believed in God. The case also invalidated provisions of laws in other states which were similar. Witnesses in courts of law need not profess a belief in God or an afterlife in order to be sworn in on the witness stand. This effectively ended "religious tests" for determining eligibility for office-holding. To have full separation of church and state, it seems absolutely necessary to remove such religious tests as a precondition for holding offices or being a witness in a courtroom.

United States v. Brown (381 US 437, 1965): Americans are protected against trial by legislative bodies in the constitutional prohibition against bills of attainder. The Supreme Court in this case found that the provision in the Landrum-Griffin Labor Act making it a crime for Communists to hold office in labor unions was a bill of attainder, and thus it was unconstitutional.

United States v. Darby Lumber Co. (312 US 100, 1941): In this case the Supreme Court upheld the Fair Labor Standards Act of 1938, which imposed restrictions on the use of child labor and which set minimum wage and maximum hour standards for industries engaged in interstate commerce.

United States v. Lovett (328 US 303, 1946): Few cases in American history have been concerned with bills of attainder. The Supreme Court found here that a legislative act which declared three public officials to be ineligible for continued governmental employment was a bill of attainder and hence unconstitional.

Waller v. Florida (397 US 387, 1970): An individual may not, under the Fifth Amendment, be tried twice for the same offense. However, an individual may be tried for the same offense by two levels of jurisdiction, the federal and the state. No distinction may be made, following this decision, between levels within a state. Thus, an individual may not be tried under city law and under state law for the same offense.

Walz v. Tax Commission (397 US 664, 1970): In determining the meaning of the "establishment clause" in the First Amendment, the Supreme Court in this case created a three-part test. The clause is designed to prevent "sponsorship, financial support, and active involvement" in religious activities. If the legislation in question does any of these three things, then it will most likely be held to be unconstitutional by the courts. The Court did uphold tax exemptions for church owned properties in the case.

Washington v. Davis (426 US 229, 1976): In this case, the Supreme Court held that laws to be invalidated by the judicial system on the grounds that they discriminate against races must be shown to have a racially discriminatory purpose. It is not enough to show that laws bear more heavily on some groups than on others or that some suffer more than others as a result of the law.

West Coast Hotel Co. v. Parrish (300 US 379, 1937): The state of Washington had enacted a minimum wage law. The Supreme Court was asked to decide if such a law was in violation of the individual's right to contract his or her services at whatever price he or she choses. The Court held that a minimum wage law does not violate the individual's right to contract under the due process clause of the Fourteenth Amendment.

Wisconsin v. Yoder (406US 205, 1972): While the Supreme Court has consistently supported the requirements of states that young people attend school for reasonable periods of time as set by the state, the Court in this case held that the Amish custom of providing only an eighth-grade education for their young had been established over three centuries, apparently without harm to the youngsters, and thus Wisconsin could not require additional education of them. One suspects that the Court found the Amish to be unusually responsible citizens whose use for additional education was limited, and thus felt that it was unreasonable to violate community standards.

Won Kim Ark v. United States (169 US 649, 1898): A child born in the United States is a citizen of the country, even if he or she is born of parents who are aliens and not themselves subject to American citizenship or in any way eligible for citizenship. The Supreme Court here applied the Fourteenth Amendment literally and thus firmed up the doctrine of *jus soli*, law of the soil, as a determination of citizenship.

Yates v. United States (354 US 298, 1957): This case mitigated the severity of the "bad tendency" doctrine of the *Dennis v. U.S.* case (341 US 494, 1951). The court held that membership in the Communist party or belief in abstract Communist revolutionary doctrine did not present a threat sufficient to cause the imprisonment of adherents.

Zenger Case: John Peter Zenger, a New York publisher, had written articles in his newspaper which were critical of the administration of Governor Cosby. Zenger was imprisoned and at his trial he attempted to show evidence that what he published was true. The evidence was not admitted. The jury nonetheless found Zenger innocent of all charges. This is healded as a milestone in the fight for freedom of the press. It undoubtedly influenced Madison when he prepared the draft of the Bill of Rights. The First Amendment provided protection to publishers and reporters who might be charged as Zenger was.

Zorach v. Clauson (343 US 306, 1952): In this case, the Supreme Court sustained the right of a state to give released time to public school children to attend religious instruction outside school property. In a prior case, *Illinois ex rel. McCollum v. Board of Education* (333 US 203, 1948) the Court had not permitted religious instruction on the premises.

10

Taxation and Fiscal Policy

Ability To Pay: In modern states, politicians often assume that the burden of taxes ought to rest on those best able to pay. In the past, the burden often fell on the poor, while the rich paid little or no taxes. Various devices are used, including graduated income taxes, to assure that the burden falls on those best able to pay.

Ad Valorem: This kind of tax levies its assessments on the value of a commodity at each step in its manufacture. As value is added to a commodity that added value in taxed. This is sometimes called a "value added tax."

Antitrust Acts: See Chapter 11, p. 159.

Assessed Valuation: This is the value assigned to property for purposes of taxation. It may represent the actual, fair market value of the property or some percentage of that value. Many items are assessed, including: homes, businesses, personal property, cars, stocks, bonds, mortgages, livestock, and machinery.

Bankruptcy: Article I, section 8 of the Constitution allows Congress to make uniform laws concerning bankruptcy. Under bankruptcy procedures, an individual seeks relief from debts that he or she cannot discharge. Once completed, bankruptcy wipes out an individual or corporate debt. Referees are appointed to pay out, from the proceeds of the sale of an individual's goods, monies to the debtors. In this way at least a portion of an individual's debts are discharged.

Benefit Theory: This theory holds that those who benefit from some governmental service ought to pay for them. The Federal Highway Act of 1965 used gasoline taxes to construct the interstate highway system. States use gasoline taxes in similar ways.

Bond: This is a certificate of indebtedness issued by a corporation, a government, or a public authority. The bond pledges repayment according to a fixed schedule, and offers interest on the money borrowed. *General obligation bonds* pledge the general taxing power of the governmental unit issuing them toward retirement of the bonds and the payment of interest. *Revenue bonds* pledge the revenues obtained from the use of a public facility that was constructed with this money toward retirement of the debt and payment of the interest. Turnpikes and parking lots are often constructed with revenue bonds. The federal government regularly issues Treasury bonds.

Borrowing Power: Article I, section 8 of the Constitution gives the Congress the power to borrow money. Money is often borrowed from the general public in the form of Treasury notes and bonds ("savings bonds" are one form). Most state constitutions require that they pay as they go, but allow short term borrowing in anticipation of taxes.

Budget: Plans for expending money are common to all levels of government, as well as to corporations and individual households. Ordinarily the executive, the president, or state governor, will prepare an executive budget document to be introduced into the legislature. The executive receives help from fiscal specialists who have prepared the executive budget based on their assessments of individual budget requests from varying departments and branches of the government. The legislature may alter the budget, it may require department heads to justify expense requests, and it may add money for expenditures of its own choosing. Departments are expected to operate within the budget allocations provided by the legislature.

Budget and Accounting Act of 1921: This law requires the president to submit an annual budget to the Congress along with an estimate of revenues to be received from all sources for the next year. It established the Bureau of the Budget to assist the president. That office has been strengthened and renamed the Office of Management and Budget (OMB). It also effectively made the president head of the national economy.

Budget and Impoundment Control Act of 1974: See Chapter 7, p. 111.

Business Cycle: These are periodic, often rhythmic, fluctuations in the economy. Laissez-faire economists considered these to be necessary adjustments in the capitalist system. Thus, periods of high employment and productivity would necessarily be followed by periods of mass unemployment and low production. Governments have taken many steps to remove these fluctuations, including spending programs and governmental controls over many sectors of the economy.

Centralized Purchasing: This function is performed for many government agencies and departments by a central purchasing agent. In the federal government the General Services Administration does mass buying, usually by competitive bid. Thus, each agency need not do its own purchasing, drawing, instead, on a central warehouse. In recent months GSA has been racked by scandal. Allegations have been made that government purchases are made at rates well above existing market prices.

Civil Aeronautics Board (CAB): Founded in 1938, this agency is charged with policing the airways. It investigates air accidents. It is a five-member independent regulatory commission and is supplemented in its work by the Federal Aviation Agency (FAA).

Clayton Act of 1914: This was a major addition to the Sherman Anti-trust Act of 1890. As amended it is still used to regulate price cutting and similar prices aimed at creating monopolies. It restricts certain corporate practices, such as the buying out of competition and the creation of interlocking directorates.

Community Action Agency: Founded in 1975 to replace similar programs under the Office of Economic Opportunity (OEO), the programs that this agency sponsors are often experimental and innovative. Federal funds are provided to state and local agencies that are designed to serve local, specialized needs. Many of its programs have been attacked as wasteful and self-serving while others have been highly successful.

Comptroller General: See Chapter 6, p. 100.

Comptroller of the Currency: This person is an official of the Treasury Department. His signature is found on our money. He supervises and examines national banks and is an ex officio member of the Federal Deposit Insurance Corporation and the Federal Savings and Loan Insurance Corporation.

Congressional Budget Office (CBO): See Chapter 7, p. 114.

Consumer Product Safety Commission: One of the most controversial of the federal regulatory agencies, it is headed by a five-member commission. It is charged with removing products that are dangerous from the market and with testing various products for safety. It is charged with helping to develop standards for safety in the manufacture and design of a variety of products. Its primary authorization comes from the Consumer Product Safety Act of 1972, but it has been given additional authority under other laws, such as the Hazardous Substances Act, the Poison Prevention Packing Act, and the Flammable Fabrics Act.

Cost-Push Inflation: Rising prices of raw materials, especially oil, and rising labor costs cause this type of inflation. In more recent years, increasing interest rates have helped to push prices upward. Governmentally mandated safety and pollution control costs fuel the flames of this form of inflation as well.

Council of Economic Advisers: Under the Employment Act of 1946 the president is required to prepare an annual economic report. Those advisers who help him in this, and in other economic areas, are to be found in the executive office as the Council of Economic Advisers.

Debt Limit: Article I, section 8 of the Constitution authorizes the Congress to borrow money. The Congress may also, by appropriate legislation, increase the size of the maximum permissible national debt. Constant governmental deficits have caused the debt ceiling to be raised many times, especially in recent years.

Deficit Financing: This occurs when income does not equal expenses. It is likely to be a permanent condition of government. The government must seek to borrow funds in the private market place, in competition with private borrowers and state and local governments. Conservatives often express this as liberal permanent prosperity through permanent deficits.

Deflation: This is the opposite of the more common change in the purchasing power of the dollar, inflation. Deflation means that the purchasing power is actually greater than it was in a previous time. Liberal economics teaches that inflation is a necessary evil because it allows industry to reasonably anticipate that greater profits will occur in the future.

Demand-Pull Inflation: This occurs when there is an excess of money available to consumers (through salaries or on credit) and a relative scarcity of goods. Consumers then bid against one another for available goods, driving prices up. This occurred at the end of the Second World War.

Department of Justice: Through its antitrust division, this department has responsibility for enforcing the Clayton and Sherman Antitrust Acts.

Direct Tax: This is a tax paid directly by individuals or corporations to the government. Income taxes are an example of a direct tax.

Earmarked Funds: Legislatures may levy certain taxes, the proceeds of which are designated ("earmarked") for specific programs. The Pitman-Robertson excise tax on firearms and ammunition is earmarked for wildlife management and restoration.

Economic Message: The Employment Act of 1946 requires the president to prepare an annual message on the economic health of the nation. He does this with the aid of his Office of Economic Advisers. The message provides an oversight on problems of unemployment, inflation, and general economic activity.

Economic Opportunity Act of 1964: A basic part of President Lyndon Johnson's Great Society, it was designed to aid young people, especially from groups having high unemployment figures, to train for and find suitable employment.

Employment Act of 1946: Designed to create high levels of employment and increase purchasing powers for average families, this act, along with the Budget and Accounting Act of 1921 makes the president titular head of the national economy. It created the Office of the Council of Economic Advisers and required the president to report annually on the state of the economy, inflation, and employment.

Excess Profits Tax: This special levy taxes profits which, by legal definition, are excessive. The special tax rate may be as high as 100 percent. One measure of profits that would normally be expected could be determined by measuring average profits of all corporations doing a certain kind of business over a base period. If, for example, the average profit was 9 percent and companies now are earning over the 9 percent, then all profits in excess of 9 percent would be "excess."

Executive Budget: The president of the United States, governors of most states, and local mayors and county executives may create proposed budgets to be submitted to the appropriate legislative body for examination, amendment, and approval. These executives may be assisted by a group of experts within the executive office, as is the case with the president who is assisted by the Office of Management and Budget. The executives screen budget requests from agencies and departments and make recommendations that are put together as the executive budget document.

Excise Tax: This is an indirect tax levied on certain classes of goods and services. In many cases, the funds taken in through excise taxes are earmarked for special purposes. An excise tax may be levied on automobile tires and the monies earmarked for highway maintenance and repair.

Fair Labor Standards Act of 1938:   This law first set a minimum hourly wage (then $0.40), set a maximum working week, and prohibited employment for children less than 16 years old for corporations doing business in interstate commerce. It was the first law of its type to be permitted by the Supreme Court.

Federal Communications Commission: The FCC has a seven-member board and is an independent regulatory agency charged with controlling most forms of communication, including radio and television. It licenses radio and television stations and assigns operating frequencies.

Federal Deposit Insurance Corporation: Along with the Federal Savings and Loan Insurance Corporation, this governmentally controlled organization insures depositors' money in federally chartered banks and savings and loan institutions. State banks may join if they so wish. It is financed by assessments on its members. Both are headed by the appropriate board which includes the comptroller of the currency and two other members. They insure accounts up to $40,000.

Federal Power Commission: This independent regulatory agency has a five-member board and is designed to control interstate sale and shipments of electricity and natural gas. It also oversees hydroelectric power facilities.

Federal Register: See Chapter 6, pp. 102, 118.

Federal Reserve Notes: This is the kind of money found today and is distinguished by the green seal. Gold notes, which had gold seals, were discontinued in 1933. Silver certificates had blue seals and were not issued after 1964. The latter two monies could be redeemed in gold and silver. U.S. Notes are a by-product of the Civil War and are no longer printed. They had a red seal.

Federal Reserve System: Created in 1933 to firm up the nation's finances, the system is divided into 12 regions, each headed by a federal reserve bank. The entire system is coordinated by a seven-member board, members being appointed by the president with the consent of the Senate. Each district has a board of directors. Six directors are appointed by the banks located within that area and three are appointed by the central board. The central board regulates the currency supply, establishes banking policy, sets ethical standards for banking, and makes major decisions on credit policies. All federally chartered banks must belong to the system; state banks may elect to purchase certain services. A certain percentage of members' deposits must be kept with the Federal Reserve. The rate is set by the central board. The system charges interest to its members on monies they borrow, and this rate has some effect on general interest rates in the nation.

Federal Trade Commission: This is a five-member independent regulatory agency charged with investigating and restricting unfair business practices. It aids in preventing those corporate practices that reduce or eliminate competition. It cooperates with the Antitrust Division of the Department of Justice in many ways.

Fiscal Policy: This term is used to describe the way the government handles its own money. The way programs are funded (or not funded) and what kinds of taxes will be levied are the kinds of fiscal policy decisions that governments make. The effects of fiscal policies are felt more readily in the economy than the effects of monetary policies.

Fiscal Year: This is a special year consisting of the usual 12 months, but it may begin on any date set by law. Funding of governmental bureaucracies and programs is made for fiscal years. The federal government begins its fiscal year on October 1 and ends it on September 30. Many states use a July 1 to June 30 fiscal year.

Full Employment: Ideally, all who are physically and mentally able to work ought to be able to find employment. If all such persons were to be employed we could say that we have achieved absolute full employment. Governments assume that, for a wide variety of reasons, absolute full employment is impossible. Thus, governments may hold that full employment has been achieved when the unemployment rate falls below a certain level, often 6 percent. Since the passage of the Employment Act of 1946, the government has been charged with some responsibility for sustaining full employment. Some "full employment" bills, such as the Humphrey-Hawkins Bill, have been introduced into the Congress. These bills frequently are designed to require the government to provide employment for those unable to secure private positions. Many such jobs would be public service positions.

General Accounting Office: See Chapter 8, p. 119.

GAO Reports: The comptroller general is required, under the Legislative Reorganization Act of 1970, to send Congress monthly reports on its activities, including copies of all reports, studies, and other materials released by the General Accounting Office.

General Services Administration: See Chapter 6, p. 103.

Government Corporations: These are a hybrid mixture of government and business. Government owns and operates some business enterprise, often in competition with, or to the exclusion of, private enterprise. The Tennessee Valley Authority (TVA) is such a government corporation, selling electric power in the Tennessee Valley. States that operate such industries find they may be taxed on these operations by the federal government.

Gross National Product (GNP): This term refers to the total value of all goods and services produced in a nation in a year. To be meaningful, the GNP must be adjusted to allow for inflation. Ideally, the GNP increases yearly, indicating great material abundance.

Impoundment: Legislatures may appropriate funds, but the executive is charged with releasing or expending these monies. If the executive refuses to spend all or most money in a certain category or for certain programs, the money is said to have been impounded. Frequently, programs will be created over the executive's objections, and his response may be impoundment. The Budget and Impoundment Control Act of 1974 is designed to check presidential impoundments at the federal level. President Nixon impounded over $18 billion during his terms of office. Presidents Jefferson and Kennedy had previously impounded monies for military programs they did not agree with.

Income Tax: Since the ratification of the Sixteenth Amendment in 1913, the federal government has been permitted to tax personal incomes. This has become a primary source of federal money. Many states and some local governments have income taxes as well. This is a part of the philosophy which holds that those with the highest incomes should bear the highest taxes. Most income taxes are graduated, with increasingly higher tax percentages being collected as incomes increase.

Incomes Policies: Some governmental programs are designed to fund a portion of the economy on a rather regular basis. Programs that are designed to sustain some individuals through governmental subsidies include: workman's compensation funds, welfare programs, medicare and medicaid medical programs, social security systems, and unemployment compensation funds. In times of high unemployment these programs may be expanded. Incomes may also be controlled by special taxes, by increasing percentages of taxes collected on higher incomes, "windfall" profits taxes, and even maximum and minimum wage standards. Voluntary and compulsory wage-price guidelines may be used to control incomes also.

Indexing: This is a contractual wage system that guarantees periodic adjustments of wages to allow for inflation. After a period of time, frequently six months or a year, wages are automatically increased to allow for inflation. These adjustments are frequently given in the same percentage as the rise in cost of living. Thus, if the cost of living has risen by 7 percent, wages will rise 7 percent.

Inflation: This term refers to the decline of the purchasing power of the dollar as compared with an earlier period. For example, the purchasing power of the dollar fell by over 50 percent from 1967 to 1978. Liberal economics assumes the necessity of inflation in a capitalist economy. It is the opposite of deflation.

Intergovernmental Tax Immunity: State governments may not tax the operations or the institutions of the federal government (*McCulloch v. Maryland*, 4 Wheaton 316, 1819). The federal government likewise does not tax the ordinary operations of state and substate governments. However, the federal government has taxed certain state industries that are not necessary and ordinary functions of state governments (*South Carolina v. United States*, 199 US 437, 1905).

Keynesian Economics: Based on the thought of John Maynard Keynes (1883–1946), especially on his ideas expressed in *The General Theory of Employment, Interest and Money* (1936), the theory is the basis of liberal economic thought. It assumed that governments should tax their citizens during periods of high employment and hold the money against high periods of unemployment when governments would spend massive amounts of money on public works projects. Keynes assumed that central economic planning was necessary. He assumed that inflation was a necessary part of the capitalist system. He believed that it was possible to stabilize the capitalist economy by governmental action, and that the fluctuations of the business cycle could be controlled, if not eliminated.

Laissez-faire Economics: This French term means "leave alone." It is associated with the economic writings of Adam Smith (1723–1790), especially his *Wealth of Nations* (1776). Governments, Smith believed, could do nothing positive with the economy, so they had simply better leave it alone. Governments that interfere least work best. Today, conservatives and some libertarians still accept his ideas. Jefferson and others extended his economic ideas to politics, holding that government should interfere with the private lives of citizens as little as possible.

Matching Funds: In this kind of financial arrangement a higher level of government will extend some help to lower levels of government. The federal government may aid state or substate governments. The states may aid their counties or cities. Local governments put up a certain percentage of the costs of a project or program and this will be matched by the higher level of government. Matching fund percentages are fixed by law, but may be more or less than 50 percent.

Medicaid: This is a social welfare program designed to help the poor meet certain medical costs. It covers those poor persons not eligible for Medicare. It was first authorized in 1965 and new federal standards were set in 1967.

Medicare: First authorized in 1965, this program was initially opposed by the American Medical Association, because, it was believed, this was the first step toward socialized medicine. It is a medical insurance program for senior citizens (over age 65). It pays certain medical costs and some nursing home care costs. It is administered by the Social Security Administration and is funded by social security funds.

Monetary Policy: The Federal Reserve System makes decisions that apply to the volume of money in circulation and to the amount of money, beyond mere replacement, to be printed by the Treasury Department. These kinds of monetary decisions will not be felt by the economy for from six to nine months after the issue is decided. Increases in the money supply are said to cause inflation, but to add to employment; decreases in the money supply are said to cause deflation (or a slowing of inflation rates) while bringing about unemployment.

Monopoly: This is a restraint of trade caused by lack of competition and the control of the market by one or a few industries. In the latter case, these industries may fix prices at an artificially high level. Because of unusual circumstances, governments may grant monopolies, as with filling stations or restaurants on limited access highways. Natural monopolies are recognized in the utility fields. When governments allow monopolies to exist, they are under grave obligation to provide adequate oversight.

National Debt: The national debt comes into existence when governmental expenditures exceed income. The government must then borrow money in competition with private enterprise and state and local governments. The Congress is authorized in Article I, section 8 of the Constitution to borrow money. It raises the national debt limit, the maximum amount the government may borrow, by legislation.

National Economic Planning: Recommended by liberal or Keynesian economists, this involves governmentally mandated allocations of precious goods and services, including labor. Government is held to be a necessary partner in the economy so much so that it may dictate long-range determinations of the use of vital resources. Conservatives and libertarians reject this as being incompatible with liberty and freedom and as a major step toward socialism.

Office of Management and Budget: This is the new title for the Bureau of the Budget. The office was created within the executive office as a source of technical aid to the president in creating his budget and as a tool for oversight of the bureaucracy.

Office of Minority Business Enterprise: This is a bureau of the Department of Commerce which aids racial and linguistic minorities in establishing and maintaining their own businesses. It offers loans and technical advice.

Performance Budget: Recommended by the First Hoover Commission Report (1949), this approach to the funding of bureaucracies and programs supported by government offers monies for total programs, judging the total program effectiveness on the basis of work performed (all activities, services, and functions). The Budget and Accounting Act of 1950 was based on performance budgeting. The assumption is that funds ought to be provided for those programs which are effective while funds would be withdrawn from those which are ineffective. All expenses, including salaries, current expenses, and the like, are drawn from a single a appropriation, instead of having separate line items for each category of expense.

Phillips Curve: In 1958 British economist A. W. Phillips offered a working hypothesis to show a correlation between unemployment/ employment and inflation/deflation. He assumed that as employment increased so did inflation; as unemployment increased, the rate of inflation decreased, and, at times, mild deflation occurred. In times of full employment, employers bid for the services of skilled workers, driving the price of labor up and accelerating inflation. In time of high unemployment, salaries need not be so high and labor costs decline decreasing the rate of inflation. Phillips concluded that full employment was incompatible with price stability.

Planning, Programming, and Budgeting System (PPBS): President Lyndon Johnson favored this form of budgeting, and President Nixon's "management by objectives" was based on it. Agencies were required to create priorities for programs and other bureaucratic expenses. The objectives of various programs were to be stated in terms of the total resources needed to carry them into execution. Agencies were to define their objectives clearly in economic terms. Whole programs were to be stated in terms of total cost. Programs could then, it was assumed, be more easily assessed by the Office of Management and Budget and by the Congress.

Political Economy: This idea assumes that government and the economy are mutually interpenetrating and mutually supportive. This science studies this inter-relationship. It assumes that there are no meaningful or definable boundaries between the two.

Postaudit: These are periodic inspections carried out by an agency of the executive or legislature to determine if monies appropriated for programs and other expenses have actually been expended for the mandated purposes. The auditing agency can determine if the problem to be solved or the program to be carried out has actually accomplished its stated purposes. Such an audit can also determine if the goods and services purchased have actually been delivered.

Preaudit: This is a check on requests for expenditures. The agency determines if the money requested seems to be within the limits set by the legislative appropriation. The auditor also determines if there is money available in the account on which the check is to be written. If the request appears to be legitimate, and if money is available, the request is approved.

Profit-Push Inflation: If only one or a few industries control a market for a type of product or service they may set artificially high prices for those services or products, thereby increasing corporate profits. Corporations may sell goods or services back and forth to one another, creating a "daisy chain" of sales. These chains are designed to give each partner a profit while raising the cost of goods. A true competitive market precludes the possibility of this kind of inflation.

Public Service Jobs: Many believe that if individuals are seeking jobs in the private sector but are unable to find work, then it is the obligation of government to create jobs for them. Such jobs will frequently be in the public sector, providing services that otherwise would not be offered. Such jobs might include: cleaning up the environment, cutting forest fire trails, building retaining walls, clearing brush from along highways, and building and maintaining public facilities. Some public service programs have provided extra manpower to local communities for fire, ambulance, and police duties.

Public Utility: This is a natural monopoly, created by governmental decree and regulated by special public regulatory bodies. Many believe that governments do not create natural monopolies, but rather recognize, by appropriate laws, their existence. They cannot exist as monopolies unless given such legal status. Governments assume that it would be useless to have several competing firms offering utility services, such as telephones, power, and water, in the same geographic area. Thus, utilities are granted monopoly status and are regulated by public utility or public services commissions.

Rebate: At times, governments may choose to refund all or a portion of some tax collected from individuals or corporations. The federal government in the past has rebated excise taxes on new automobiles and portions of individual income taxes. President Carter's first tax proposals in 1977 emphasized tax rebates instead of permanent tax reductions.

Recession: This is the modern term for an economic slowdown. In prior years other terms had been used, such as depression or panic. One indication of a recession would be a decline in the gross national product.

Regressive Taxation: If one assumes that taxes ought to fall most heavily on those best able to pay, then taxes that fall equally on all, or taxes that fall most heavily on those least able to pay, are regressive. Progressive taxes are based on the ability to pay. A true regressive tax falls more heavily, or proportionately more heavily, on the poor. A food tax is a relatively regressive form of taxation as the poor are forced to spend proportionately more of their income on food.

Regulatory Tax: Most taxes are levied to raise revenue. In this form of tax, however, the focus of attention is on the desired effect rather than on the raising of revenue. Such taxes may be imposed to curtail a certain activity, such as a tax imposed by the federal government on state bank notes. The purpose of that tax was to destroy state bank notes rather than to raise money. A tariff may be levied on foreign goods to protect American industries rather than to seek monies collected from the tax.

Restraint of Trade: Capitalism is assumed to operate best and most efficiently when it is competitive and the market is open to all who produce a certain type of goods or service. Those factors that alter or change this free competition are said to operate in restraint of trade. Some such operations include: interlocking directorates, price cutting, price fixing, and merging with competitors. The Sherman and Clayton Acts seek to control business operations that restrain or eliminate competition.

Revenue Sharing: A higher level of government may seek to distribute a portion of its income or existing assests with a lower level of government. Commonly, the federal government shares a portion of its income with state and local governments. This practice was authorized under the State and Local Fiscal Assistance Act of 1972 and is called the General Revenue Sharing Program (GRS). Revenue sharing grants money to state and local governments without attaching conditions and thus differs from specific grants given under the grants-in-aid programs wherein conditions of construction and performance are required.

Sales Tax: This is a tax levied on the wholesale or, more commonly, the retail, price of goods and services. It is collected by the seller on the final price of the goods or services. There is no national sales tax, but most states obtain much of their funding from such a tax. A sales tax may be levied on certain goods or it may be levied on all, or nearly all, goods and services.

Sectors: These are major divisions of political and/or economic activity within the nation. One often refers to capitalist enterprises as the "private sector." Governments are commonly called the "public sector." Some liberal and radical analyses assume that distinctions between the two are only artificial, not real, divisions. Conservatives and libertarians generally assume that the divisions between the two are real.

Securities and Exchange Commission: This is a five-member independent regulatory commission created by the Securities Exchange Act of 1934 to watch over, and set standards for, the selling of stocks and other, similar securities. It has jurisdiction over several other laws, including the Securties Act of 1933 and the Public Utility Holding Company Act of 1935. It seeks to prevent the sale of valueless ("blue sky") investments.

Self-Fulfilling Economic Prophecy: There is an underlying psychological assumption made here that people will act as they are told to act. If the nation is told to expect good times, the people will purchase goods and service and invest money. Corporations will expand their activities and merchants will increase their stocks. All of these things will then provide good times. If, conversely, people are convinced that bad times lie ahead they will save their money, waiting to buy goods until a later date.

Merchants will not restock their shelves and businesses will restrict investments. All of these things will tend to produce recessions and depressions. Thus, the prophecy will fulfill itself because of what it has caused to happen.

Severance Tax: This is a tax levied on raw materials at the time they are removed from their natural state. Several states tax coal and other raw materials at the time they are prepared for market. There have been several proposals for national severance taxes on coal, with the money earmarked for restoration of strip mines and closing of abandoned deep mines.

Sherman Antitrust Act of 1890: As amended, this is the basic law that seeks to control monopolistic practices in the marketplace. It seeks to break up cartels and monopolies that operate in restraint of trade. After initial failures, it has worked well in its avowed purpose.

Sixteenth Amendment: Adopted in 1913, this alteration of the Constitution allowed for direct taxes to be levied on personal and corporate incomes. It altered Article I, section 9, of the Constitution which required that taxes be levied according to the population of states.

Small Business Adminstration: First authorized in 1953 and fully funded in 1958, this agency was designed to provide loans to business enterprises that had been denied conventional loans from commercial establishments. It provides small businesspersons with disaster aid, certain types of technical expertise, and help in obtaining government contracts.

Social Security Act of 1935: See Chapter 9, p. 176.

Standing Appropriation: Taxes are frequently levied for a particular purpose with those monies all being earmarked for that use. Gasoline taxes may be used for highway maintenance and construction. These standing appropriations remain in force until repealed.

Subsidy: Governments are frequently asked to underwrite the costs of some business venture. Such monies, when appropriated, are called subsidies. At times, the public purpose may be affected by subsidies. Government may underwrite some portion of the cost of a new ocean liner with the attached condition that it be built so that it may be converted to military use in event of war. Some foreign governments may subsidize the costs of trade goods to better their foreign exchange position or decrease their balance of trade deficits.

Tax Exemption: This is an immunity granted to a person or institution from certain types of taxes. Most educational, scientific, charitable, and civic organizations are granted immunities from many taxes. Most, if not all, their incomes may be exempted from federal income taxes. Special tax exemptions may be granted to veterans, the elderly, the poor, or the handicapped.

Treasurer of the United States: This person heads this Department of the Treasury, a Cabinet level position created in 1789 to assist the president in many fiscal matters. He manages the national debt, collects many taxes and internal revenues, and signs our money. He supervises the operations of the U.S. Mint, which coins money, and the Bureau of Printing and Engraving, which prints paper money. The Secret Service comes under his jurisdiction.

Value-Added Tax: This is a new name for the *ad valorem* tax that has been used in Europe for many decades. It taxes goods at each step of production and thus is an indirect sales tax.

CASES

Ashwander v. T.V.A. (297 US 288, 1936): See Chapter 8, p. 154.

Bailey v. Drexel (259 US 20, 1922): This case established the principle that the federal government has a power to tax which is broader than its power to regulate. The Congress may establish its taxing powers in areas wholly beyond its power to regulate. When it chooses to tax in an area wherein it may not regulate, it must clearly establish that its purpose is to raise revenue and not to regulate through taxation. The true purpose of the law is thus crucial to the courts when they judicially review such legislation. A revenue-raising tax is permitted in many areas where a regulatory tax would not be permitted.

Knox v. Lee (12 Wallace 457, 1871): In this and similar cases, the Supreme Court recognized the power of Congress to establish the value of our money, and its power to make a number of things, paper money included, the legal tender of the land. The states are forbidden to make anything but gold and silver legal tender, but the Congress is not subjected to that limitation. The power Congress has to coin money includes the power to print paper money.

Massachusetts v. Mellon (262 US 447, 1923): See Chapter 3, p. 43.

McCulloch v. Maryland (4 Wheaton 316, 1819): See Chapter 3, pp. 36, 43.

Pollock v. Farmers Loan and Trust Co. (158 US 601, 1895): In this case the Supreme Court struck down laws authorizing federal income taxes. It was invalidated by the ratification of the Sixteenth Amendment, which authorized the federal collection of such taxes.

Steward Machine Co. v. Davis (301 US 548, 1937): See Chapter 3, p. 45.

U.S. v. Butler (297 US 1, 1937): See Chapter 3, p. 45.

Veazie Bank v. Fenno (8 Wallace 544, 1869): The Congress wished to drive state bank notes out of existence, and replace them with federal paper money. It thus levied an annual regulatory tax of 10 percent on all outstanding notes. The Supreme Court recognized this tax as a regulatory tax (and not one designed to raise revenue primarily) and allowed such activity in areas proper to the purpose of Congress.

Welton v. Missouri (91 US 275, 1876): See Chapter 3, p. 46.

11

International and Military Affairs

Absolute Economic Advantage: Based on the economic thought of Adam Smith, this theory assumes that each major nation possesses some absolute (not merely relative) economic advantage in the manufacture of one or more products. Each nation should then concentrate on the production of those goods and services for which it has such an absolute advantage. Goods that the nation can produce less efficiently should be imported from those nations that manufacture them at such an absolute economic advantage. This free trade of goods and services creates an interdependent world trade system wherein the nations would choose to live in peace and prosperity instead of being at war with one another.

Agency for International Development (AID): This is a semi-independent arm of the U.S. State Department designed to grant technical assistance and economic aid to foreign states. It was created in 1961 under the AID Act, as a part of President Kennedy's New Frontier programs related to foreign countries known as the "Alliance for Progress." It was financed with large sums of money under Kennedy and Lyndon Johnson, but its funds have been cut considerably since 1968.

Aggression: The world community seems to be unable to arrive at a definition of aggression that suits even most members. To political scientists who need to deal only with abstractions, aggression is the unprovoked attack on the homes, persons, and properties of people living in another state by a sovereign power. Both the United Nations and the League of

Nations condemned aggression. The Korean police action is the one forceful act by international organization designed to stop an act of aggression.

Alliance: Sovereign states frequently enter into treaties of mutual assistance with one another to provide mutual defense against acts of aggression by outside powers. Such bipartisan or multipartisan arrangements are called alliances. Occasionally, the term will be used in a non-military context, such as in the "Alliance for Progress." Examples of mutual defense alliances are NATO and SEATO.

Alliance for Progress: This term covers the majority of foreign aid programs announced in 1961 by President Kennedy as the international phase of the New Frontier. It specifically has been applied to inter-American relations. All Western Hemisphere powers except Cuba have participated in Alliance for Progress programs.

Ambassador: This is the title given to the ranking diplomat sent to represent a state in a foreign state. Occasionally, it is used as the title of the ranking diplomat sent to some nonsovereign or international or multinational meeting or organization. In the United States, ambassadors are nominated by the president and must be approved by two-thirds of the Senate. In the past ambassadors were often appointed to fulfill political debts. Today, most are career and highly trained diplomats.

Antidumping Act of 1921: This act, as amended, is the basic tool used by the government to prevent the importation of cheaply priced foreign goods in competition with more costly American-made goods. Many foreign nations pay labor at rates far below the salaries paid to American workers and thus are able to undersell American-made goods. Some foreign governments subsidize the prices of goods sent abroad in order to gain foreign exchanges. The act is designed to protect the jobs of American workers and American industries.

ANZUS: This is the multipartite agreement for mutual assistance and protection signed by the United States, Australia and New Zealand in 1951. It recognizes the interdependence of the English speaking nations in the Pacific Ocean.

Appeasement: This term is universally associated with the policies of British Prime Minister Neville Chamberlain in granting territorial demands of Hitler rather than using force to stop his aggression. It is properly used to describe the policies of states in granting the demands of any potential aggressor rather than using force to stop the aggression. Today, diplomats often feel that if they make concessions to potential enemies in negotiating treaties, they will be charged with taking the route of appeasement.

Arbitration: As in its domestic use, arbitration in the international arena suggests the use of impartial and disinterested judges or referees to settle disputes. In many ways the various international and regional courts are courts of arbitration because they lack the power to enforce their judgments. Many disputes are settled by arbitration and many more could be settled if sovereign states would allow the use of this device.

Attache: These are minor diplomats who are stationed at embassies or consulates to provide assistance in a variety of matters. They are frequently career diplomats or civil servants. Frequently, they are stationed at embassies at the request of foreign governments. Technical assistance provided by attaches includes military advice.

Autarky: This is the formal term used to describe a policy of establishing economic self-sufficiency. It is opposed to such ideas as free trade and absolute or comparative economic advantage. A national practicing autarky seeks to provide itself with all the goods and services needed by the state and its citizens. This is considered especially advantageous in war time. With modern technology most modern, industrial states can synthesize many, if not all, those things that they do not have naturally. Other vital materials may be kept by governments in strategic stockpiles.

Balance of Power: This is an older theory of international relations, practiced by the states of Europe during the 18th and 19th centuries. These nations sought to establish an equilibrium between the two competing camps, with England traditionally playing the role of balancing agent. World War I marked the end of the classic balance of power in Europe. Today, one might speak more reasonably of a "balance of terror."

Balance of Terror: The world is divided primarily into two competing camps, the capitalist and the Communist. Each has the wherewithal to destroy the other, and, perhaps, also the entire world. Each camp has nuclear weapons with ballistic missile delivery systems. Each camp holds the other in terror. President Eisenhower's secretary of state, John Foster Dulles, developed the basic American strategy out of the balance of terror: no modern nation would risk all-out, nuclear war. Thus, the United States had merely to maintain its nuclear superiority over its enemies and no future world war would be fought. No nation could expect to fight and win a nuclear war, and thus they would not risk mutual destruction.

Balance of Trade: Ideally, each nation ought to export as many goods and services as it imports. Few nations achieve such a balance. Most nations import more than they export (negative or unfavorable trade balance) while a few export more than they import (favorable trade balance). Unfavorable trade balances may undermine confidence in, and erode the value of, the nation's money. Favorable trade balances tend to strengthen a nation's money on the international market.

Battle Act: See *Mutual Defense Assistance Control Act of 1951*, Chapter 11, p. 223.

Bipartisan Foreign Policy: While political parties may argue over domestic policies, they tend to agree on foreign policy matters. This seems to be generally true irrespective of the politics of the president and of the majority of Congress. In times of international turmoil, especially in war time, partisan politics are forgotten and both parties tend to support a unified foreign policy. One indication of this bipartisanship is seen by the fact that less than 1 percent of all treaties negotiated by all presidents have been rejected by the Senate. There is usually bipartisan support given to alliances and to our action in the United Nations and in other international or regional organizations.

Central Intelligence Agency: The CIA functions under the National Security Council, an executive department. It is headed by a director appointed by the president with the consent of the Senate. It coordinates all American intelligence operations and evaluates the data collected by them. Since it was charged with planning assassinations of foreign leaders and with domestic surveillance, it has been carefully watched over by the select congressional committee. Its budget and operations are still secret, even from most members of the Congress.

Central Treaty Organization (CENTO): Formerly known as the Bagdad Pact, CENTO is a multiparty mutual defense and mutual assistance treaty involving the nations of the Middle East. Members include Great Britain, Turkey, Pakistan, and Iran. It is supported military and financially by the United States.

Charge d'Affaires: This is a person who is temporarily in charge of a diplomatic mission in a foreign nation when an ambassador is not present. This person assumes responsibility when an ambassador has been withdrawn, has died, or when the office is vacant. At times an ambassador may be withdrawn to show his or her nation's displeasure with some policy of the foreign nation, but a charge d'affaires is maintained so that the diplomatic mission is not wholly closed and relations are not completely severed.

Civil Defense: Most modern nations have created emergency and disaster-preparedness units which can act in a variety of emergencies. They are primarily designed to provide basic services in the event of a war, but they can be mobilized to handle a variety of other disasters. In the United States, the civil defense system is managed by the Defense Civil Preparedness Agency, part of the Department of Defense. It maintains a shelter system, and emergency food and water supplies. Using volunteers, it provides training in a variety of emergency skills and it cooperates with adjunct agencies such as the American Red Cross, and ambulance and fire departments.

Civilian Control of the Military: The Founding Fathers warned against the evils of an unrestrained military establishment and many objected to a standing army. They demanded republican safeguards from what they considered a potentially dictatorial power, a strong and uncontrolled military. Thus, civilian control over the military was guaranteed by making the president the head of the nation's armed forces; by giving Congress control over the military budget; and by limiting military appropriation to a maximum of two years. The military was further limited by guaranteeing the people the right to keep and bear arms and by granting the states the right to keep militia (Second Amendment). Under the Third Amendment troops may not ordinarily be stationed in private homes. Statutory laws have required that civilians head certain departments, such as the Department of Defense. An example of the civilian control of the military can be found in the firing of General MacArthur by President Truman during the Korean War.

Collective Security: In theory, all states have renounced the use of war and aggression in foreign policy. The idea of collective security, as found in the U.N. Charter, suggests that all nations are peace-loving, and that they would take immediate action against any aggressor. No acts of aggression would then take place, for all nations would fear the collective power of the whole community of nations. Only rarely can international bodies agree on what is aggressive behavior. Some nations then seek protection through regional collective security arrangements such as ANZUS or NATO.

Comity: The nations of the world extend certain courtesies to one another, such as immunity to diplomatic personnel. These acts are collectively known as comity. While not ordinarily guaranteed under enforcable international law, they are based in the good will of nations.

Comparative Economic Advantage: Based on the economic theories of David Ricardo, the theory of comparative economic advantage assumes that each nation can produce certain goods and services more efficiently than other products. A nation ought to concentrate on the production of such items, trading these in the international market for other goods and services which it produces less efficiently. It further assumes that few nations possess an absolute advantage in the production of some items, as compared with other nations. It opposes economic self-sufficiency [autarky].

Competing Ideologies: This is primarily associated with the Soviet Marxist ideology as taught by Nikita Khrushchev. He held that there were two competing forms of economic thought, communism and capitalism, and that communism would defeat capitalism in peaceful competition because communism is more efficient. The United States has also attempted to export its capitalist ideology, claiming that it is more efficient and better suited to maintaining freedom. In reality most of the competition between the two competing ideologies has been of a military nature.

Consulate: These are offices established by sovereign states in major cities of the world to aid their nationals who travel in foreign nations, to promote trade, and to assist in other areas of foreign relations. They are subordinate to embassies and are staffed by career diplomats.

Counterinsurgency: This is a military type of operation directed against revolutionary and terrorists groups that threaten political regimes and lives and property of citizens. It is one of the primary roles assigned to national guard and army units in many nations. The United States frequently aids in training foreign military and paramilitary units in counterinsurgency warfare.

Declaration of War: This is a formal notification by one sovereign state to another that a state of war exists between them. Theoretically, all wars are to be declared prior to the commencement of hostilities, but this is not always done. In the United States, the president is charged with addressing the Congress in joint session to ask for a declaration of war if he deems it necessary. We have frequently done this even after we have been attacked, as in the case of the declaration of war against Japan after Pearl Harbor.

De Facto Recognition: New states come into existence, usually as a result of the withdrawal of a colonial power, or after they have separated from an existing state. Once they have established sovereign power, most nations of the world recognize that, in fact, a new state has been born or that, in fact, a new regime has taken control, as is the case after a successful revolution or seizure of power. Even if a state withholds formal or legal recognition, as the United States did with China after the Chinese revolution was completed in 1949, it must still recognize that, by fact and deed, the new regime or state exercises the major aspects of sovereignty.

De Jure Recognition: This is the formal or legal recognition of the sovereignty of a new regime or state by a foreign power. It is generally accompanied by the exchange of ambassadors. *De Jure* recognition may take place long after a regime has established control over the land and its people.

Devaluation: The currency of one nation is related, for purposes of relative valuation, to either gold or the currency of one or more other sovereign states. Since the gold standard has been abandoned by most states, currencies are most frequently valued relative to other currencies. A nation that has long-run trade deficit will frequently find its currency devalued on foreign money exchanges. Many nations allow their currencies to "float," meaning that they do little or nothing to maintain its value while allowing other nations to determine the relative value of their currency. In recent years the American dollar has been devalued against the Japanese yen, reflecting, among other things, the trade deficit we have with Japan. A government may choose, on its own, to try to reduce imports and increase exports, by devaluing its currency.

Detente: This French term is used to describe an atmosphere of mutual understanding between two sovereign states. It is an atmosphere that permits mutual trade, conclusion of treaties, and general agreement on many matters of mutual concern.

Diplomacy: This ancient art is aimed at concluding peaceful relations among the world community of nations. If carried on by heads of state, it is called summit diplomacy. If negotiated by deputy heads of state, it is known as subsummit diplomacy. Diplomacy is best left to the professionals, either in foreign affairs or state department offices, or to special negotiators. Some states have mastered diplomacy to such a degree that, by diplomatic skills, they have actually increased their power. Wars occur when traditional diplomacy fails.

Domino Theory: Credited to President Eisenhower, this theory holds that if one nation of Asia were to fall to communism, the others would fall, one after another, "Like a row of dominoes." It is a part of the theory of the containment of communism. The theory was accepted by Presidents Kennedy and Johnson who tried to prevent the first domino, South Vietnam, from falling to Communist aggression.

Executive Agreement: See Chapter 5, p. 80.

Extradition: This is the process of rendering up alleged criminals and fugitives from justice from one sovereign state to another. Extradition is usually established by treaty. States may refuse to deliver such persons, especially if they are held to be political refugees fleeing from oppression. Within the 50 states this process is correctly called rendition.

Favorable Balance of Trade: Sovereign nations trade goods and services with other sovereign nations. If a state sells more goods and services than it purchases on the foreign market, it is said to have established a favorable trade balance. A favorable trade balance tends to strengthen a nation's currency.

Foreign Aid: This is a kind of international charity given by the richer nations to the poorer ones. In granting foreign aid, states may require certain performances by the nation benefiting from the aid, such as guarantees of human rights. Aid may be given in money, as goods and services, or as military or technical advice. The United States has long granted aid to underdeveloped and emerging nations.

Free Trade: Associated with the economic theories of Adam Smith (1723–1790) the idea advanced here is that nations ought to avoid placing trade restrictions, such as tariffs or quotas, on goods imported from foreign nations. Locally produced goods and services should be required to compete with foreign items in a free and unrestricted market. It is opposed to protectionism, wherein artifical trade barriers are erected by governmental action. Free trade would force nations to pursue their absolute economic advantages.

Gulf of Tonkin Resolution: This joint resolution of Congress underwrote President Johnson's use of American forces in Southeast Asia, especially in South Vietnam. Recent publication of the "Pentagon Papers" has indicated that information provided by the Johnson administration related to how and why we became involved there was in error.

Hegemony: This term describes the considerable influence exercised by one nation over one or more other nations. There are mininations throughout the world which owe their existences to the support and protection of a major power. To the degree that these major states exercise control over their client states they can be said to be exercising hegemony over them.

Immunity: A part of comity, diplomatic immunity means that foreign diplomats, staff, and their families cannot be prosecuted under the laws of their host state unless special permission is granted from their home nation. It also allows their embassies to be free from governmental interference and searches.

Intelligence: This is the process of fact-finding and information gathering carried on by one sovereign state in regard to another sovereign nation. Most information is gathered by analyzing foreign newspapers, journals, public and private documents, and other published sources. Some information is gathered clandestinely by "cloak and dagger" methods and spying. The Central Intelligence Agency (CIA) is the principal department concerned with intelligence in this nation.

International Court of Justice: Commonly called the World Court, this tribunal is a part of the United Nations. It was established in 1945 and sits at the Hague, Netherlands. It has 15 judges appointed by the General Assembly of the United Nations. It has little power to enforce its decisions other than moral persuasion. It may give advisory opinions to the United Nations or its agencies and it may interpret the U.N. Charter. Primarily, it seeks to interpret that body of international morality called international law.

international Law: This is a body of knowledge which seeks to regulate the conduct of sovereign nations and to establish peace through law. It consists of the practices of nations, treaties and other international acts, and the U.N. Charter. To some degree it is established by the learned writings of international law scholars. Excepting its use in domestic courts, there really is no power to be used to enforce its provisions.

Internationalism: This theory rejects the one-state self-sufficiency of isolationism and holds that all states are part of a great international community wherein members have grave obligations to other states. It generally accepts the idea of containment of aggression and peace through collective security. It practices foreign aid to less fortunate states and cooperates with international organizations, such as the United Nations. Many believe that one day, inevitably, sovereign states will be replaced with one world government.

Isolationism: This theory rejects internationalism and formal ties with foreign states. It holds that each nation must exist as a separate, sovereign entity. It rejects international organizations and international law, except as used in domestic courts. It holds that each state has obligations only to its own people, and thus it practices charity in the international sphere only when it chooses to do so. The geographical separation of this nation from Asia and Europe allowed us to practice isolationism with little difficulty during the interwar period.

League of Nations: Founded by the victorious allies (United States, Britain, France and Italy) after World War I as a means of preventing future wars, the League ranks as the first major collective security arrangement in the modern world. Although it was based on suggestions made during the war by President Woodrow Wilson, the United States was not among the 63 nations that joined. It had an assembly, a world court (Permanent Court of International Justice), and a secretariat, all of which were quite similar to their counterparts in the United Nations. By the mid-1930s it had failed as a result of several unchecked incidents of aggression (Japan in Manchuria in 1931 and Italy in Abyssinia in 1935), growing Fascist, Nazi, and Japanese aggressive tactics, and general apathy of its members. Some of its adjunct organizations survive and its spirit is today found in the United Nations.

Levees en Masse: This principle of international law allows local citizens to resist, as an unorganized army, invasion or aggression, terrorism, or revolutionary movements. This is a part of the idea of the local militia or the citizen-soldier principle. It is practiced today by citizen-soldiers in Israel on a regular basis.

Limited War: Wars have traditionally been fought to a final conclusion, to victory or defeat. Modern strategists predict the use of wars for limited purposes as an alternative to nuclear holocaust. The police action in Korea was designed only to free South Korea, not to liberate North Korea or to destroy Communist China. Some limited wars may be planned only to give token resistance to an invading enemy.

Marshall Plan: See Chapter 5, p. 84.

Mediation: An international leader may choose to try to end war or other conflict between two sovereign states by negotiating and by mediating the dispute. President Theodore Roosevelt won a Nobel Peace Prize for mediating the war between Japan and Russia in 1905.

Military Government: The military is usually disinterested in the politics of a nation, but it may choose to move in and assume power if it believes that a revolution is about to create anarchy. In many underdeveloped and emerging nations, political power will often rest on the support of the military. Military governments seldom do more than maintain the status quo for a period of time, returning power to civil governments when the crisis has passed. Military governments are frequently charged with violations of human rights in that they may seek to destroy revolutionary movements and terrorism.

Military-Industrial Complex: This term was coined by President Eisenhower to describe the relationship between the Pentagon (armed force) and industrial leaders (corporations) which seeks to spend ever more money on weapons systems. The increased budget gives the Pentagon power and it gives corporations large profits.

Militia: These are the citizen-soldiers of a state. They receive some basic military training, and can be mobilized quickly in an emergency. Many of the Founding Fathers felt that the militia ought to be the primary defense of the state and opposed a standing army.

Mobilization: Frequently associated with the calling of people to arms in order to meet the enemy, actually the term implies the mustering of resources of many kinds, people included, to meet any emergency. One may mobilize precious resources after a natural disaster. The Office of Emergency Preparedness is used to mobilize disaster services.

Monroe Doctrine: Actually prepared by Secretary of State John Quincy Adams, this famous "doctrine" was given by President Monroe on December 2, 1823, as a part of his State of the Union message. It has been added to and interpreted by nearly every president since Monroe. It closed the Western Hemisphere to colonization and aggressive actions, including the reclamation of former colonies, by European powers. It provided a special interest zone for the United States, the Western Hemisphere, and, at the same time, restricted our active foreign relations rather effectively to this hemisphere. Originally, it was backed by British sea power.

Most Favored Nation: Most nations import substantial amounts of goods and services from other nations. Frequently, tax structures are set in such a way as to permit several different levels of taxation on the same type of goods. Most favored nation status guarantees that the tax to be levied will be the lowest rate accorded any foreign nation on a given good or service.

Multinational Corporation: In the past the word "cartel" was used to describe a corporation that had major offices, and conducted business, in several or many foreign nations. More recently, the term "multinational corporation" has been used. Some liberal and radical analyses of American foreign relations have concluded that our foreign policy is dictated by such corporations in keeping with their economic interests.

Mutual Defense Assistance Control Act of 1951: Commonly known as the Battle Act, this law prohibited trade with Communist nations in strategic goods and services, Further, it prohibited most trade with other nations engaged in trade of strategic goods with Communist block countries. The president is authorized to make certain exceptions.

Mutual Deterrence: This theory was developed under President Truman and was perfected by President Nixon's secretary of defense, Melvin Laird. It holds that atomic weapons are the ultimate weapons which cannot be countered. The United States, and all other nations that possess nuclear weapons, will never make war on one another because of the fear of mutual destruction. So long as we retain an arsenal of nuclear weapons and a system capable of delivering these to the enemy's homeland, war will be averted. This nearly makes the foot soldier and most conventional weapons systems obsolete.

National Guard: This term refers to the enrolled and trained militia, as opposed, on the one hand, to standing armies, and, on the other hand, to unenrolled citizen-soldier militias. Most nations have some sort of trained militia system. Many are trained in counterinsurgency warfare and in civic actions projects, such as road and bridge construction. In the United States the militia system is given to the states, although the national guard units may be called into federal service.

Nationalization: Many multinational corporations invest in facilities in emerging nations. Local industries are owned by local or foreign investers. Radical changes in political regimes or systems may bring about public ownership of such industrial facilities through the process of nationalization.

National Interest: Developed from the political philosophy of Niccolo Machiavelli (1426–1527), this theory holds that there is a definable national interest which ought to be served by domestic, and especially foreign policy. The national interest is what is in the best interests of the people and their political system, and it differs from one state to another. The national interest of one state may clash directly with the same national interest of another state, leading to war. Today, political scientists are uncertain as to the definition of the national interest or its usefulness as an explanatory term.

Neutral: In wartime a neutral is a state that is not involved in the war on either side. Some states like Switzerland have declared their permanent neutrality in all wars. Such neutrality, of course, can be violated by an aggressor at any time. In the modern world many "third world nations" have declared themselves to be uninvolved in the ideological and economic, and, possibly, military, struggles between the capitalist and Communist blocs.

Nixon Doctrine: Sometimes called the "Guam Doctrine" because it was first suggested at a press conference on that island in 1969, the doctrine as fully developed limits American aid and involvement in wars to allied states. Nixon indicated that, after the Vietnam War, the United States would rarely, if ever, commit American combat troops to contain

Communist expansion. He invited other nations to ally themselves with us, promising to protect them under our "nuclear umbrella" if they were threatened with nuclear aggression. Although we would try to aid all nations resisting aggression from communism, following the Truman Doctrine, we expected that they would provide the maximum effort from their own resources.

North Atlantic Treaty Organization (NATO): This mutual defense pact was created by the North Atlantic Treaty of 1949 as a anti-Communist, defensive alliance, including, principally, the United States and its Western European allies. Members include: United States, Belgium, Canada, Denmark, Netherlands, Iceland, Italy, Luxemburg, West Germany, Greece, Turkey, Portugal, Norway, and Great Britain. France withdrew in 1966. Greece effectively withdrew in 1974. NATO spawned other multilateral mutual-defense pacts such as SEATO, ANZUS, and CENTO. The Warsaw Pact among Communist states in East Europe and USSR was a reaction to NATO.

No Win War: This is a war for limited objectives, but it differs from limited wars because the nations supporting one side are prepared to lose the war if necessary. This kind of war generally involves major foreign powers that are supporting two sides in a basically civil war. Many hold that Secretary of State Henry Kissinger was quite prepared to lose the war in South Vietnam, although he was committed to making some military commitments in order to impress our allies and show that we honored treaty obligations wtih our allies. There is much in many of Dr. Kissinger's books (published before he assumed national office) which would justify this conclusion, for he speaks of wars we can "afford to lose."

Organization of American States (OAS): This regional organization includes Western Hemisphere powers, principally the United State and 21 Central and Latin American states. It was created by the Bogota Conference of 1948 to provide for peaceful relations and peaceful settlement of disputes among members. The OAS implemented the Pact of Rio of 1947, which is a mutual defense alliance among OAS membership. The OAS backed, generally, American intervention in the Dominican Republic in 1965.

Petrodollars: This term refers to money earned by the sale of oil by those emerging nations belonging to the Organization of Petroleum Exporting Countries (OPEC). Many of these states have accumulated billions

of dollars in foreign exchange from the advanced nations that are dependent on them for oil. Some petro-dollars are invested in land, bonds, and
stocks in industrial nations, while other monies are used to buy goods,
services, technical aid, and military hardware.

Police Action: This term is used often to describe military action
against an aggressor which is something less than war. United Nations
involvement in Korea is often described as a police action, although many
found it difficult to distinguish from a real war.

Policy of the Containment of Communism: The general policy
of containing communism and preventing its expansion into new areas is
associated with President Truman's secretary of state, Dean Acheson. It
was perfected by President Eisenhower's secretary of state, John Foster
Dulles. One assumption made here is that if communism is contained, it
will collapse from internal pressures and revolutions. By containing communism, Dulles hoped to encourage revolutions in Communist bloc nations. One such revolution occurred in Hungary in 1956, but the United
States was unable or unwilling to capitalize on it. One might view this
containment theory in terms of geopolitics. Communism controls the
"heartland" of the World Island (that is, Europe-Asia-Africa). The United
States sought to control the rimland of the World Island by ringing the
"heartland" with bases from Norway to Korea. The wars in Korea and
Vietnam may be viewed as necessary actions in the containment theory.

Quid pro Quo: This Latin term means "this for that." In international negotiations one must give up something in order to get something
else. If progress is to be made in international affairs states must be prepared to bargain with one another in a "take and give" arrangement.

Rio Pact of 1947: Formerly known as the Inter-American Treaty of
Reciprocal Assistance, this multipartite arrangement is a mutual-defense
treaty for the Western Hemisphere nations, including the United States
and 21 Central and Latin American states. Cuba was expelled in 1962 for
promoting Communist aggression against its neighbors. Several nations
objected to the 1965 invasion of the Dominician Republic by the United
States, with the nominal cooperation of most members, to quell a possible
Communist revolution.

Sanction: Especially designed to discourage aggression, sanctions
are acts taken against an aggressor by other nations of the world community or by international organizations, but short of war. Sanctions usually

involve embargoes against shipments of strategic goods and services to aggressors. The League of Nations sought to contain Fascist aggression in Ethopia and Japanese aggression against China (Manchuria) by using sanctions. These actions were ineffective. Sanctions may also be used against states that repress human rights, as in the case of American embargoes against certain types of trade with Rhodesia.

Southeast Asia Treaty Organization (SEATO): This organization was created by the Southeast Asia Collective Defense Treaty of 1954, and its membership include United States, Great Britain, New Zealand, France, Pakistan, Australia, Philippines, and Thailand. It was created as a necessary part of the containment of communism, and of the ringing of Communist states, by mutual-defense alliances and was the handiwork of President Eisenhower's secretary of state, John Foster Dulles. American involvement in Vietnam could be justified, in part, by secret (protocol) portions of SEATO. Some SEATO members sent token forces to Vietnam under the treaty.

Sovereignty: See Chapter 1, p. 17.

Strategic Arms Limitations Talks (SALT): In 1969 the United States and the Soviet Union began negotiations aimed at limiting weapons systems within these two sovereign states by treaty arrangement. Between 1969 and 1972 some progress was made and a treaty concluded (SALT I). The guidelines for SALT II were established by President Nixon and Soviet First Party Secretary Brezhnev in 1973. These are the first halting step toward major disarmament and toward defusing the nuclear threat.

Strategic Stockpiling: Most modern nations realize that they must have certain supplies of raw materials accumulated in case of an international emergency, such as war; or in case those nations producing these materials should interrupt deliveries. They also realize that they must retain supplies of vital and scarce materials, such as gold, in case of some emergency. Thus, governments maintain and control significant amounts of such goods as their strategic stockpiles.

Strategy: This involves broad and general planning of courses of action to be used by nation-states in international affairs. The containment of communism has been one broad strategy to which this nation is committed. In military affairs, strategy involves long-range and broad planning in the use of the nation's armed forces. In this nation, the president plans strategy with his key military and civilian advisers, as in the National Security Council.

Tactics: This is the science of deploying troops and using equipment in individual battles or military engagements. It occurs on a much smaller scale than strategy. Officers of the armed forces are trained in tactics.

Theory of Convergence: This theory teaches that the United States and the Soviet Union, or, alternately, the capitalist and socialist states, are daily growing more alike in their political, social, and economic philosophies. At some future date the two systems will reach a point of convergence at which time they will be indistinguishable from one another. This is caused by the fact that they must handle similar problems and use similar technologies. Capitalist states use more centralized economic planning and allocation of goods and services each year. The Communist states, especially since the introduction of the Lieberman Reforms in the Soviet Union and the Sik reforms in Eastern Europe, have moved toward a consumer-oriented market system.

Third World: This term is used to describe the neutral or uncommitted nations, generally underdeveloped and emerging states. They belong to neither the Communist nor the capitalist bloc. Some members of the Organization of Petroleum Exporting Countries (OPEC) are included in the "Third World," but generally these nations are quite poor, having a low per capita income. Many consider the third world to have as many as 100 members, many of these being mininations. These nations have begun to exercise some power in the United Nations, especially in the General Assembly where they can command a majority.

Trade Reform Act of 1974: This act has tended to weaken the Mutual Defense Assistance Control Act of 1951 (Battle Act) by allowing more latitude in trade with Communist bloc nations. It was designed primarily to allow presidents considerable latitude in dealing with foreign tates in trade negotiations. The president is permitted to raise or lower many tariffs in order to deal with foreign leaders. He is permitted to eliminate tariffs to encourage free trade with developing nations, and he may eliminate trade quotas. President Nixon was permitted to grant most favored nation status to the Soviet Union, provided it allowed free emigration of Jews to Israel. The act gave the president special tools to deal with industries and workers injured by imports of cheap foreign goods and sought to punish OPEC nations by withdrawing "most favored nation" status from them.

Treaty: A form of international act, a treaty pledges two or more nations to certain specified conditions. There are many ways to view treaties. *Bilateral treaties* are negotiated between two sovereign states. *Multipartite treaties* involve several nations. Some treaties sponsored by international organizations are called *declarations*, such as the United Nations Declaration on Human Rights. *Trade treaties* set conditions for the exchange of goods among nations. *Defense treaties* provide for mutual aid in war time. *Treaties of friendship* merely pledge states to act in good faith toward one another. Other treaties may provide for extradition of alleged criminals, cultural exchanges, foreign aid, technical assistance, or military help.

Truman Doctrine: When Communist expansion into Eastern Europe after World War II seemed to threaten the whole of Europe and Asia, President Truman announced that the United States would offer aid to any nation attempting to resist Communist aggression. After the announcement was made on March 12, 1947, the Congress appropriated $400 million to aid Greece and Turkey in repressing Communist revolutionaries. It has been mitigated by the Nixon Doctrine.

United Nations: Created by multipartite agreement in 1945 in San Francisco, this organization was designed to replace the League of Nations as a forum for discussion among the nations of the world. It was to be a collective security arrangement designed to respond to acts of aggression. Its charter outlaws war and requires its members to seek peaceful solutions to problems. It has a *Secretariat*, which provides the clerical and book-keeping functions of the United Nations. This division is headed by a *Secretary-General* who is the chief administrative office of the organization. He is selected by the General Assembly. He may place items on the agenda of the *Security Council.* This portion of the United Nations has five permanent members (China, USSR, United States, France, and Great Britain) and ten nonpermanent members which are chosen by the General Assembly for two-year terms. The five permanent members have a veto power. Chapter 7 of the U.N. Charter gives the Security Council primary responsibility for recommending action against aggressors and for defining aggression. Because of the deadlock brought about by the veto power of the permanent members, most responsibility has fallen on the *General Assembly.* In this major forum all nations who are members of the United

Nations are represented and each state has but one vote. It selects members to serve on other U.N. divisions, elects the ten nonpermanent members of the Security Council, and elects the Secretary General. It now considers matters of war and aggression (if the Security Council fails to act) under the "Uniting for Peace" resolution. It controls the U.N. budget and receives reports of committees. Most items may be passed by simple majority, but some major items require a two-thirds majority of those present and voting. It has sponsored many declarations (really multipartite treaties) such as those against genocide and for human rights. There is an associated court which interprets the U.N. Charter and international law, the *International Court of Justice*. It has a number of specialized agencies, dealing with a wide variety of matters of international concern. A few of these would include: the *International Labor Organization (ILO)*, which gathers data on the condition of the world's working population, and makes appropriate recommendation; the *World Health Organization (WHO)*, which collects information on diseases and helps to combat special illnesses; *Trusteeship Council*, which supervises certain territories administered under U.N. mandate by U.N. members; *Economic and Social Council (ECOSOC)*, which attempts to upgrade the world's standard of living and promote justice; *International Trade Organization (ITO)*, which attempts to encourage mutual interdependence of nations through free trade; and, the *Food and Agricultural Organization (FAO)*, which promotes good farming practices and encourages the use of modern and superior seeds and fertilizers. The United Nations is headquartered in New York City and the representatives are accorded diplomatic immunity by the United States. It issues its own stamps. It lost much credibility in the Western World when the General Assembly voted to condemn Zionism as a form of racism. It has sponsored police actions in Korea and in the Congo. It budget is underwritten by its members, with the United States paying a significant portion of its costs.

United States Arms Control and Disarmament Agency (USACDA): Headed by a director appointed by the president with the consent of the Senate, USACDA is an independent agency charged with developing strategies to ease the pressures of the arms race among world powers. Much of its research has been used in developing strategies used in SALT I and II.

12

State and Local Government

Alderman: This is an old English term for a member of a city council. At one time, some cities had bicameral governing bodies and one house was frequently called the Board of Aldermen. Generally, an alderman is selected to represent one ward in the single-member districts of cities.

Annexation: As cities grow new space is needed for homes and industrial sites. One way that cities acquire additional space is by annexing land from townships and counties. The procedures required for obtaining additional space are outlined in state codes, but may include direct permission of the legislature and the courts. Hearings are frequently held on proposed annexations.

Attorney General: The title of this office may vary, but this frequently used term describes the highest legal offices of a state. In most states the office is elective. In some states this office coordinates the efforts of local prosecutors. In some states the office may enpanel a state-wide grand jury. The attorney general may represent the state in cases brought against it or its officers in civil or criminal courts. The office may issue advisory opinions to state and local officers. Although these opinions may be overturned by subsequent court action, they do carry a force of law until overturned.

Boro: This is the modernized spelling of the English "borough" and it describes an incorporated municipality that is smaller than a city. In Alaska the term describes larger geographic areas and is somewhat like the term "county" elsewhere.

Burgess: This term was once used to describe the mayor of a small incorporated area. It is seldom used today.

Charter: This is the basic law under which local governments operate. They are created by state legislatures and may apply to all areas of one type or to one city or county only. Occasionally, state legislatures may empower special groups to create charters, although these are ordinarily subject to legislative approval. In *home rule charters* local citizens or their elected representatives draw up special charters for their own area, pursuant to legislative approval. Few small local governmental entities, such as villages, have written charters.

Circuit Court: In those states that call their county commissioners a county court, the term describes the lowest level of the courts of record. In other cases it may be used to describe a specialized court of record.

City: A larger metropolitan area than a town, boro, or village, this term is used to describe an incorporated municipal area. There are about 20,000 cities in America, making up about a quarter of all local governmental bodies. Usually, a city offers a wide variety of services, including fire and police protection, water, and sewage and waste disposal. Many cities operate under home rule charters, giving them considerable freedom of action.

City Council: Cities are commonly governed by elected, representive bodies called city councils. The relationship of such bodies to the executive (often, the mayor) is described in the city charter. They may provide certain oversight functions in regard to city departments and bureaucracies. They may be elected at-large or from single or multiple member districts (wards). When a city manager is hired, they oversee his work.

City-County Relations: Ordinarily cities exist within counties and the citizens may be taxed, at least to some degree, by both entities. When the two are separated, the city dwellers may only be taxed and administered by the city. On the other hand, cities and counties may wish to consolidate services, especially in areas with high population density. In some cases of consolidation it is impossible to determine where one body ends and the other begins. The city of Philadelphia is coextensive with that county.

Classification: State legislatures may group cities or counties according to population for the purpose of enacting laws, setting salary scales, and granting charters. Classifications are based on population sizes or densities. Legislative acts may permit certain powers to be exercised by some areas and not by others. Occassionally, an entity of a certain type may constitute the only member of that classification.

Commission Plan: This is a type of city or county government in which legislative and executive functions are merged in a single body called a commission. Frequently the members are elected on a nonpartisan basis. The commissioners head and serve on administrative boards created by the commission, its charter, or its enabling legislation.

Commonwealth: This term, used in several states, is another name used in place of the word "state." Puerto Rico is a "free commonwealth" which is associated with the United States.

Conference of Commissioners on Uniform State Laws: Created in 1892, this body of lawyers works to secure uniformity in several areas of law within the 50 states.

Consolidation: Two or more units of substate government may be joined to form a single unit in an act called consolidation. At times, this is done by legislative act and at other times it may be accomplished through the judicial process. Many school districts have been consolidated in recent years. Many feel that the number of local units of local government should be consolidated for greatest efficiency.

Constitution: Each state operates under a written constitution. These documents prescribe the form state governments must take and they outline the duties, functions, and responsibilities of the states. They also create the relationships states have with substate governments. They are longer than our federal Constitution and are more frequently amended. Many contain bills of rights.

Constitutional Convention: This is a body selected by popular vote or appointed by another appropriate body to rewrite the state's constitution. Over 200 constitutional conventions have been held in the 50 states. Several states require the electorate to be polled on the ballot periodically to inquire into the necessity of holding a constitutional convention.

Wholesale revision of state constitutions has been popular in recent years, leading to commission recommendations for piecemeal changes.

Constitutional Officer: State constitutions prescribe that certain offices shall be created and filled, commonly by election or by appointment by the governor with the consent of the state senate. Commonly, attorneys general and secretaries of state are constitutional offices.

Coroner: This office is ordinarily a county-wide elective one in which the office holder assumes responsibility for investigating all violent deaths, and all deaths that occur under mysterious or suspicious circumstances. Coroners are not required to be physicians. Many of their duties have been given over to trained forensic pathologists known as medical examiners. Coroners may hold formal hearings, known as coroner's juries, to investigate and make conclusions about violent deaths.

Council of State Governments: This is a form of municipal government where in an elected city council hires a professional city administrator. A mayor may be chosen, but if there is such an office, the duties would be ceremonial as the manager is really the executive. Many believe this to be the ideal form for small to medium size city administration.

Council of Governments: These regional, substate governmental councils have developed as the result of federal incentives to take a broad area approach to many problems, such as solid waste disposal and water purity. Many councils have been created as a result of federal programs that mandate these councils as the designated agency through which federal funds are channeled to local governments. Technically voluntary associations, they possess a measure of power because of federal supports. They add another layer to government above cities, townships, and counties, and below states.

County: These legal divisions of state government are found in nearly every state. In Lousiana, counties are called "parishes." Connecticut recently (1959) abolished its counties and Rhode Island has never had counties. Alaska has created rather unique units of local government called "boroughs." Local officials such a sheriffs are elected in counties and, throughout most of the nation, these units are the backbone of local government. They have such powers as are given them by state constitutions and legislatures.

County Clerk: Commonly an elected local official, the county clerk serves as the secretary to the county commissioners and performs a wide variety of other clerical jobs, such as the issuance of local licenses and permits. He or she is the keeper of "vital statistics."

County Commissioners: These are the elected officials who serve as the governing body of a county. In some areas, following the practice in colonial Virginia, they are called the "county court" although they have few judicial duties. In other areas they are called "county boards" or "boards of supervisers." Commonly, they levy taxes, supervise local officials, and govern the county.

County Manager: Patterned after city-manager plans of municipal administration, this system of county government provides for professional and full-time management of county government. County commissioners may hire (and fire) the manager. The commissioners commonly head bureaus and departments of county government while the manager provides day-to-day administration. This plan has been nearly as successful as the city-manager system.

County Seat: This is the county equivalent of a "capital." It is the place where the county court and principal offices of the county are to be found.

County Treasurer: In those areas without home rule charters, Dillon's rule provides basic guidance in interpreting the functions and duties of municipalities. The rule holds that there are no implied powers in municipal corporations. They have only such powers as are expressly granted them by state constitutions and laws, and those absolutely necessary for them to carry out their functions as municipalities. Whenever there is doubt, the doubt is resolved in favor of the state and against the municipality.

District Magistrate: Known in some areas as "justice of the peace," officers are the lowest level of the court system. Many states now require extensive training for district magistrates, whereas the justices of the peace were most often untrained in the law. They are elected commonly in units smaller than counties (sometimes called magisterial districts). They handle many summary offenses, such as traffic tickets. They may also handle small claims and some civil cases and certain misdemeanors.

General Law: Such laws apply to all citizens of a state. They are different from laws made applicable only to certain classes of substate governments. The overwhelming bulk of state laws is of a general type.

Governor: This is the principal executive officer of a state. Governors are popularly elected in all 50 states. They have most of the powers held by the president of the United States, including veto, appointment, and removal from office.

Home Rule: State legislatures may give counties and/or cities the power to control many of their own affairs by authorizing the creation of charters. Home rule is permitted in most of the 50 states. The basic assumption made here is that local governments are frequently in the best position to determine what the needs of the people are. Home rule reduces the work of state legislatures. Ordinarily a local group is elected to draft a home rule charter which is then presented to the voters for their approval.

Housing and Community Development Act of 1974: This act authorized extension of urban development programs by revising and consolidating a number of existing programs for community development. It continued public housing programs (urban and rural), mortgage credit programs, and cash subsidies for low-income, nonpublic housing. Monies given under block grants here may be used for urban renewal, recreational facilities, housing code enforcement, water and sewage facilities, and comprehensive planning.

Incorporation: Cities and towns are municipal corporations, except in New England. In the past incorporated areas were given special legal considerations not available to unincorporated areas, but this distinction is rapidly disappearing as unincorporated areas now participate in many programs heretofore reserved for municipal corporations. Only incorporated cities are eligible for home rule charters ordinarily, although counties are unincorporated and are granted home rule charters in many states.

Initiative: This popular, democratic device permits citizen groups to present legislation for approval in cases where the legislature has not acted. Although it is permitted in only a few states, it is a handy way to permit direct democracy. The way it functions is set by law. Ordinarily, signatures are gathered by the concerned group equal to a certain percentage of the registered voters (or, alternately, a certain percentage of those who voted in a specified, recent election). Once the appropriate signatures have been gathered and verified, the proposition is either voted on by the state legislature or by the electorate in the next available election.

Item Veto: While all state governors share the veto power with the president, only a few state governors are permitted to disapprove portions of a bill, while retaining the rest. Ordinarily, line item veto is permitted only in the original state budget and may not be used in general legislation or in supplemental or deficiency appropriations. The legislature may vote to over-ride, as in the case of normal type of veto. The presence of line item veto in a state constitution ordinarily marks the system as one maintaining a strong executive. Some mayors have line item veto, generally applicable only to the budget.

Justice of the Peace: This is the lowest level of the state judiciary. The office is ordinarily elected by voters in districts smaller than counties. The more modern term for the trained minor judiciary is district magistrate.

Legislative Auditor: In those states wherein the state auditor does only preaudit, the legislature may create an office to do postaudit, commonly called the legislative auditor. The preaudit of some state auditors serves merely to indicate if the requested appropriation has funds available and if the expense request seems appropriate for that account. The postaudit of the legislative auditor provides a final check on whether the monies have been expended lawfully and as the legislature had intended when putting the money in the state budget. Such postaudit is a final check on the executive branch.

Lieutenant Governor: This office serves much the same purpose in states that the vice-presidency serves in our national government. In the event of the death, impeachment, or resignation of the governor, the lieutenant governor assumes that office. He or she presides over the state senate and may be assigned other tasks by the state constitution, by law, or by the governor. In states without lieutenant governors those in line to replace the governor may include: president of state senate, president pro tempore of state senate, speaker of state house, and secretary of state. The office of lieutenant governor is elective. In some states he or she may run as a team with the governor; in others each is elected separately, thus allowing for the possibility that each may be of a different political party.

Local Option: Ordinarily associated with permission or refusal to allow the sale of liquor in a substate governmental area (county or town or city), the broad meaning of the term is that local units of government are permitted to make certain policy decisions with respect to their own areas, and without regard to other areas. The local option must be permitted by state law or state constitution and is decided by referendum.

Magisterial District: This is the territory served by a local, lower level judicial office (justice of the peace, district magistrate). It often corresponds to no other political district (e.g., county or city), although it seldom would cross county boundaries. Magisterial districts may be used for other purposes, such as for establishing voting precincts.

Mayor: This is the principal executive officer of a city or town, although in certain council-manager plans the duties may be only ceremonial. The duties and powers vary considerably, depending on population sizes. In some cities, such as New York, the powers are greater than for certain state governors. In some areas mayors may have, or have had, basic low-level responsibilities.

Mayor-Administrator Plan: In this form of municipal government, a professional administrator is hired, under control of the elected mayor, to manage city government. The mayor still makes major policy decisions, but is freed from the ordinary routine by the administrator. This system may or may not include an elected council with some degree of power and responsibility. It is a form of strong mayor government.

Mayor-Council Plan: Under this form of municipal government, the city council operates as a legislature while the mayor serves as the chief executive. It thus preserves traditional executive-legislation division and checks and balances. It may be formed as either a strong or a weak mayor system.

Megalopolis: This term describes the huge urban population, covering the eastern seaboard area from Richmond, Virginia, to north of Boston, Massachusetts. It is roughly 500 miles from north to south and 200 miles from east to west and covers over 30 major metropolitan areas.

Metropolitan Area: This term describes a city and its immediate residential neighbors. In many ways, these metropolitan areas transcend ordinary boundaries and consume all those who enjoy a greater sense of commonality and community. It is largely a cultural unit with the core city at its center. By 1975 there were over 250 metropolitan areas in the United States. The Census Bureau requires that the core city have a population of at least 50,000 to be considered a metropolitan area.

Metropolitan Government: First used in Miami-Dade County, Florida, in this country, this plan projects the consolidation of most or all government services within a metropolitan area into a single unit. The plan would negate tax differences within such an area and would provide uniform area planning and development. It presumably would promote greater efficiency in local government.

Optional Charter: Many states permit local governments to have home rule merely by adopting one of several alternative charters created by the state. This is a middle ground between complete legislative domination and complete local option on a self-made charter.

Ordinance: This is the law created by a local unit of government ordinarily enacted by county commissioners or city councils. Such laws must comply with state constitutions and laws and be within the limits of their charters.

Piecemeal Change: Voters in recent years have seldom been receptive to completely new constitutions in the states or city charters. They have been nearly as reluctant to make major changes in these basic documents. Consequently, much change has had to come by single amendments, frequently of limited scope. Such changes may, in the long run, produce major changes.

Planning: In the past far too much unplanned change has taken place at every level of governmental concern. Many leaders have recognized that unplanned change can have many detrimental effects on society and the environment. The science of planning seeks ways to control change and to limit its negative side effects. Planning may be of many types, including: social, economic, physical, demographic, and environmental. Practiced by professionals, planning draws on many sciences, including: geography, economics, engineering, history, architecture, sociology, geology, agriculture, life and medical sciences, and biology. Planning is carried out by the federal government to some degree, but is most often found at the state, regional, and local level. Planning is best when accompanied by development.

Precinct: There are largely urban divisions wherein people vote and where divisions are made for purposes of electing local officers, such as city council seats.

Prothonotary: This local officer (ordinarily elected) is used in some states, notably in Pennsylvania, as clerk of the local courts. The prothonotary keeps many of the court records and prepares the docket, has certain other clerical functions, and is, or retains, a notary public, primarily for use of other county officials.

Public Service District: This term describes a special unit of local government, permitted by state legislatures, and created by one or more units of local government to provide some public service, such as water, sewage, or solid waste disposal. Units of government may create several such authorities which perform different services but which coexist in the same, or approximately the same, geographic area.

Regionalism: The federal government has encouraged the growth of intermediate government or quasigovernment units between cities and counties on the one hand and states on the other hand. They have probably been most successful in the planning field and as conduits for federal funds in certain program areas. Many believe that regional governments will one day take the place of township, county, and other local governments.

Recall: This popular, democratic device permits the voters to force a state or local governmental official to return to the area that elected him or her and to stand, once again, for voter approval (or disapproval) before the official's term of office has expired. Only a few states have the legislation necessary to permit recall. In those states permitting recall, a petition must be drawn up and signed by a certain percentage of the voters in the area (or a percentage of those who voted in a recent or a specified election). If the petition finds sufficient support and is verified by the appropriate state agency, the official must stand for a special election, usually, as "Shall Joe Doe be retained as (office specified)?" If a majority of those who voted wish to remove the official, then he or she is removed from office.

Referendum: In this practice a constitutional amendment or law is placed before the electorate for approval or rejection. A petition signed by a certain percentage of the eligible voters (or of the voters who participated in a specified election) may be used to force placement of an issue on the ballot, or the issue may be recommended by the state legislature. Nearly every state uses *constitutional referendum* to approve changes in the state constitution or to adopt a new constitution. Many states require that certain issues or constitutional amendments or bonded indebtedness be approved by more than a simple majority of the voters (often by 60 percent of those voting). Bond issues are frequently approved by popular vote and voted on in a *statutory referendum*.

Register and Recorder of Deeds: This local, often county, official (ordinarily elected) is responsible for recording and preserving deeds and other documents involved with real estate and land ownership.

Revenue Sharing: Under this plan, a portion of revenue from a higher governmental authority is given over, usually without restriction, to a lower level of government. The federal government has, since 1972, shared its moneys with states and local governments under the State and Local Fiscal Assistance Act. Initially, some $30 billion was to be shared over a five-year period under the General Revenue Sharing Program. The idea was popularized by Professor Walter Heller's book, *New Dimensions of Political Economy*.

School Board: Most often filled by popular, nonpartisan (or bipartisan election wherein one may cross-file) election, this body makes the general policy for a school system. It hires (and removes) major school administrators and may grant teachers tenure or leaves of absence, and select regular and substitute teachers. In some states school districts are fiscally independent of other governmental authorities, having the power to tax and to borrow moneys (The latter sometimes requires voter approval by referendum).

Secretary of State: This office is found in most states (39), with the office holder being elected in some and appointed by the governor in others. In several states, the secretary of state is in line to succession to the governor's office should it fall vacant. He or she is the keeper of the state seal and the official designated to receive certain legal papers, including subpoenas, for out-of-state corporations.

Sheriff: The sheriff is the principal law enforcement officer of a county, and is nearly universally elected. In some states, following early practices in Virginia, the sheriff is also the county treasurer. He may conduct sales of goods to satisfy certain types of debts and may serve civil and criminal warrants.

Sinking Fund: This is a special fund, set aside out of revenues, to be invested and used toward the redemption of debts or bond issues. In several states the state sinking fund commission administers these monies for state and local governmental agencies.

Solicitor: Substate governmental authorities frequently retain the services of an attorney to advise them on the law and to represent them in legal actions. These officers are commonly known as solicitors or corporation counsels or city's attorneys.

Special Act: Occasionally, legislatures will create laws applicable only to one unit of substate government. These special acts were used more commonly in the late 19th century than they are today.

Special Authority: These special units of substate government are created to accomplish some specialized task, such as running municipal airports, maintaining recreational facilities, or providing a public service. They are occasionally used to avoid debt limitations imposed on local governments by state constitutions.

State Aid: Monies are appropriated by states for the use of local governments, school districts, and special authorities. These grants sustain many local activities that counties and cities cannot afford.

State Auditor: This constitutional officer is found in most states, and is frequently elected, but may be appointed by the governor. In some states the state auditor is known as the comptroller. Some auditors have preaudit duties while others perform postaudit and act as watchdogs over public expenditures. In those states where the auditor performs only preaudit there is frequently a legislative auditor appointed to perform the postaudit of accounts.

State Treasurer: The state treasurer is a constitutional officer, commonly elected, but sometimes appointed, who keeps accounts of state funds. He or she may be charged with investing surplus state monies and state retirement funds and his or her signature is frequently required on state checks.

Strong Mayor Plan: Under this plan for municipal government the mayor has complete executive authority, including the power of veto over the city council. The mayor is ordinarily elected by the voters, and generally has the power to create an executive budget. He or she assumes responsibility for day-to-day administration and supervision of city employees, and may be assisted by a professional manager who relieves the mayor of some mundane duties and functions.

Superintendent of Schools: This state official may be elected, but is more commonly appointed by the governor. The office may be created by statute, but is frequently a constitutional office. The superintendent supervises the state school system, and may have responsibility for supervising colleges, universities, trade and technical schools, and/or community colleges. This office generally sets standards for teacher educational requirements and school curriculum.

Superviser: In those states having townships, the supervisers serve as the directing board. In the past their duties were commonly confined to road construction and maintenance, but today they frequently make up and administer multimillion dollar budgets, and control major programs of many kinds.

Tax Limitation: State constitutions may set specified limits on the amount of taxes or tax rates used by states, cities, townships and/or counties. "Proposition 13" in California sets specific real estate tax rates and appraisals.

Tax Collector: Officers may be elected or hired under competitive bid system to collect taxes for units of substate government. They are commonly paid a small percentage of the taxes collected.

Torrens System: This is a system of land title registration created by Robert R. Torrens and used in several states. Upon payment of a fee, a purchaser obtains a valid land title. Subsequent valid claims are compensated out of an insurance fund maintained by the fees.

Town: Small urban areas, ordinarily incorporated, are called town throughout the United States. In New England the term is used to designate both urban and rural areas under a government, commonly a town meeting government, a form of direct democracy wherein all citizens are eligible to participate directly.

Townships: Some 16 states subdivide counties into smaller components called townships. These are unincorporated areas that traditionally had responsibility principally for road maintenance. Today they have multimillion dollar budgets and manifold responsibilities. Incorporated areas (cities and towns) are excluded from townships. Townships supervisers are elected to administer these units.

Uniform State Law: Within the United States there is a wide diversity of laws dealing with specific subject areas. Acts that are classified as misdemeanors in some areas are felonies in other jurisdictions. The requirements for commercial operations or home building or lending money vary considerably. The Conference of Commissioners on Uniform State Laws and other organizations, including the American Bar Association, have attempted to create model laws in many areas which they hope might be universally adopted by state legislatures. Some organizations have created model, uniform municipal codes dealing with many subjects of local interest and control.

Unitary Government: The federal courts have consistently assumed that the relationship between state governments and their local components is unitary, not federal. The cities, townships, counties, and other substate governmental units have no reserved powers. These units may be altered or abolished by state legislatures or by amending the state constitution. Their powers exist only as given by the states.

Urban County Plan: In major metropolitan areas many municipal services and functions may be transferred to county governments under this plan. A county-wide emergency telephone system may be used to summon help. County-wide sewage and water systems may be created. Police systems may be consolidated under county control. Separate governments may be retained while services and functions are consolidated.

Village: This is one name for a small municipal corporation. In some states villages are unincorporated whereas in other states villages may be recognized as the smallest incorporated unit of government. Many areas used the term "town" instead of village.

Vital Statistics: These are the records of marriages, divorces, births, and deaths maintained in counties, frequently by the office of the county clerk.

Ward: This is a division of a city and is used for electing city council members and for establishing voting precincts. Frequently, political party committee persons are elected in wards.

Weak Mayor Plan: Under this plan for municipal government, the mayor must share executive functions with city council. The mayor's powers of appointment and removal are weak or nonexistent. Frequently, the voters must use the long ballot and elect a number of city department heads. The mayor has no veto power or limited veto power. The council shares in making up the budget and administering it.

Zoning: This requires that a unit of substate government, ordinarily a municipal corporation, subdivide the land under its control into units whose use is designated by law (e.g., residential, commercial, industrial). The zoning law is administered frequently by a zoning commission which may have the power to grant variances to the code. Zoning laws may specify the type, height, architecture, or cost of buildings to be constructed in certain areas.

CASES

Avery v. Midland County, Texas (390 US 474, 1968):   In this case the Supreme Court applied the "one man, one vote" principle to local elections for township supervisers.

Baker v. Carr (369 US 186, 1962):   See Chapter 4, p. 71.

Cohens v. Virginia (6 Wheaton 264, 1821):   See Chapter 8, p. 155.

Colgrove v. Green (328 US 549, 1946):   In this early case the Supreme Court held that malapportionment of state legislative districts was a political, not a judicial, problem and thus could not be reviewed by the federal courts. This was overturned in *Baker v. Carr* in 1962.

Euclid v. Amber Realty Co. (272 US 365, 1926):   The Supreme Court held here that zoning laws were permitted as a police function of local communities to protect health, safety, and the welfare of the citizens of the community.

German Alliance Insurance Co. v. Lewis (233 US 389, 1914): The Supreme Court here upheld state regulation of the insurance business, reasoning that this was legitimate since the business tended to be semimonopolistic. The regulation of insurance was akin to the regulation of public utilities, something already permtted to the states.

Sturges v. Crowninshield (4 Wheaton 122, 1819): The Supreme Court held that states might enact state bankruptcy laws which, if they did not impair obligation of contract, would be valid until superseded by federal legislation.

Texas v. White (7 Wallace 700, 1869): See Chapter 3, p. 45.

Wabash, St. Louis and Pacific Railroad v. Illinois (118 US 557, 1886): The Supreme Court decided here that the states were without the constitutional power to regulate interstate rates of railroads passing through their jurisdiction, even if the federal government had not acted in this area.

The Declaration of Independence

When in the Course of human events, it becomes necessary for one people to dissolve the political bands which have connected them with another, and to assume among the Powers of the earth, the separate and equal station to which the Laws of Nature and of Nature's God entitle them, a decent respect to the opinions of mankind requires that they should declare the causes which impel them to the separation.

We hold these truths to be self-evident, that all men are created equal, that they are endowed by their Creator with certain unalienable Rights, that among these are Life, Liberty and the pursuit of Happiness. That to secure these rights, Governments are instituted among Men, deriving their just powers from the consent of the governed, That whenever any Form of Government becomes destructive of these ends, it is the Right of the People to alter or to abolish it, and to institute new Government, laying its foundation on such principles and organizing its powers in such form, as to them shall seem most likely to effect their Safety and Happiness. Prudence, indeed, will dictate that Governments long established should not be changed for light and transient causes; and accordingly all experience hath shown, that mankind are more disposed to suffer, while evils are sufferable, than to right themselves by abolishing the forms to which they are accustomed. When a long train of abuses and usurpations, pursuing invariably the same Object evinces a design to reduce them under absolute Despotism, it is their right, it is their duty, to throw off such Government, and to provide new Guards for their future security.—Such has been the patient sufferance of these Colonies; and such is now the necessity which constrains them to alter their former Systems of Government. The history of the present King of Great Britain is a history of repeated injuries and usurpations, all having in direct object the establishment of an absolute Tyranny over these States. To prove this, let Facts be submitted to a candid world.

He has refused his Assent to Laws, the most wholesome and necessary for the public good.

He has forbidden his Governors to pass Laws of immediate and pressing importance, unless suspended in their operation till his Assent should be obtained; and when so suspended, he has utterly neglected to attend to them.

He has refused to pass other Laws for the accommodation of large districts of people, unless those people would relinquish the right of Representation in the Legislature, a right inestimable to them and formidable to tyrants only.

He has called together legislative bodies at places unusual, uncomfortable, and distant from the depository of their Public Records, for the sole purpose of fatiguing them into compliance with his measures.

He has dissolved Representative Houses repeatedly, for opposing with manly firmness his invasions on the rights of the people.

He has refused for a long time, after such dissolutions, to cause others to be elected; whereby the Legislative Powers, incapable of Annihilation, have returned to the People at large for their exercise; the State remaining in the mean time exposed to all the dangers of invasion from without, and convulsions within.

He has endeavoured to prevent the population of these States; for that purpose obstructing the Laws of Naturalization of Foreigners; refusing to pass others to encourage their migration hither, and raising the conditions of new Appropriations of Lands.

He has obstructed the Administration of Justice, by refusing his Assent to Laws for establishing Judiciary Powers.

He has made Judges dependent on his Will alone, for the tenure of their offices, and the amount and payment of their salaries.

He has erected a multitude of New Offices, and sent hither swarms of Officers to harass our People, and eat out their substance.

He has kept among us, in times of peace, Standing Armies without the Consent of our legislature.

He has affected to render the Military independent of and superior to the Civil Power.

He has combined with others to subject us to a jurisdiction foreign to our constitution, and unacknowledged by our laws; giving his Assent to their acts of pretended legislation:

For quartering large bodies of armed troops among us:

For protecting them, by a mock Trial, from Punishment for any Murders which they should commit on the Inhabitants of these States:

For cutting off our Trade with all parts of the world:

For imposing taxes on us without our Consent:

For depriving us in many cases, of the benefits of Trial by Jury:

For transporting us beyond Seas to be tried for pretended offences:

For abolishing the free System of English Laws in a neighbouring Province, establishing therein an Arbitrary government, and enlarging its Boundaries so as to render it at once an example and fit instrument for introducing the same absolute rule into these Colonies:

For taking away our Charters, abolishing our most valuable Laws, and altering fundamentally the Forms of our Governments:

For suspending our own Legislature, and declaring themselves invested with Power to legislate for us in all cases whatsoever.

He has abdicated Government here, by declaring us out of his Protection and waging War against us.

He has plundered our seas, ravaged our Coasts, burnt our towns, and destroyed the lives of our people.

He is at this time transporting large armies of foreign mercenaries to compleat the works of death, desolation and tyranny, already begun with circumstances of Cruelty & perfidy scarcely paralleled in the most barbarous ages, and totally unworthy the Head of a civilized nation.

He has constrained our fellow Citizens taken Captive on the high Seas to bear Arms against their Country, to become the executioners of their friends and Brethren, or to fall themselves by their Hands.

He has excited domestic insurrections amongst us, and has endeavoured to bring on the inhabitants of our frontiers, the merciless Indian Savages, whose known rule of warfare, is an undistinguished destruction of all ages, sexes and conditions.

In every stage of these Oppressions We have Petitioned for Redress in the most humble terms: Our repeated Petitions have been answered only by repeated injury. A Prince, whose character is thus marked by every act which may define a Tyrant, is unfit to be the ruler of a free People.

Nor have We been wanting in attention to our British brethren. We have warned them from time to time of attempts by their legislature to extend an unwarrantable jurisdiction over us. We have reminded them of the circumstances of our emigration and settlement here. We have appealed to their native justice and magnanimity, and we have conjured them by the ties of our common kindred to disavow these usurpations, which, would inevitably interrupt our connections and correspondence. They too have been deaf to the voice of justice and of consanguinity. We must, therefore, acquiesce in the necessity, which denounces our Separation, and hold them, as we hold the rest of mankind, Enemies in War, in Peace Friends.

We, therefore, the Representatives of the United States of America, in General Congress, Assembled, appealing to the Supreme Judge of the world for the rectitude of our intentions, do, in the Name, and by Authority of the good People of these Colonies, solemnly publish and declare, That these United Colonies are, and of Right ought to be Free and Independent States; that they are Absolved from all Allegiance to the British Crown, and that all political connection between them and the State of Great Britain, is and ought to be totally dissolved; and that as Free and Independent States, they have full Power to levy War, conclude Peace, contract Alliances, establish Commerce, and to do all other Acts and Things which Independent States may of right do. And for the support of this Declaration, with a firm reliance on the Protection of Divine Providence, we mutually pledge to each other our Lives, our Fortunes and our sacred Honor.

The Constitution of the United States

We the people of the United States, in Order to form a more perfect Union, establish Justice, insure domestic Tranquility, provide for the common defence, promote the general Welfare, and secure the Blessings of Liberty to ourselves and our Posterity, do ordain and establish this CONSTITUTION for the United States of America.

ARTICLE I

Section 1. All legislative Powers herein granted shall be vested in a Congress of the United States which shall consist of a Senate and House of Representatives.

Section 2. The House of Representatives shall be composed of Members chosen every second Year by the People of the several States, and the Electors in each State shall have the Qualifications requisite for Electors of the most numerous Branch of the State Legislature.

No Person shall be a Representative who shall not have attained to the Age of twenty-five Years, and been seven Years a Citizen of the United States, and who shall not, when elected, be an inhabitant of that State in which he shall be chosen.

Representatives and direct Taxes shall be apportioned among the several States which may be included within this Union, according to their respective Numbers, which shall be determined by adding to the whole Number of free Persons, including those bound to Service for a Term of Years and excluding Indians not taxed, three fifths of all other Persons. The actual Enumeration shall be made within three Years after the first Meeting of the Congress of the United States, and within every subsequent Term of ten Years, in such Manner as they shall be Law direct. The Number of Representatives shall not exceed one for every thirty Thousand, but each State shall have at Least one Representative; and until such enumeration shall be made, the State of New Hampshire shall be entitled to chuse three, Massachusetts eight, Rhode-Island and Providence Plantations one, Connecticut five, New-York six, New Jersey four, Pennsylvania eight, Delaware one, Maryland six, Virginia ten, North Carolina five, South Carolina five, and Georgia three.

When vacancies happen in the Representation from any State, the Executive Authority thereof shall issue Writs of Election to fill such Vacancies.

The House of Representatives shall chuse their Speaker and other Officers; and shall have the sole Power of Impeachment.

Section 3. The Senate of the United States shall be composed of two Senators from each State, chosen by the Legislature thereof, for six Years; and each Senator shall have one Vote.

Immediately after they shall be assembled in Consequence of the first Election, they shall be divided as equally as may be into three Classes. The Seats of the Senators of the first Class shall be vacated at the Expiration of the second Year, of the second Class at the Expiration of the fourth Year, and of the third Class at the Expiration of the sixth Year, so that one-third may be chosen every second Year; and if Vacancies happen by Resignation, or otherwise, during the Recess of the Legislature of any State, the Executive thereof may make temporary Appointments until the next Meeting of the Legislature, which shall then fill such Vacancies.

No Person shall be a Senator who shall not have attained to the Age of thirty Years, and been nine Years a Citizen of the United States, and who shall not, when elected, be an Inhabitant of that State in which he shall be chosen.

The Vice President of the United States shall be President of the Senate, but shall have no vote, unless they be equally divided.

The Senate shall chuse their other Officers, and also a President pro tempore, in the absence of the Vice President, or when he shall exercise the Office of the President of the United States.

The Senate shall have the sole Power to try all Impeachments. When sitting for that purpose, they shall be on Oath or Affirmation. When the President of the United States is tried, the Chief Justice shall preside: And no person shall be convicted without the Concurrence of two thirds of the Members present.

Judgment in Cases of Impeachment shall not extend further than to removal from Office, and disqualification to hold and enjoy any Office of honor, Trust, or Profit under the United States: but the Party convicted shall nevertheless be liable and subject to Indictment, Trial, Judgment, and Punishment, according to Law.

Section 4. The Times, Places and Manner of holding Elections for Senators and Representatives, shall be prescribed in each state by the Legislature thereof; but the Congress may at any time by Law make or alter such Regulations, except as to the Places of Chusing Senators.

The Congress shall assemble at least once in every Year, and such Meeting shall be on the first Monday in December, unless they shall by Law appoint a different Day.

Section 5. Each House shall be the Judge of the Elections, Returns and Qualifications of its own Members, and a Majority of each shall constitute a Quorum to do Business; but a smaller number may adjourn from day to day, and may be authorized to compel the Attendance of absent Members, in such Manner, and under such Penalties, as each House may provide.

Each House may determine the Rules of its Proceedings, punish its Members for disorderly Behavior, and, with the Concurrence of two thirds, expel a Member.

Each House shall keep a Journal of its Proceedings, and from time to time publish the same, excepting such Parts as may in their Judgment require Secrecy; and the Yeas and Nays of the Members of either House on any question shall, at the Desire of one fifth of those Present, be entered on the Journal.

Neither House, during the Session of Congress, shall, without the Consent of the other, adjourn for more than three days, nor to any other Place than that in which the two Houses shall be sitting.

Section 6. The Senators and Representatives shall receive a Compensation for their Services, to be ascertained by Law, and paid out of the Treasury of the United States. They shall in all Cases, except Treason, Felony, and Breach of the Peace, be privileged from Arrest during their Attendance at the Session of their respective Houses, and in going to and returning from the same; and for any Speech or Debate in either House, they shall not be questioned in any other Place.

No Senator or Representative shall, during the Time for which he was elected, be appointed to any civil Office under the Authority of the United States, which shall have been created, or the Emoluments whereof shall have been increased, during such time; and no Person holding any Office under the United States shall be a Member of either House during his continuance in Office.

Section 7. All Bills for raising Revenue shall originate in the House of

Representatives; but the Senate may propose or concur with Amendments as on other bills.

Every Bill which shall have passed the House of Representatives and the Senate, shall, before it become a Law, be presented to the President of the United States; If he approve he shall sign it, but if not he shall return it, with his Objections, to that House in which it shall have originated, who shall enter the Objections at large on their Journal, and proceed to reconsider it. If after such Reconsideration two thirds of that House shall agree to pass the bill, it shall be sent, together with the objections, to the other House, by which it shall likewise be reconsidered, and if approved by two thirds of that House, it shall become a Law. But in all such Cases the Votes of both Houses shall be determined by Yeas and Nays, and the Names of the Persons voting for and against the Bill shall be entered on the Journal of each House respectively. If any Bill shall not be returned by the President within ten Days (Sundays excepted) after it shall have been presented to him, the Same shall be a Law, in like Manner as if he had signed it, unless the Congress by their Adjournment prevent its Return, in which Case it shall not be a Law.

Every Order, Resolution, or Vote to which the Concurrence of the Senate and House of Representatives may be necessary (except on a question of Adjournment) shall be presented to the President of the United States; and before the Same shall take Effect, shall be approved by him, or being disapproved by him, shall be repassed by two thirds of the Senate and House of Representatives, according to the Rules and Limitations prescribed in the Case of a Bill.

Section 8. The Congress shall have Power To lay and Collect Taxes, Duties, Imposts and Excises, to pay the Debts and provide for the common Defence and general Welfare of the United States; but all Duties, Imposts and Excises shall be uniform throughout the United States;

To borrow money on the credit of the United States;

To regulate Commerce with foreign Nations, and among the several States, and with the Indian Tribes;

To establish an uniform Rule of Naturalization, and uniform Laws on the subject of Bankruptcies throughout the United States;

To coin Money, regulate the Value thereof, and of foreign Coin, and fix the Standard of Weights and Measures;

To provide for the Punishment of counterfeiting the Securities and current Coin of the United States;

To establish Post Offices and post Roads;

To promote the Progress of Science and useful Arts, by securing for limited Times to Authors and Inventors the exclusive Right to their respective Writings and Discoveries;

To constitute Tribunals inferior to the Supreme Court;

To define and punish Piracies and Felonies committed on the high Seas, and Offences against the Law of Nations;

To declare War, grant Letters of Marque and Reprisal, and make Rules concerning Captures on Land and Water;

To raise and support Armies, but no Appropriation of Money to that Use shall be for a longer Term than two Years;

To provide and maintain a Navy;

To make Rules for the Government and Regulation of the land and naval forces;

To provide for calling forth the Militia to execute the Laws of the Union, suppress Insurrections and repel Invasions;

To provide for organizing, arming, and disciplining the Militia, and for governing such Part of them as may be employed in the Service of the United States, reserving to the States respectively, the Appointment of the Officers, and the Authority of training the Militia according to the discipline prescribed by Congress;

To exercise exclusive Legislation in all Cases whatsoever, over such District (not exceeding ten Miles square) as may, be Cession of particular States, and the acceptance of Congress, become the Seat of Government of the United States, and to exercise like Authority over all Places purchased by the Consent of the Legislature of the States in which the Same shall be, for the Erection of Forts, Magazines, Arsenals, dock-Yards, and other needful Buildings;—And

To make all Laws which shall be necessary and proper for carrying into Execution the foregoing Powers, and all other Powers vested by this Constitution in the Government of the United States, or in any Department or Officer thereof.

Section 9. The Migration or Importation of such Persons as any of the States now existing shall think proper to admit, shall not be prohibited by the Congress prior to the Year one thousand eight hundred and eight, but a tax or duty may be imposed on such Importation, not exceeding ten dollars for each Person.

The privilege of the Writ of Habeas Corpus shall not be suspended, unless when in Cases of Rebellion or Invasion the public Safety may require it.

No Bill of Attainder or ex post facto Law shall be passed.

No capitation, or other direct, Tax shall be laid unless in Proportion to the Census or Enumeration herein before directed to be taken.

No Tax or Duty shall be laid on Articles exported from any State.

No Preference shall be given by any Regulation of Revenue to the Ports of one State over those of another: nor shall Vessels bound to, or from, one State, be obliged to enter, clear, or pay Duties in another.

No Money shall be drawn from the Treasury, but in Consequence of Appropriations made by Law; and a regular Statement and Account of the Receipts and Expenditures of all public Money shall be published from time to time.

No Title of Nobility shall be granted by the United States: And no Person holding any Office of Profit or Trust under them, shall, without the Consent of the Congress, accept of any present, Emolument, Office, or Title, of any kind whatever, from any King, Prince, or foreign State.

Section 10. No State shall enter any Treaty, Alliance, or Confederation; grant Letters of Marque and Reprisal; coin Money; emit Bills of Credit; make any Thing but gold and silver Coin a Tender in Payment of Debts; pass any Bill of Attainder, ex post facto Law, or Law impairing the Obligation of Contracts, or grant any Title of Nobility.

No State shall, without the Consent of the Congress, lay any Imposts or Duties on Imports or Exports, except what may be absolutely necessary for executing its inspection Laws: and the net Produce of all Duties and Imposts, laid by any State on Imports or Exports, shall be for the use of the Treasury of the United States; and all such Laws shall be subject to the Revision and Control of the Congress.

No State shall, without the Consent of Congress, lay any duty of Tonnage, keep Troops, or Ships of War in time of Peace, enter into any Agreement or Compact with another State, or with a foreign Power, or engage in War, unless actually invaded, or in such imminent Danger as will not admit of delay.

ARTICLE II
Section 1. The executive Power shall be vested in a President of the United States of America. He shall hold his Office during the Term of four years, and, together with the Vice-President, chosen for the same Term, be elected, as follows:

Each State shall appoint, in such Manner as the Legislature thereof may direct, a Number of Electors, equal to the whole Number of Senators and Representatives to which the State may be entitled in the Congress; but no Senator or Representative, or Person holding an Office of Trust or Profit under the United States, shall be appointed an Elector.

The Electors shall meet in their respective States, and vote by Ballot for two persons, of whom one at least shall not be an Inhabitant of the same State with themselves. And they shall make a List of all the Persons voted for, and of the Number of Votes for each; which List they shall sign and certify, and transmit sealed to the Seat of the Government of the United States, directed to the President of the Senate. The President of the Senate shall, in the Presence of the Senate and House of Representatives, open all the Certificates, and the Votes shall then be counted. The Person having the greatest Number of Votes shall be the President, if such Number be a Majority of the whole Number of Electors appointed; and if there be more than one who have such Majority, and have an equal Number of Votes, then the House of Representatives shall immediately chuse by Ballot one of them for President; and if no Person have a Majority, then from the five highest on the List the said House shall in like Manner chuse the President. But in chusing the President, the Votes shall be taken by States, the Representation from each State having one Vote; a quorum for this Purpose shall consist of a Member or Members from two-thirds of the States, and a Majority of all the States shall be necessary to a Choice. In every Case, after the Choice of the President, the Person having the greatest Number of Votes of the Electors shall be the Vice President. But if there should remain two or more who have equal votes, the Senate shall chuse from them by Ballot the Vice-President.

The Congress may determine the Time of chusing the Electors, and the Day on which they shall give their Votes; which Day shall be the same throughout the United States.

No person except a natural-born Citizen, or a Citizen of the United States, at the time of the Adoption of this Constitution, shall be eligible to the Office of President; neither shall any Person be eligible to that Office who shall not have attained to the Age of thirty-five years, and been fourteen Years a Resident within the United States.

In Case of the Removal of the President from Office, or of his Death, Resignation, or Inability to discharge the Powers and Duties of the said Office, the same shall devolve on the Vice President, and the Congress may by Law provide for the Case of Removal, Death, Resignation, or Inability, both of the President and Vice President, declaring what Officer shall then act as President, and such Officer shall act accordingly, until the disability be removed, or a President shall be elected.

The President shall, at stated Times, receive for his Services a Compensation, which shall neither be increased nor diminished during the Period for which he shall have been elected, and he shall not receive within that Period any other Emolument from the United States, or any of them.

Before he enter on the execution of his Office, he shall take the following Oath or Affirmation:—"I do solemnly swear (or affirm) that I will faithfully execute the Office of President of the United States, and will, to the best of my Ability, preserve, protect, and defend the Constitution of the United States."

Section 2. The President shall be Commander in Chief of the Army and Navy of the United States, and of the Militia of the several States, when called into the actual Service of the United States; he may require the Opinion, in writing, of the principal Officer in each of the executive Departments, upon any subject relating to the Duties of their respective Offices, and he shall have Power to Grant Reprieves and Pardons for Offences against the United States, except in Cases of Impeachment.

He shall have Power, by and with the Advice and Consent of the Senate, to make Treaties, provided two thirds of the Senators present concur; and he shall nominate, and by and with the Advice and Consent of the Senate, shall appoint Ambassadors, other public Ministers and Consuls, Judges of the supreme Court, and all other Officers of the United States, whose Appointments are not herein otherwise provided for, and which shall be established by Law: but the Congress may by Law vest the Appointments of such inferior Officers, as they think proper, in the President alone, in the Courts of Law, or in the Heads of Departments.

The President shall have Power to fill up all Vacancies that may happen during the Recess of the Senate, by granting Commissions which shall expire at the End of their next Session.

Section 3. He shall from time to time give to the Congress Information of the State of the Union, and recommend to their Consideration such Measures as he shall judge necessary and expedient; he may, on extraordinary occasions, convene both Houses, or either of them, and in Case of Disagreement between them, with respect to the Time of Adjournment, he may adjourn them to such Time as he shall think proper; he shall receive Ambassadors and other public Ministers; he shall take Care that the Laws be faithfully executed, and shall Commission all the Officers of the United States.

Section 4. The President, Vice President and all civil Officers of the United States, shall be removed from Office on Impeachment for, and Conviction of, Treason, Bribery, or other high Crimes and Misdemeanors.

ARTICLE III

Section 1. The judicial Power of the United States, shall be vested in one supreme Court, and in such inferior Courts as the Congress may from time to time ordain and establish. The Judges, both of the supreme and inferior Courts, shall hold their Offices during good Behaviour, and shall, at stated Times, receive for their Services, a Compensation, which shall not be diminished during their Continuance in Office.

Section 2. The judicial Power shall extend to all Cases, in Law and Equity, arising under this Constitution, the Laws of the United States, and treaties made, or which shall be made, under their Authority;—to all Cases affecting ambassadors, other public ministers and consuls;—to all cases of admiralty and maritime Jurisdiction;—to Controversies to which the United States shall be a Party;—to Controversies between two or more States;—between a State and Citizens of another State;—between Citizens of different States,—between Citizens of the same State claiming Lands under Grants of different States, and between a State, or the Citizens thereof, and foreign States, Citizens or Subjects.

In all Cases affecting Ambassadors, other public Ministers and Consuls, and those in which a State shall be Party, the supreme Court shall have original Jurisdiction. In all the other Cases before mentioned, the supreme Court shall have appellate Jurisdiction, both as to Law and Fact, with such Exceptions, and under such Regulations as the Congress shall make.

The trial of all Crimes, except in Cases of Impeachment, shall be by Jury; and such Trial shall be held in the State where the said Crimes shall have been committed; but when not committed within any State, the Trial shall be at such Place or Places as the Congress may by Law have directed.

Section 3. Treason against the United States, shall consist only in levying War against them, or in adhering to their Enemies, giving them Aid and Comfort. No Person shall be convicted of Treason unless on the Testimony of two Witnesses to the same overt Act, or on Confession in open Court.

The Congress shall have power to declare the Punishment of Treason, but no Attainder of Treason shall work Corruption of Blood, or Forfeiture except during the Life of the Person attainted.

ARTICLE IV

Section 1. Full Faith and Credit shall be given in each State to the public Acts, Records, and judicial Proceedings of every other State. And the Congress may by general Laws prescribe the Manner in which such Acts, Records and Proceedings shall be proved, and the Effect thereof.

Section 2. The Citizens of each State shall be entitled to all Privileges and Immunities of Citizens in the several States.

A Person charged in any State with Treason, Felony, or other Crime, who shall flee from Justice, and be found in another State, shall on demand of the executive Authority of the State from which he fled, be delivered up, to be removed to the State having Jurisdiction of the crime.

No Person held to Service or Labour in one State, under the Laws thereof, escaping into another, shall, in Consequence of any Law or Regulation therein, be discharged from such Service or Labour, but shall be delivered up on Claim of the Party to whom such Service or Labour may be due.

Section 3. New States may be admitted by the Congress into this Union; but no new State shall be formed or erected within the Jurisdiction of any other State; nor any State be formed by the Junction of two or more States, or parts of States, without the Consent of the Legislatures of the States concerned as well as of the Congress.

The Congress shall have Power to dispose of and make all needful Rules and Regulations respecting the Territory or other Property belonging to the United States; and nothing in this Constitution shall be so construed as to Prejudice any Claims of the United States, or of any particular State.

Section 4. The United States shall guarantee to every State in this Union a Republican Form of Government, and shall protect each of them against Invasion; and on Application of the Legislature, or the Executive (when the Legislature cannot be convened) against domestic Violence.

ARTICLE V

The Congress, whenever two-thirds of both Houses shall deem it necessary, shall propose Amendments to this Constitution, or, on the Application of the Legislatures of two-thirds of the several States, shall call a Convention for proposing Amendments, which, in either Case, shall be valid to all Intents and Purposes, as part of this Constitution, when ratified by the Legislatures of three-fourths of the several States, or by Conventions in three-fourths thereof, as the one or the other Mode of Ratification may be proposed by the Congress; Provided that no Amendment which may be made prior to the Year One thousand eight hundred and eight shall in any Manner affect the first and fourth Clauses in the Ninth Section of the first Article; and that no State, without its Consent, shall be deprived of its equal Suffrage in the Senate.

ARTICLE VI

All Debts contracted and Engagements entered into, before the Adoption of this Constitution, shall be as valid against the United States under this Constitution, as under the Confederation.

This Constitution, and the Laws of the United States which shall be made in Pursuance thereof; and all Treaties made, or which shall be made, under the Authority of the United States, shall be the supreme Law of the Land; and the Judges in every State shall be bound thereby, any Thing in the Constitution or Laws of any State to the Contrary notwithstanding.

The Senators and Representatives before mentioned, and the Members of the several State Legislatures, and all executive and judicial Officers, both of the United States and of the several States, shall be bound by Oath or Affirmation to support this Constitution; but no religious Test shall every be required as a qualification to any Office or public Trust under the United States.

ARTICLE VII
The Ratification of the Conventions of nine States shall be sufficient for the Establishment of this Constitution between the States so ratifying the same.

Done in Convention by the Unanimous Consent of the States present the Seventeenth Day of September in the Year of our Lord one thousand seven hundred and Eighty seven, and of the Independence of the United States of America the Twelfth. In Witness whereof We have hereunto subscribed our names.

Articles in Addition to, and Amendment of, the Constitution of the United States of America. Proposed by Congress, and Ratified by the Legislatures of the Several States, Pursuant to the Fifth Article of the Original Constitution.

AMENDMENT I [1791]
Congress shall make no law respecting an establishment of religion, or prohibiting the free exercise thereof; or abridging the freedom of speech, or of the press; or the right of the people peaceably to assemble, and to petition the Government for a redress of grievances.

AMENDMENT II [1791]
A well regulated Militia, being necessary to the security of a free State, the right of the people to keep and bear Arms shall not be infringed.

AMENDMENT III [1791]
No Soldier shall, in time of peace, be quartered in any house, without the consent of the Owner, nor in time of war, but in a manner to be prescribed by law.

AMENDMENT IV [1791]
The right of the people to be secure in their persons, houses, papers, and effects, against unreasonable searches and seizures, shall not be violated, and no Warrants shall issue, but upon probable cause, supported by Oath or affirmation, and particularly describing the place to be searched, and the persons or things to be seized.

Section 2. Congress shall have power to enforce this article by appropriate legislation.

AMENDMENT XIV [1868]

Section 1. All persons born or naturalized in the United States, and subject to the jurisdiction thereof, are citizens of the United States and of the State wherein they reside. No State shall make or enforce any law which shall abridge the privileges or immunities of citizens of the United States; nor shall any State deprive any person of life, liberty, or property, without due process of law; nor deny to any person within its jurisdiction the equal protection of the laws.

Section 2. Representatives shall be apportioned among the several States according to their respective numbers, counting the whole number of persons in each State, excluding Indians not taxed. But when the right to vote at any election for the choice of electors for President and Vice-President of the United States, Representatives in Congress, the Executive and Judicial officers of a State, or the members of the Legislature thereof, is denied to any of the male inhabitants of such State, being twenty-one years of age, and citizens of the United States, or in any way abridged, except for participation in rebellion, or other crime, the basis of representation therein shall be reduced in the proportion which the number of such male citizens shall bear to the whole number of male citizens twenty-one years of age in such State.

Section 3. No person shall be a Senator or Representative in Congress, or elector of President and Vice-President, or hold any office, civil or military, under the United States, or under any State, who, having previously taken an oath, as a member of Congress, or as an officer of the United States, or as a member of any State legislature, or as an executive or judicial officer of any State, to support the Constitution of the United States, shall have engaged in insurrection or rebellion against the same, or given aid or comfort to the enemies thereof. But Congress may by a vote of two-thirds of each House, remove such disability.

Section 4. The validity of the public debt of the United States, authorized by law, including debts incurred for payment of pensions and bounties for services in suppressing insurrection or rebellion, shall not be questioned. But neither the United States nor any State shall assume or pay any debt or obligation incurred in aid of insurrection or rebellion against the United States or any claim for the loss or emancipation of any slave; but all such debts, obligations, and claims shall be held illegal and void.

Section 5. The Congress shall have the power to enforce, by appropriate legislation, the provisions of this article.

Amendment XV [1870]
Section 1. The right of citizens of the United States to vote shall not be denied or abridged by the United States or by any State on account of race, color, or previous condition of servitude—
Section 2. The Congress shall have power to enforce this article by appropriate legislation.

AMENDMENT XVI [1913]
The Congress shall have power to lay and collect taxes on incomes, from whatever source derived, without apportionment among the several States, and without regard to any census or enumeration.

AMENDMENT XVII [1913]
The Senate of the United States shall be composed of two Senators from each State, elected by the people thereof, for six years; and each Senator shall have one vote. The electors in each State shall have the qualifications requisite for electors of the most numerous branch of the State legislatures.

When vacancies happen in the representation of any State in the Senate, the executive authority of such State shall issue writs of election to fill such vacancies: *Provided,* That the legislature of any State may empower the executive thereof to make temporary appointments until the people fill the vacancies by election as the legislature may direct.

This amendment shall not be so construed as to affect the election or term of any Senator chosen before it becomes valid as part of the Constitution.

AMENDMENT XVIII [1919]
Section 1. After one year from the ratification of this article the manufacture, sale, or transportation of intoxicating liquors within, the importation thereof into, or the exportation thereof from the United States and all territory subject to the jurisdiction thereof for beverage purposes is hereby prohibited.
Section 2. The Congress and the several States shall have concurrent power to enforce this article by appropriate legislation.
Section 3. This article shall be inoperative unless it shall have been ratified as an amendment to the Constitution by the legislatures of the several States, as provided in the Constitution, within seven years from the date of the submission hereof to the States by the Congress.

AMENDMENT XIX [1920]
The right of citizens of the United States to vote shall not be denied or abridged by the United States or by any State on account of sex.

AMENDMENT V [1791]

No person shall be held to answer for a capital or otherwise infamous crime, unless on a presentment or indictment of a Grand Jury, except in cases arising in the land or naval forces, or in the Militia, when in actual service in time of War or public danger; nor shall any person be subject for the same offence to be twice put in jeopardy of life or limb; nor shall be compelled in any criminal case to be a witness against himself, nor be deprived of life, liberty, or property, without due process of law; nor shall private property be taken for public use, without just compensation.

AMENDMENT VI [1791]

In all criminal prosecutions, the accused shall enjoy the right to a speedy and public trial, by an impartial jury of the State and district wherein the crime shall have been committed, which district shall have been previously ascertained by law, and to be informed of the nature and cause of the accusation; to be confronted with the witnesses against him; to have compulsory process for obtaining witnesses in his favor, and to have the Assistance of Counsel for his defence.

AMENDMENT VII [1791]

In suits at common law, where the value in controversy shall exceed twenty dollars, the right of trial by jury shall be preserved, and no fact tried by a jury, shall be otherwise reexamined in any Court of the United States, than according to the rules of the common law.

AMENDMENT VIII [1791]

Excessive bail shall not be required, nor excessive fines imposed, nor cruel and unusual punishments inflicted.

AMENDMENT IX [1791]

The enumeration in the Constitution, of certain rights, shall not be construed to deny or disparage others retained by the people.

AMENDMENT X [1791]

The powers not delegated to the United States by the Constitution, nor prohibited by it to the States, are reserved to the States respectively, or to the people.

AMENDMENT XI [1798]

The Judicial power of the United States shall not be construed to extend to any suit in law or equity, commenced or prosecuted against one of the

United States by Citizens of another State, or by Citizens or Subjects of any Foreign State.

AMENDMENT XII [1804]

The Electors shall meet in their respective States and vote by ballot for President and Vice-President, one of whom, at least, shall not be an inhabitant of the same State with themselves; they shall name in their ballots the person voted for as President, and in distinct ballots the person voted for as Vice-President, and they shall make distinct lists of all persons voted for as President, and of all persons voted for as Vice-President, and of the number of votes for each, which lists they shall sign and certify, and transmit sealed to the seat of the government of the United States, directed to the President of the Senate;—The President of the Senate shall, in the presence of the Senate and House of Representatives, open all the certificates and the votes shall then be counted;—The person having the greatest number of votes for President, shall be the President, if such number be a majority of the whole number of Electors appointed; and if no person have such majority, then from the persons having the highest numbers not exceeding three on the list of those voted for as President, the House of Representatives shall choose immediately, by ballot, the President. But in choosing the President, the votes shall be taken by states, the representation from each state having one vote; a quorum for this purpose shall consist of a member or members from two-thirds of the states, and a majority of all the states shall be necessary to a choice. And if the House of Representatives shall not choose a President whenever the right of choice shall devolve upon them, before the fourth day of March next following, then the Vice-President shall act as President, as in the case of the death or other constitutional disability of the President.—The person having the greatest number of votes as Vice-President, shall be the Vice-President, if such number be a majority of the whole number of Electors appointed, and if no person have a majority, then from the two highest numbers on the list, the Senate shall choose the Vice-President; a quorum for the purpose shall consist of two-thirds of the whole number of Senators, and a majority of the whole number shall be necessary to a choice. But no person constitutionally ineligible to the office of President shall be eligible to that of Vice-President of the United States.

AMENDMENT XIII [1865]

Section 1. Neither slavery nor involuntary servitude, except as a punishment for crime whereof the party shall have been duly convicted, shall exist within the United States, or any place subject to their jurisdiction.

Congress shall have power to enforce this article by appropriate legislation.

AMENDMENT XX [1933]

Section 1. The terms of the President and Vice-President shall end at noon on the 20th day of January, and the terms of Senators and Representatives at noon on the 3d day of January, of the years in which such terms would have ended if this article had not been ratified; and the terms of their successors shall then begin.

Section 2. The Congress shall assemble at least once in every year, and such meeting shall begin at noon on the 3rd day of January, unless they shall by law appoint a different day.

Section 3. If, at the time fixed for the beginning of the term of the President, the President elect shall have died, the Vice-President elect shall become President. If a President shall not have been chosen before the time fixed for the beginning of his term, or if the President elect shall have failed to qualify, then the Vice-President elect shall act as President until a President shall have qualified; and the Congress may by law provide for the case wherein neither a President elect nor a Vice-President elect shall have qualified, declaring who shall then act as President, or the manner in which one who is to act shall be selected, and such person shall act accordingly until a President or Vice-President shall have qualified.

Section 4. The Congress may by law provide for the case of the death of any of the persons from whom the House of Representatives may choose a President whenever the right of choice shall have devolved upon them, and for the case of the death of any of the persons from whom the Senate may choose a Vice-President whenever the right of choice shall have devolved upon them.

Section 5. Sections 1 and 2 shall take effect on the 15th day of October following the ratification of this article.

Section 6. This article shall be inoperative unless it shall have been ratified as an amendment to the Constitution by the legislatures of three-fourths of the several States within seven years from the date of its submission.

AMENDMENT XXI [1933]

Section 1. The eighteenth article of amendment to the Constitution of the United States is hereby repealed.

Section 2. The transportation or importation into any State, Territory, or possession of the United States for delivery or use therein of intoxicating liquors, in violation of the laws thereof, is hereby prohibited.

Section 3. This article shall be inoperative unless it shall have been ratified as an amendment to the Constitution by conventions in the several States, as provided in the Constitution, within seven years from the date of the submission hereof to the States by the Congress.

AMENDMENT XXII [1951]

No person shall be elected to the office of the President more than twice, and no person who has held the office of President, or acted as President, for more than two years of a term to which some other person was elected President shall be elected to the office of the President more than once.

But this Article shall not apply to any person holding the office of President when this Article was proposed by the Congress, and shall not prevent any person who may be holding the office of President, or acting as President, during the term within which this Article becomes operative from holding the office of President or acting as President during the remainder of such term.

AMENDMENT XXIII [1961]

Section 1. The District constituting the seat of Government of the United States shall appoint in such manner as the Congress may direct:

A number of electors of President and Vice President equal to the whole number of Senators and Representatives in Congress to which the District would be entitled if it were a State, but in no event more than the least populous State; they shall be in addition to those appointed by the States, but they shall be considered, for the purposes of the election of President and Vice President, to be electors appointed by a State; and they shall meet in the District and perform such duties as provided by the twelfth article of amendment.

Section 2. The Congress shall have power to enforce this article by appropriate legislation.

AMENDMENT XXIV [1964]

Section 1. The right of citizens of the United States to vote in any primary or other election for President or Vice President, for electors for President or Vice President, or for Senator or Representative in Congress, shall not be denied or abridged by the United States or any State by reason of failure to pay any poll tax or other tax.

Section 2. The Congress shall have the power to enforce this article by appropriate legislation.

AMENDMENT XXV [1967]

Section 1. In case of the removal of the President from office or his death or resignation, the Vice President shall become President.

Section 2. Whenever there is a vacancy in the office of the Vice President, the President shall nominate a Vice President who shall take the office upon confirmation by a majority vote of both houses of Congress.

Section 3. Whenever the President transmits to the President pro tempore of the Senate and the Speaker of the House of Representatives his written declaration that he is unable to discharge the powers and duties of his office, and until he transmits to them a written declaration to the contrary, such powers and duties shall be discharged by the Vice-President as Acting President.

Section 4. Whenever the Vice President and a majority of either the principal officers of the executive departments, or of such other body as Congress may by law provide, transmit to the President pro tempore of the Senate and the Speaker of the House of Representatives their written declaration that the President is unable to discharge the powers and duties of his office, the Vice President shall immediately assume the powers and duties of the office as Acting President.

Thereafter, when the President transmits to the President pro tempore of the Senate and the Speaker of the House of Representatives his written declaration that no inability exists, he shall resume the powers and duties of his office unless the Vice President and a majority of either the principal officers of the executive department, or of such other body as Congress may by law provide, transmit within four days to the President pro tempore of the Senate and the Speaker of the House of Representatives their written declaration that the President is unable to discharge the powers and duties of his office. Thereupon Congress shall decide the issue, assembling within 48 hours for that purpose if not in session. If the Congress, within 21 days after receipt of the latter written declaration, or, if Congress is not in session, within 21 after Congress is required to assemble, determines by two-thirds vote of both houses that the President is unable to discharge the powers and duties of his office, the Vice President shall continue to discharge the same as Acting President; otherwise, the President shall resume the powers and duties of his office.

AMENDMENT XXVI [1971]

Section 1. The rights of citizens of the United States, who are eighteen years of age or older, to vote shall not be denied or abridged by the United States or any state on account of age.

Section 2. The congress shall have the power to enforce this article by appropriate legislation.

Index